Innovation in Carrier Aviation

Thomas C. Hone, Norman Friedman, and
Mark D. Mandeles

Tom Hone: "To Bailey Siletchnik, whom I could only beat at Scrabble by cheating."

Norman Friedman: "To my wife Rhea, without whom nothing would be possible."

Mark Mandeles: "To Laura."

Contents

List of Figures and Tables		v
List of Acronyms and Abbreviations		vii
Acknowledgments		xi
Foreword, *by Carnes Lord*		xiii
Introduction		1
CHAPTER ONE	BuAer before World War II	11
CHAPTER TWO	BuAer in World War II	23
CHAPTER THREE	The Potential of the Big Bomber	35
CHAPTER FOUR	Royal Navy Wartime Experience and Analysis	45
CHAPTER FIVE	Adopting Jet Engines	53
CHAPTER SIX	British and American Prospects after the War	69
CHAPTER SEVEN	The Flexdeck	89
CHAPTER EIGHT	Catapults: Choosing an Option under Pressure	99
CHAPTER NINE	Analysis	123
Conclusion		157
APPENDIX A	The Physics of Jet Propulsion	173

APPENDIX B	The Impact of Jet Aircraft on Carriers	177
APPENDIX C	Problem Solving within Bureaucracies	181
APPENDIX D	Chronology	185

Bibliography 193
About the Authors 197
Index 199
The Newport Papers 219

List of Figures and Tables

Figures

FIGURE 1-1	Fighter Speed, in Knots, for Selected Fighters—Royal Navy, U.S. Navy, and Imperial Japanese Navy	14
FIGURE 1-2	Service Ceiling, in Feet, for Selected Fighters—Royal Navy, U.S. Navy, and Imperial Japanese Navy	15
FIGURE B-1	Stall Speed vs. Prototype Year	178
FIGURE B-2	Takeoff Weight vs. Year	179
FIGURE B-3	Roll at 25 Knots WOD vs. Year	180

Tables

TABLE 2-1	Characteristics of Aircraft to Replace the SB2C	24
TABLE 2-2	BuAer's Fighter Aircraft Characteristics, 1936–43	26
TABLE 2-3	Comparison of Navy Aircraft with Army 1942 Models	27
TABLE 2-4	Catapults Developed by the Naval Aircraft Factory, 1936–45	29
TABLE B-1	Carrier Fighter-Bomber/Attack Aircraft at the End of World War II	177
TABLE B-2	Weight Comparison	178

List of Acronyms and Abbreviations

A	**Adm.**	Admiral
	AEW	airborne early warning
	ALCO	American Locomotive Company
B	**BuAer**	Bureau of Aeronautics
	BuOrd	Bureau of Ordnance
	BuShips	Bureau of Ships
C	**CCA**	carrier-controlled approach
	Capt.	Captain
	Cdr.	Commander
	CIC	combat information center
	CinC	Commander in Chief
	CINCPAC	Commander in Chief, U.S. Pacific Fleet [in World War II]
	CNO	Chief of Naval Operations
	CNR	Chief of Naval Research
	CO	Commanding Officer
	CV	aircraft carrier
	CVAN	attack aircraft carrier, nuclear-powered
D	**DCNO (Air)**	Deputy Chief of Naval Operations for Air
	DCNO (Logistics)	Deputy Chief of Naval Operations for Logistics
	DNC	Director of Naval Construction
E	**EIC**	Engineer-in-Chief

F	**FAA**	Fleet Air Arm
	FBC	Future Building Committee
	ft./sec.	feet per second
	FY	fiscal year
G	*g*	acceleration of gravity
	GE	General Electric
	GLOMB	glider bomb
H	**hp**	horsepower
	HTP	hydrogen peroxide
I	**IJN**	Imperial Japanese Navy
J	**JATO**	jet-assisted takeoff
L	**lb.**	pound
	LSO	landing signal officer
	Lt.	Lieutenant
	Lt. Cdr.	Lieutenant Commander
M	**MAP**	Ministry of Aircraft Production
	MIT	Massachusetts Institute of Technology
	Mod.	modification
	mph	miles per hour
N	**NACA**	National Advisory Committee for Aeronautics
	NAD	Naval Aircraft Department
	NAMC	Naval Air Material Center

	NATO	North Atlantic Treaty Organization
	NDRC	National Defense Research Committee
	ONI	Office of Naval Intelligence
	OPNAV	Office of the Chief of Naval Operations
	OSD(NA)	Office of the Secretary of Defense (Net Assessment)
	PRO	Public Records Office
	psi	pounds per square inch
	R&D	research and development
	RAE	Royal Aircraft Establishment
	RAF	Royal Air Force
	repr.	reprinted by
	RG	record group
	RN	Royal Navy
	SAM	surface-to-air missile
	SCB	Ship Characteristics Board
	TACAN	Tactical Air Navigation
	USAF	U.S. Air Force
	USN	U.S. Navy
	WOD	wind over the deck

Acknowledgments

Our main sources for the study were Royal Navy records held by the Public Records Office (PRO), U.S. Navy papers held by the National Archives and by the Aviation History Office of the Naval History and Heritage Command, records of the Grumman Aircraft Corporation held in the Northrop Grumman archives, memoirs of Royal Navy (RN) and U.S. Navy (USN) personnel, memoirs of American aviation engineers, and oral histories of Americans involved in the development of jet aircraft and modern carrier aviation. We also consulted books and articles that were well researched.

In obtaining this material, we were assisted by the following individuals: Dr. Evelyn Cherpak, of the Naval War College; Dr. Curtis Utz and Dr. Timothy Francis, of the Naval History and Heritage Command; Dr. Hill Goodspeed, of the Naval Aviation Museum in Pensacola, Florida; Lt. Cdr. Peter J. Hardy, RN (Ret.), of HMS *Heron;* and Ms. Susan Dearing, of the Fleet Air Arm Museum. All were generous with their time and their expertise. None bears responsibility for any errors in this study.

Vice Adm. Robert Dunn, USN (Ret.), also read an early draft of the study and alerted us to several sources we had missed, including *Farnborough and the Fleet Air Arm,* by Geoffrey Cooper. Professor Donald Chisholm of the Naval War College and Dr. Jeffrey G. Barlow of the Naval History and Heritage Command also shared their insights.

Ms. G. F. Siletchnik of the Naval Undersea Warfare Center graciously constructed the graphs in appendix B. Mr. Trent Hone organized the manuscript.

The study on which this monograph is based was commissioned by the Office of the Secretary of Defense (Net Assessment) in the fall of 2006 as part of that office's long-standing support for studies of military innovation. In some sense, the OSD(NA) project was a follow-on to an earlier study by the present coauthors, published in 1999 as *American & British Aircraft Carrier Development, 1919–1941* by the Naval Institute Press.

In the mid-1980s, Andrew Marshall, the director of the Office of Net Assessment in the Office of the Secretary of Defense, encouraged a number of investigators to examine cases of innovation in the U.S. armed forces and in the armed forces of other countries. His encouragement, coupled with the financial support of his office, led to a number of studies, among which was the book *American & British Aircraft Carrier Development,*

1919–1941 (Annapolis, Md.: Naval Institute Press, 1999), written by the authors of the study that you are about to read.

The success of *American & British Aircraft Carrier Development, 1919–1941* led Mr. Marshall to ask whether we might examine the development of the modern aircraft carrier after World War II. We already knew that the three essential innovations—the steam catapult, the angled flight deck, and the optical landing aid—had been developed first in Great Britain for and by the Royal Navy. Then all three innovations had been picked up by the U.S. Navy.

But why, Mr. Marshall wanted to know, had the Royal Navy developed these innovations *first*? He asked us to come together and answer that question, as well as the related question of how these innovations were "transferred" so quickly to the U.S. Navy. Mr. Marshall's interest was in the process of innovation and in how innovations spread. We have tried to find answers to his questions.

In the late spring of 2006, the authors presented Net Assessment with a proposal. In the fall of 2006, Net Assessment agreed to fund research by Dr. Friedman and Dr. Mandeles. At the same time, the Naval War College agreed to allow Dr. Hone to devote some of his effort as a faculty member to the study. The written result of the research conducted by these three analysts—delayed by some unanticipated obstacles—is in the pages that follow.

Foreword

In a widely noted speech to the Navy League Sea-Air-Space Expo in May 2010, Secretary of Defense Robert M. Gates warned that "the Navy and Marine Corps must be willing to reexamine and question basic assumptions in light of evolving technologies, new threats, and budget realities. We simply cannot afford to perpetuate a status quo that heaps more and more expensive technologies onto fewer and fewer platforms—thereby risking a situation where some of our greatest capital expenditures go toward weapons and ships that could potentially become wasting assets." Secretary Gates specifically questioned whether the Navy's commitment to a force of eleven carrier strike groups through 2040 makes sense, given the extent of the anticipated superiority of the United States over potential adversaries at sea as well as the growing threat of antiship missiles. Though later disclaiming any immediate intention to seek a reduction in the current carrier force, Gates nevertheless laid down a clear marker that all who are concerned over the future of the U.S. Navy would be well advised to take with the utmost seriousness.

We may stand, then, at an important watershed in the evolution of carrier aviation, one reflecting not only the nation's current financial crisis but the changing nature of the threats to, or constraints on, American sea power, as well as—something the secretary did not mention—the advent of a new era of unmanned air and sea platforms of all types. Taken together, these developments argue for resolutely innovative thinking about the future of the nation's carrier fleet and our surface navy more generally.

In *Innovation in Carrier Aviation,* number thirty-seven in our Newport Papers monograph series, Thomas C. Hone, Norman Friedman, and Mark D. Mandeles examine the watershed period in carrier development that occurred immediately following World War II, when design advances were made that would be crucial to the centrality in national-security policy making that carriers and naval aviation have today. In those years several major technological breakthroughs—notably the jet engine and nuclear weapons—raised large questions about the future and led to an array of innovations in the design and operational utilization of aircraft carriers.

Central to this story is the collaboration between the aviation communities in the navies of the United States and Great Britain during these years, building on the intimate relationship they had developed during the war itself. Strikingly, the most important of these innovations, notably the angled flight deck and steam catapult, originated with the British, not the Americans. This study thereby also provides interesting lessons for the U.S. Navy today with respect to its commitment to maritime security cooperation in the context of its new "maritime strategy." It is a welcome and important addition to the historiography of the Navy in the seminal years of the Cold War.

CARNES LORD
Director, Naval War College Press
Newport, Rhode Island

Introduction

This study is about innovations in carrier aviation and the spread of those innovations from one navy to the navy of a close ally. The innovations are the angled flight deck; the steam catapult; and the mirror and lighted landing aid that enabled pilots to land jet aircraft on a carrier's short and narrow flight deck.

This study is different from our previous study of innovation in the development and use of aircraft carriers, *U.S. & British Aircraft Carrier Development, 1919–1941*, which compared innovation in carrier aviation in the U.S. Navy and the Royal Navy in the years before World War II. At the time, the U.S. Navy and the Royal Navy were competitors. The two navies did not share technical information and in fact worked to hide their advances from one another, despite the fact that they had cooperated closely during World War I. Only in the winter of 1940–41 was there a renewal of the close professional contact between the naval aviators of the two nations that had first blossomed in 1918. Those initial cooperative relations grew into a very strong relationship during World War II, when British carriers were often equipped with mostly U.S.-made aircraft and many British pilots trained in the United States.

After World War II the cooperation continued, and as we show in the pages to follow, it had major benefits for both navies—but especially for the U.S. Navy, which had the resources to construct the large carriers and carrier aircraft that came to be seen as "the world standard" starting in the mid-1950s. Indeed, the cooperation between the U.S. Navy and the Royal Navy after World War II facilitated an eventual dramatic improvement in the USN's carrier aviation, as we shall show.

Though this is a study of innovations and the diffusion of innovations, it is really a study of professional people—civilian and military pilots, civilian and military engineers, and leaders of military and civilian organizations. The effort to put modern jet aircraft on aircraft carriers depended on courageous, dedicated, and clever individuals in both Great Britain and the United States. These individuals did their work within organizations established to develop and field modern naval aircraft, especially the U.S.

Navy's Bureau of Aeronautics (BuAer), along with its industrial suppliers, and—in Great Britain—the Royal Aircraft Establishment, the Royal Navy, the Ministry of Aircraft Production, and British aircraft manufacturers. In addition, the key players—individuals and organizations—in our story acted within different legal and official requirements, especially regulations and the laws governing the spending of public funds on military procurement and research and development. Finally, the innovators in both the United States and Britain needed the support of the major political institutions of their respective countries.

There are, then, three lenses through which we examine the events central to this story. The first lens focuses our attention on the role of individual perception and analysis. Why and when did innovators identify their problems and take action to solve them? Why was it that the three essential innovations were developed in Britain *first*? Why didn't the U.S. Navy develop these innovations first, or at least in parallel with the Royal Navy? How and why did these innovations spread from the Royal Navy to the U.S. Navy? The second lens focuses on what happens inside an organization. It's not enough for an innovator to come up a new idea or with a new application of an existing technology. The leaders of the innovator's organization need to recognize that the innovation solves a problem or shortfall, and then they need to support its development and demonstration. These leaders need to do this despite the press of everyday affairs—despite the attention they must devote to routine matters that require their attention. The third lens examines the interplay of institutions that contain the organizations in which the innovators worked. These institutions and interconnections include the U.S. Navy, the Royal Navy, and the processes by which civilian political institutions (such as the U.S. Congress) influenced naval policy.

The Importance of the Past as Prologue

In World War II, the aircraft carrier proved itself as the dominant naval weapon, especially in the U.S. campaign against Japan in the Pacific. When World War II began in 1939, no navy that fielded carriers possessed more than a limited number of them. The U.S. Navy, for example, had five first-line carriers. By the end of October 1942, only three of the five were still afloat. But a huge construction program pumped out a *fleet* of American carriers by war's end: seventeen large new carriers (with another seven to follow after the war), eight light carriers (with another two under construction), and seventy-seven escort carriers (an additional seven would be completed after the war). There were also three new armored-flight-deck carriers under construction for the U.S. Navy, giving it both the largest and the most modern carrier force by 1946.

Cooperation between the carrier forces of the U.S. Navy and the Royal Navy had begun in the winter of 1940, when the RN invited the USN to send observers to its carriers. These observers reported that the Royal Navy had combined radar warning with the control of defensive fighters by specially trained naval personnel in "fighter direction" ships (usually carriers) to blunt Italian air attacks against RN carriers in the Mediterranean. In the USN, using the radar-equipped carrier *Yorktown* in exercises in July and August 1941, then–rear admiral William Halsey and his staff validated the RN's approach and laid the foundations for what became a very effective form of fleet air defense by the summer of 1944.[1]

Equally important were technical contacts between the two governments, especially the "Tizard Mission" of September 1940. Sir Henry Tizard, who had been a pilot in World War I and had later been instrumental in the development and construction of Britain's air-defense radars in the late 1930s, led a delegation of British technical experts to Washington to reveal to the War and Navy departments a number of new devices, including the cavity magnetron and Frank Whittle's turbojet engine. This exchange was "much more than a means for transferring hardware; it also involved the exchange of intellectual property of all types."[2] Tizard's mission did more than set the stage for a variety of scientific and technical cooperative efforts. It also set a precedent of cooperation that persisted even after the war was over.

The British and French governments had already been purchasing U.S.-made aircraft, starting in 1939. However, with "the passage of the Lend-Lease Act in 1941 and the Defense Aid program which grew out of that legislation, the United States government undertook the financing and direction of the production of planes for the use of our allies-to-be."[3] But production of planes for the Royal Navy and sharing of scientific and technical information were only part of the story of close cooperation between the USN and the RN during the war. The U.S. Navy also trained a number of RN Fleet Air Arm pilots.

This effort was sponsored in the summer of 1941 by the Navy's senior aviator, Rear Adm. John H. Towers, then chief of the Bureau of Aeronautics. Towers went so far as to make sure that Fleet Air Arm recruits sent to the United States had access to the latest and best training aircraft, even if it meant shortchanging U.S. Navy needs. The result of this program was significant: "The Towers scheme was hugely important to the Fleet Air Arm. By November 1944 it was providing 44 percent of the pilots required by the Royal Navy. In particular, the Fleet Air Arm had come to rely on the scheme to turn out the pilots needed to fly the American aircraft on which it increasingly depended."[4] The results of this training program, coupled with U.S. aircraft provided through Lend-Lease, can also be illustrated by considering British carrier attacks against Japanese-controlled oil production facilities in Sumatra in January 1945. In one attack, of the

124 British carrier aircraft involved only twelve had been developed and produced in the United Kingdom. All the rest had been produced in the United States, and most of those were flown by Fleet Air Arm pilots trained in the United States.[5]

After the war, Fleet Air Arm pilots who had been trained in the United States formed a club called the "British Pensacola Veterans." There is evidence that many members of the club strongly supported "the Anglo-American special relationship, especially during the tensions of the Cold War. That special relationship was not just a matter of national self-interest and formal alliances: it existed in the hearts and minds of individuals."[6] It was also deliberately fostered by officers on both sides, especially Admiral Towers, who, according to his biographer Clark Reynolds, had "such great respect" for the Royal Navy.[7]

After World War II

The situation in naval aviation after World War II was in three important ways similar to that after World War I. First, the huge increase in research and development (R&D) spending during the war had produced a fistful of important aviation innovations, including effective jet engines, ballistic missiles, cruise missiles, air-launched rockets, ground-based radars to track aircraft, new aircraft designs (such as the delta wing), airborne radars, and improved facilities at existing and war-built R&D centers. Second, rapid demobilization after war's end had sent masses of former servicemen back into civilian life and had cut dramatically the output from aircraft manufacturers while slashing the sizes of their workforces. Third, spending on defense declined severely just as senior military officers wished to invest in the new technologies produced by wartime R&D.

Again, as after World War I, there was a national-level argument in the United States over how military aviation should be organized. The U.S. Army's aviators won their campaign to have Congress create a separate aviation service, and the U.S. Air Force (USAF) was formally established in 1947. Thereafter in the years immediately after World War II the Air Force and Navy disputed the future role and organization of military aviation in deadly earnest, and the status of carrier aviation was always at or near the center of these disputes.

One factor, however, was entirely new: the introduction of nuclear weapons. For a time after World War II, it looked as though nuclear weapons had changed the whole face of war. Given the great size and weight of the first generation of nuclear weapons, it was clear that only large aircraft could carry them; therefore aircraft carriers and their planes seemed irrelevant, even useless. The debate over which military arm should carry nuclear weapons began almost immediately after their first use in August 1945 and continued throughout the period that we examine (1945–55). This debate strongly affected the development of U.S. carrier aviation.[8]

As a reaction to the increasing importance of its own aviation arm, the Navy during World War II had restructured its own aviation organization. In Washington, in a major organizational change, staff elements of BuAer had been reassigned to the Office of the Chief of Naval Operations (OPNAV). This reorganization moved Navy aviation in a direction almost opposite to that taken after World War I. When the Bureau of Aeronautics was created in 1921, its official responsibilities had included developing requirements for new aircraft; drawing up the Navy's budget for aircraft procurement, maintenance, training, and R&D; manufacturing specialized components and even whole aircraft at the Naval Aircraft Factory in Philadelphia, Pennsylvania; and creating and controlling the training (and to some degree the promotion) of naval aviators. These broad powers made the chief of the bureau one of the most visible and influential Navy officers in Washington.

It was many of these responsibilities that were transferred out of BuAer during and immediately after World War II, and the bureau was left mainly with the functions of procuring aircraft and aircraft ordnance, setting the Navy's aviation research agenda, and working with the Navy's Bureau of Ships (BuShips) to plan the design of new aircraft carriers and the modifications of existing carriers. In short, OPNAV removed most of BuAer's policy-making authority, as well as the responsibility to search for or create the evidence that would support Navy aviation policies. As we shall show, these changes in structure and authority moved BuAer personnel away from thinking about aviation *operations* and focused their professional attention on developing and procuring high-performance aircraft. That change in focus also altered the way that senior officers in OPNAV and members of Congress would assess the work done by BuAer and its industry contractors.

The period after World War II was therefore extraordinary in many ways—indeed, in more ways than had been true of the period immediately after World War I. The level of uncertainty for naval aviation personnel was incredibly high. Could surface ships survive nuclear attack? Would high-speed, high-endurance submarines drive surface warships from the oceans? Would developments in radar lead to the invention of "death rays" that would kill the pilots of high-flying aircraft? Could a carrier's interceptors defend it against attacks by supersonic bombers? If the Soviet Union—whose primary military power rested in its army and land-based air forces—posed a grave danger to the United States, was a powerful navy even needed, or should scarce defense resources go to the Air Force and Army?

In November 1946, Vice Adm. Robert B. Carney, Deputy Chief of Naval Operations for Logistics, noted in an "eyes only" memorandum to the Chief of Naval Operations, Adm. Chester Nimitz, that "current trends in the weight, size, speed, and characteristics of aircraft may have a serious adverse effect on the utility of existing carriers and even on the overall importance of carrier aviation in the future."[9] That was a formal way of saying, "Carrier aviation—our most powerful tool in the Pacific in World War II—will pass its prime as an operational tool unless carriers grow as new aircraft grow."

Even before Carney penned his concerns to Nimitz, John L. Sullivan, Acting Secretary of the Navy, had urged President Harry Truman to allow the Navy to convert its large carrier force to a nuclear strike force by altering the carriers and their largest attack aircraft to deliver existing nuclear weapons.[10] At about the same time, a note circulated inside OPNAV suggesting that the Royal Navy was preparing to modify at least some of its carriers so that they could launch and recover the very heavy bombers required to lift large nuclear weapons like that used against Nagasaki in August 1945.[11] What this sort of evidence shows is that the level of strategic and technological uncertainty was so great right after World War II as to be almost overwhelming at times. Naval personnel in both the United States and Great Britain had to attempt to see their way forward in the face of numerous technological, strategic, political, and financial challenges.

From our perspective, what makes this period so interesting (and also so difficult to study) is the lack of "main organizational players" in the U.S. Navy of the kind that we discovered in doing the research for our earlier book. In the 1920s and '30s, the Bureau of Aeronautics was a strong bureaucratic actor within the Navy and the key obstacle to the unification of all military aviation in one executive department. In the 1920s especially, BuAer was markedly experimental, supporting the installation of aircraft on submarines, aircraft carriers, surface ships (mostly cruisers and battleships), and even on aircraft-carrying rigid airships. After 1943, however, BuAer lost its commanding position in the Washington arena, and the process of making naval aviation policy became shared among different Navy offices. The "paper trail" of decisions is therefore harder to follow.

Obscuring the decision-making process even more for the postwar years was the decline in the influence of the Navy's General Board and of the Naval War College. The former was a focal point of decision making in the years between World War I and World War II. The board, which reported directly to the Secretary of the Navy, reviewed the rationales for ship designs, which meant that it also reviewed the linkages between any major innovation and the military requirements it was designed to meet. The secret hearings held by the General Board were forums where major strategic, operational, and technical issues were discussed by senior officers and technical experts. The board survived efforts of Fleet Adm. Ernest J. King—Navy commander in chief and Chief of

Naval Operations during the war—to eliminate it entirely, but it lost its standing as the place where serious issues were discussed, argued about, and then (usually) resolved through a process of weighing hard evidence. As a result, the postwar discussions among officers from BuAer, the Bureau of Ships (which designed carriers), and OPNAV did not match the quality of the board's prewar proceedings.

The Naval War College, in Newport, Rhode Island, had pioneered war gaming even before World War I, but under post–World War I presidents such as Rear Admirals William S. Sims and William V. Pratt the college explored the possibilities of naval (especially carrier) aviation in a deliberate and disciplined manner that produced hypotheses that often framed the annual "fleet problems." But during World War II, the responsibility for solving operational and tactical naval problems shifted to the fleet commands, especially to the Pacific Fleet in Hawaii. For example, the concept of the combat information center (CIC) for U.S. Navy carriers grew from experiments in the summer of 1941 and from experience in the battles of Coral Sea and Midway in 1942.[12] The CIC for surface ships was first developed by an officer serving on a destroyer in the fighting around Guadalcanal in the fall of 1942 and was then strongly supported by Admiral Nimitz, and—very soon thereafter—CIC procedures were taught to new personnel in schools adjacent to the combat zone by the combat veterans themselves.[13] Because of the rise in the influence and responsibility of the Pacific Fleet staff, the Naval War College did not regain in 1946 the responsibility it had had before World War II as the source of systematic and innovative tactical and operational thinking. Thus by 1946 three of the four "players" critical to innovation in Navy aviation before World War II (BuAer, the Naval War College, and the General Board) had lost their functions, and that loss had deprived the Navy of a major innovative "tool."

But the changes had not all been for the worse. In World War II, naval aviators in the U.S. Navy and the Royal Navy again worked closely together and began a process of reciprocal visits and exchanging information that would help both services over the next ten years. The U.S. Navy also came out of the war with a powerful, *experienced* carrier force and a cadre of officers confident enough to take on the challenges posed by nuclear weapons and new technologies, such as jet propulsion. Finally, technologies pioneered in World War II, especially jet propulsion, aircraft designed for supersonic flight, and electronics, challenged the imaginations of the foremost aircraft designers and aircraft propulsion engineers in U.S. industry. These individuals sought ever greater aircraft performance within the boundaries set by available and future technology, and the best naval aviators in both the United Kingdom and the United States shared their enthusiasm.

The Plan of the Monograph

Readers will have to tolerate our tacking back and forth as we trace all the threads and outline their interrelationships. Ours is a complex story. Pieces of it have been told before—for example, in retired Vice Adm. Jerry Miller's *Nuclear Weapons and Aircraft Carriers: How the Bomb Saved Naval Aviation,* published by the Smithsonian Institution in 2001, and aeronautical engineer Tommy H. Thomason's *U.S. Naval Air Superiority* and *Strike from the Sea.* But to our knowledge no one has up to now put the pieces together in the way that we will in the pages to follow.

We will take major issues one at a time, from the development of reliable and powerful jet engines to the work of engineers trying to design and install on carriers the catapults and arresting gear required to launch and recover ever heavier and faster aircraft. We will also link these issues. When we began this study, we thought that those linkages would stand out once we examined the material available in archival and other sources. For example, we had read in several places that when British naval aviators showed their counterparts in the U.S. Navy the concept of the angled flight deck, the Americans saw its value almost immediately and embraced it. That seemed to make the process of adopting an innovation within the U.S. Navy straightforward. But matters turned out to be more complex than that, as we shall show.

Notes

1. Thomas C. Hone, Norman Friedman, and Mark D. Mandeles, *American & British Aircraft Carrier Development, 1919–1941* (Annapolis, Md.: Naval Institute Press, 1999), pp. 67–68. See also "Radar Doctrine, U.S. Pacific Fleet," *Pacific Fleet Tactical Bulletin no. 6-41,* from CinC, U.S. Pacific Fleet, to Pacific Fleet (December 31, 1941), in Pacific Fleet Tactical Bulletins 1941 folder, World War II Command File, Pacific Fleet, box 250, National Archives.
2. David Zimmerman, *Top Secret Exchange: The Tizard Mission and the Scientific War* (Montreal: McGill–Queen's Univ. Press and Alan Sutton, 1996), p. 193.
3. History Unit, DCNO (Air), "Aviation Procurement, 1939–1945, Part II," *Monographs in the History of Naval Aviation* 19 (1946), p. 30.
4. Gilbert Guinn and G. H. Bennett, *British Naval Aviation in World War II: The US Navy and Anglo-American Relations* (London: Tauris Academic Studies, 2007), p. 21.
5. Ibid., p. 144.
6. Ibid., p. 165.
7. Clark G. Reynolds, *Admiral John H. Towers: The Struggle for Naval Air Supremacy* (Annapolis, Md.: Naval Institute Press, 1991), p. 419. See also Alan P. Dobson, *U.S. Wartime Aid to Britain, 1940–1946* (New York: St. Martin's, 1986).
8. See Jeffrey G. Barlow, *Revolt of the Admirals: The Fight for Naval Aviation, 1945–1950* (Washington, D.C.: Naval Historical Center, 1994), and Vice Adm. Jerry Miller, USN (Ret.), *Nuclear Weapons and Aircraft Carriers: How the Bomb Saved Naval Aviation* (Washington, D.C.: Smithsonian Institution Press, 2001).
9. Carney to Nimitz, memorandum, 25 November 1946, subject "Merger Discussions," file 31 (Memos, CNO, Personal, 1942–47), box 2, Records of the Immediate Office of

the CNO, Naval Historical Center, Washington, D.C.
10. Sullivan to Truman, draft letter, 24 July 1946, Op-602/cmf, Serial 0014P602, (SC) A-23, Naval Aviation History Office, Washington Navy Yard, Washington, D.C.
11. Copy memo, no date, no number, Naval Aviation History Office.
12. Norman Friedman, *Network-centric Warfare: How Navies Learned to Fight Smarter through Three World Wars* (Annapolis, Md.: Naval Institute Press, 2009), pp. 58–59.
13. Joseph C. Wylie, Jr., "The Reminiscences of Rear Admiral Joseph C. Wylie, Jr." (Annapolis, Md.: U.S. Naval Institute Press, 2003), pp. 38–39.

BuAer before World War II

Before World War II, the Bureau of Aeronautics was a unique institution within the Navy. Its leaders were charged with developing and procuring aircraft; training pilots, crewmen, and maintenance personnel; working with Army aviators and the National Advisory Committee on Aeronautics to advance aviation research; and codifying aviation combat doctrine and routine flying procedures. Command of BuAer was in the hands of Navy officers, almost all of whom were qualified pilots.

As in the case of the Navy's Bureau of Ordnance (BuOrd), officers in charge of and manning the divisions of BuAer came from service in the fleet and returned to fleet assignments when their tours in the bureau were over. Also like BuOrd, BuAer had charge of a large government-owned industrial establishment, in BuAer's case the Naval Aircraft Factory in Philadelphia. But BuAer's primary aircraft suppliers were private firms, such as Grumman, Douglas, Consolidated, Curtiss, and Martin. The Naval Aircraft Factory built aircraft and other equipment (such as catapults) that the privately owned industrial base could not or would not provide.[1] To get high-performance aircraft, BuAer's basic strategy was to promote the development of high-horsepower aircraft engines and then invite the private aircraft manufacturers to build various types of planes around them. BuAer's periodic design competitions had led to improved piston-engine fighters and bombers for the Navy's carriers.

In 1937, what might be called the "aviation community"—composed of civilian and military pilots, engineers in the aircraft industry, a few scientists in universities such as the Massachusetts Institute of Technology (MIT), and aircraft and airline industry executives—was still relatively small. Officers in BuAer often were friends of their counterparts in industry. The exchange of information among them was usually rapid and informal, despite government regulations that formalized the process for procuring aircraft. In just a few years, this community would swell with a new generation of pilots, engineers, technical specialists, and executives. Within a decade, officers and civilian engineers in the U.S. Navy would be set on the task of bringing jet aircraft into the Navy's carrier force. None of these people could see that future in 1937—or even in 1940. Almost all were focused on developing, fielding, and flying the latest piston-engine planes.

In 1937, BuAer was led by a rear admiral. His immediate deputy was a Navy captain. Below them in the hierarchy were two major organizational branches—the Executive Branch, with divisions for planning, training, and Marine Corps aviation, and a Material Branch, with divisions for engineering, maintenance, lighter-than-air vehicles, and procurement. BuAer also contained an administrative section and a financial division. In January 1937, the Plans Division developed the requirements for new aircraft, in consultation with the Engineering Division. Working with the Flight Division, the officers in these other two offices served as intermediaries between the fleet and the aircraft production firms, translating fleet requirements into specifications that the Procurement Division would issue as the bases for periodic design competitions.[2]

Using this organization, the Navy had taken carrier aviation from its infancy to its adolescence. In the early 1920s, simulations at the Naval War College based on BuAer projections had shown the military potential of a "pulse" of striking power delivered by a carrier's planes. By 1929, using for the first time in a major fleet exercise the big carriers (and converted battle cruisers) *Saratoga* and *Lexington,* carrier commanders had shown that the potential of carriers suggested by the Naval War College simulations was attainable.[3] After that, what the Navy's aviators wanted from their bureau was more powerful aircraft with longer ranges. With two new carriers *(Yorktown* and *Enterprise)* under construction in 1937, officers like Cdr. Marc A. Mitscher, who headed BuAer's Flight Division, were working to provide them the best possible airplanes.

Both new carriers were designed for the pattern of flight operations first worked out on the experimental carrier *Langley* in 1925. Aircraft returning to the ship were taken aboard over the stern, then pushed forward to a "deck park" near the bow. A wire barrier was then hoisted into place behind the parked aircraft. It protected the aircraft in the deck park from being damaged by any plane that missed the cross-deck arresting-gear wires while attempting a landing. Once all planes were aboard, they were moved back to the after end of the flight deck and readied for their next sorties.[4]

Rapid Progress in Aircraft Performance Just before the War

Navy aviation benefited from the rolling cycle of war games, fleet exercises, and aircraft improvements in a number of ways. One of the most important was in the procurement of aircraft from private manufacturers. For example, the first carrier *(Ranger)* designed as such from the beginning was not large enough to carry the torpedo planes that had been flown from the much larger converted battle cruisers *Lexington* and

Saratoga. In 1934, therefore, as a means to give *Ranger* a serious strike capability, BuAer asked various manufacturers to submit designs for a new dive-bomber. Northrop won the competition in 1935 with its design of what became the XBT-1. This aircraft reached operational squadrons in April 1938. A modified version of this plane would become the famous Douglas SBD Dauntless of World War II fame.[5]

In 1931, when *Ranger*'s design was approved, the potential of torpedo planes seemed to be very limited. Yet the fleet problems suggested that an effective torpedo plane, operated in conjunction with bombers and fighters, posed a distinct threat to even the largest ships. Moreover, advances in aircraft engine technology indicated to officers in BuAer and to the members of the General Board that an improved torpedo plane could be built. Accordingly, BuAer issued a solicitation for torpedo plane designs in 1934. The strongest response to the solicitation was a design by Douglas Aircraft of the Navy's first monoplane attack aircraft—later christened the TBD Devastator. Though limited in range when carrying a thousand-pound torpedo, when it appeared the plane seemed a good match for the new carriers *Yorktown* and *Enterprise*.

The rapidly improving performance of radial air-cooled piston engines for carrier aircraft in the 1930s led to dramatic changes in aircraft performance, as illustrated by the following two charts. Figure 1-1 shows the steep increase in fighter speed from 1927 to 1941 for the three navies (USN, RN, and Imperial Japanese Navy) that possessed carriers. Figure 1-2 depicts the increase in service ceiling for selected fighters over the same period. This performance increase gave carrier aircraft dramatically improved fighting power.

Incremental improvements in engine horsepower, the switch from biplanes to monoplanes, and the effectiveness of hydraulic aircraft controls and streamlining yielded dramatic improvements in performance.[6] The fleet problems showed that it was essential for the Navy to take advantage of these improvements.

To do that, BuAer sponsored another dive-bomber design competition in 1938. The winners were the Curtiss XSB2C-1 and the Brewster XSB2A-1. The first became the well-known SB2C Helldiver, which was to be produced in great quantities in World War II. The Brewster design was developed as the SB2A Buccaneer, which was ordered as a prototype in April 1939, produced in limited quantities during the war, and never saw combat.

The dive-bomber competition was followed by one in 1939 for a new torpedo bomber. That competition produced two rival designs: Grumman's XTBF-1 Avenger and Chance Vought's XTBU-1 Sea Wolf (which was eventually produced by Consolidated Aircraft). Grumman signed the contract to produce the Avenger prototype in 1940, and the aircraft made its first flight in August 1941. The Sea Wolf's loaded weight was greater than

FIGURE 1-1
Fighter Speed, in Knots, for Selected Fighters—Royal Navy, U.S. Navy, and Imperial Japanese Navy

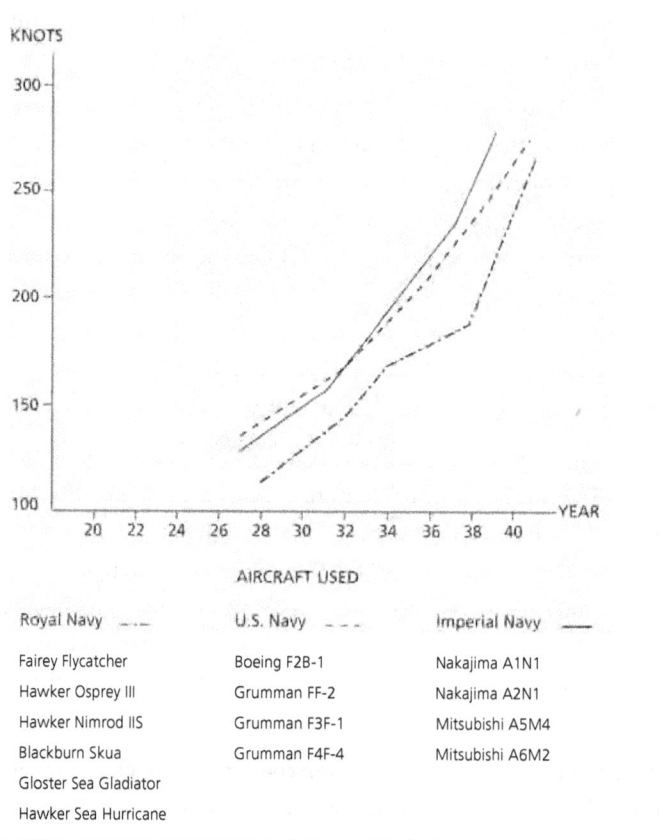

Source: Norman Friedman, *Carrier Air Power* (New York: Rutledge, 1981), app. 2.

the Avenger's, and its range with a torpedo was less, so the Avenger design was chosen by BuAer's evaluators as the basis of the bulk of Navy carrier heavy strike aircraft production during World War II. As in the case of the dive-bombers, the growth in capability from 1934 to 1939 was impressive. The Devastator design of 1934 could range only seven hundred miles carrying a thousand-pound torpedo. The TBF Avenger (the 1939 design) could fly 1,200 miles with a bomb or torpedo load of 1,600 pounds.[7]

Holding to its three-year dive-bomber design cycle, BuAer sponsored a third dive-bomber competition in 1941, before the United States entered World War II. Two prototypes came out of this competition: the Curtiss XSB3C-1 and the Douglas XSB2D-1. Curtiss stopped development of its prototype at the end of 1942. Douglas signed a contract in 1941 for the development of its prototype and flew the plane for the first time

FIGURE 1-2
Service Ceiling, in Feet, for Selected Fighters—Royal Navy, U.S. Navy, and Imperial Japanese Navy

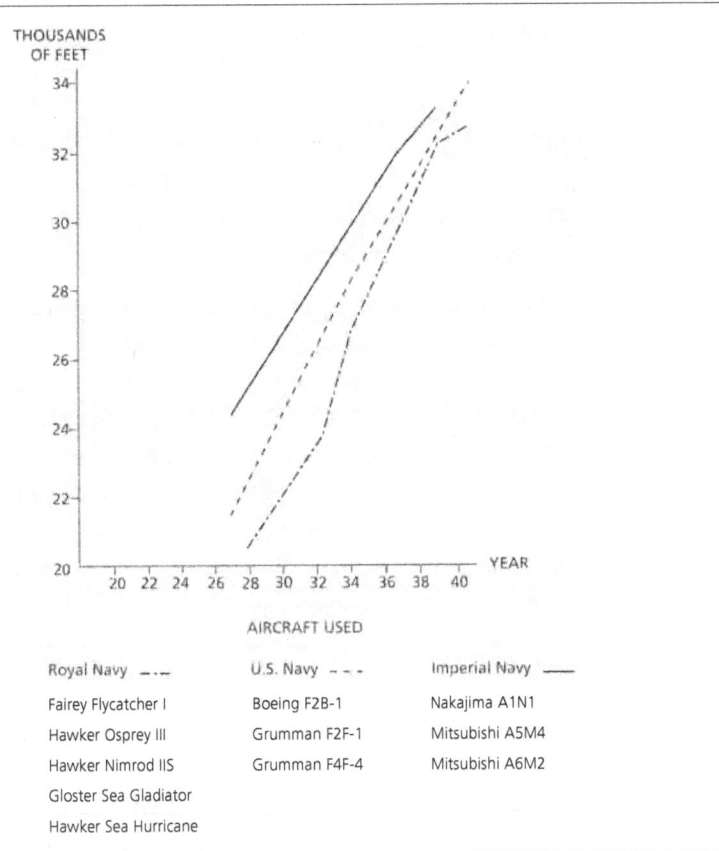

Source: Friedman, Carrier Air Power, app. 2.

in April 1943, as the BTD-1. A modification of the BTD-1 eventually became the XBT2D-1 Sky Pirate in 1944, and a further modification of the Sky Pirate became the famous Douglas AD-1 Skyraider, ordered into production in April 1945. The process created in the 1920s to tap the results of war games and fleet exercises to set the requirements for new aircraft had worked.

Challenges to BuAer Starting in 1941

By 1941, Marc Mitscher had been promoted to captain and was assistant chief of BuAer under the bureau's nationally known head, Rear Adm. John Towers. Other younger aviation pioneers had also been promoted. Alfred M. Pride, a catapult designer, was now a commander and the staff officer representing Rear Admiral Towers on the Aeronautical

Board, where his task was to facilitate Army–Navy cooperation. Capt. DeWitt Ramsey was head of the Plans Division in BuAer; his counterpart in the Procurement Division was Cdr. Lawrence Richardson. Mitscher, Ramsey, and Richardson were part of an "inner circle" advising BuAer chief Towers, along with Capt. Sidney Kraus, head of the Material Branch in BuAer, and up-and-coming Lt. George Anderson, who would eventually (in 1961) become Chief of Naval Operations.[8] A bright young engineer by the name of George Spangenberg worked directly under William Z. Frisbie, the respected head of the Design Coordination and Contract Airplane Design section in BuAer's Engineering Division. Spangenberg described Frisbie "as the senior technical advisor to the command structure of the Bureau of Aeronautics."[9]

These officers and civilians were preoccupied with the tasks of preparing the U.S. Navy for participation in a coalition that would fight and win World War II. Some numbers reveal the extent to which Navy and Marine Corps aviation changed between 1937 and 1941. In 1937 the Navy had 972 combat aircraft, 113 transport and utility planes, and 161 trainers.[10] The figures for 1941 were 1,774, 183, and 1,444, respectively. In 1937 the Navy had 1,260 pilots; the Marines had 142. In 1941, the Navy had 4,112 pilots, and the Marines had 480.[11] When Rear Admiral Towers was appointed chief of BuAer in June 1939, he had under his command sixty-six officers and 171 civilians. By the summer of 1941, he had 176 officers and 518 civilians, many of them crammed into the rather primitive BuAer spaces in "Main Navy" on Constitution Avenue in Washington, D.C.[12]

Towers and his subordinates faced wide-ranging and ambitious requirements. They had simultaneously to ramp up the production of aircraft, recruit and train hundreds of new pilots, construct new bases for training and for combat use, and find ways to distribute the aircraft being produced among the Army, Navy, and foreign buyers (then mainly Great Britain, France, and China). They also had to fund research and development of new aviation technologies. All of this had to be done in peacetime, often against strong congressional opposition. In 1940, for example, Admiral Towers could not persuade Congress to fund a five-year program of Navy aeronautical research, "especially in the revolutionary field of jet propulsion."[13]

Selected Navy officers discovered just how important that research could be, when they were briefed by Sir Henry Tizard and his colleagues in Washington in September 1940. The "Tizard Mission" showed the Americans a working cavity magnetron. The Naval Research Laboratory had already developed and tested lower-power air search radars, so the American officers and scientists knew how important the cavity magnetron was. (To exploit its potential, the Americans would set up what became known as the Radiation Laboratory at MIT. Together, researchers at the laboratory and engineers in such firms as General Electric would develop and produce a series of effective microwave radars.) Tizard's staff also showed their American counterparts the specifications of the turbojet engine developed by Frank Whittle. That led the National Advisory Committee for Aeronautics (NACA) to cooperate with the Army and Navy in expanding the limited research into jet propulsion starting in the summer of 1941.[14]

The key point, however, is that American army and naval aviators and their civilian colleagues had their hands full in 1941. In his detailed biography of BuAer chief Towers, historian Clark Reynolds notes that "Towers was lukewarm to diverting funds, personnel, and precious time to unproved concepts."[15] Given all the work Towers and his command had to do to prepare for war, the admiral's reluctance to support "unproved concepts" should come as no surprise. Towers, his subordinates, and their successors in BuAer faced a huge task—acquiring thousands of first-rate aircraft and the pilots to man them, as well as the maintenance personnel to support a huge naval air force. The 1,774 combat aircraft force of 1941 mushroomed to one of 29,125 combat aircraft by 1945. The number of Navy pilots jumped from 4,112 in 1941 to 49,819 in 1945, and the number of Marine pilots increased from 480 to 10,276 in the same time period. The number of enlisted personnel needed to support this dramatic growth went from 13,691 (both Navy and Marines) in 1941 to 337,718 in 1945.[16]

The First Signs of an Impending Crisis

The Bureau of Aeronautics had developed "standard operating procedures" in the years before World War II to harness the skills of scientists, engineers, and airplane manufacturers on behalf of carrier aviation. BuAer's design competitions and its investments in piston-engine development promoted incremental but dramatic improvement in the performance of fighter and attack aircraft. Yet the process of learning to operate these constantly improving aircraft from carriers, and then using the planes to defeat an enemy, was dogged by great uncertainty.

For example, in 1935 and 1936 there was a serious debate among carrier aviators about the proper design of fighter aircraft for carrier squadrons. Carriers were mainly offensive weapons. In 1935 and 1936 (and even in the spring of 1941), no navy knew how to protect a carrier from an effective strike staged by opposing carrier-based bombers. If a carrier had lots of fighters for defense, then its strike potential went down. If its strike potential—indicated by the number of bombers and torpedo planes it carried—was high, then its airborne defense was weak. Navy aerial strike doctrine in 1935 was clear: "In naval warfare control of the air is obtained through destruction of the enemies [sic] carriers, tenders, and bases, as his air strength can be reduced much more effectively in this manner than by attrition in the air."[17] That implied using fighters as escorts for the bombers and not as defensive weapons, especially given the fact that existing fighters were hardly faster than the bombers they were supposed to shoot down.

At the same time, the fleet's aviators wanted BuAer to continue fighter development "in order to be in a position to capitalize on it should developments warrant."[18] As the commander of the fleet's carrier squadrons put it in a memorandum to the Commander in Chief, U.S. Fleet, in April 1936, "The need for speed [in fighters] cannot be overstressed. It is the first and fundamental requirement in a fighting airplane and no other characteristic is of equal importance in the design."[19] Put another way, "protection of aircraft formations is not an efficient or desirable use of single-seat [fighters]."[20] The U.S. fleet commander in chief, Adm. Joseph M. Reeves, endorsed the letter with these comments: "I agree with every word. Sound, logical & unanswerable."[21] In May 1936, Admiral Reeves sent a confidential letter to the Chief of Naval Operations, through the chief of BuAer, stating his views in strong language: "No fleet commander can give carrier space and personnel to squadrons of so-called fighters that cannot destroy enemy planes and are equally worthless for other uses. And yet, no fleet commander can submit passively to the attacks of enemy bombers. *THE FLEET MUST HAVE AIRPLANES THAT CAN FIGHT OTHER AIRPLANES.*"[22] The Naval War College war games and the actual fleet problems had led Reeves to this insight.

BuAer's response, however, was not initially positive. Officers in the Plans and Engineering divisions took issue with the commander in chief's argument as they reviewed his proposal in late May and June 1936. Commander Mitscher, then head of the Flight Division in BuAer, summed up the bureau's concerns by saying that "one fighter squadron per carrier should be discontinued until this argument is settled. Keep sufficient fighters on say [sic] two carriers to carry on the development."[23] To keep development alive, the Plans Division of BuAer asked the Engineering Division in October 1936 to conduct a preliminary design study of a supercharged twin-engine, heavily armed fighter.[24] Rear Adm. Arthur B. Cook, BuAer's chief, took the next step in February 1937, by directing the assistant chief of BuAer to plan on developing a "two-engine single seat fighter."[25] Accordingly, the bureau issued a "Request for Competitive Designs and Proposals" to industry in March 1937 that called for a two-engine, single-seat fighter with four .50-caliber guns, a landing speed of 65 mph, and an economical speed range of a thousand miles.[26]

Industry's response was not seen as satisfactory. Part of the difficulty lay with the bureau, as Captain Kraus, head of the Material Branch, pointed out to the assistant chief of BuAer on 23 July 1937: "The maximum speed of prospective shore-based bombers is derived from supercharging at high altitude. In order to utilize carrier-based fighters against them, the fighters must be supercharged to equivalent altitude. The Bureau design of two-engined fighters did not adopt this means of obtaining performance."[27] However, the basic problem wasn't BuAer's. Instead, it was the fleet's. Fleet air commanders wanted the landing speed of carrier aircraft kept to 65 mph *without power*—that is, the pilot, on getting the "cut" signal from the landing signal officer, was supposed to shut down his engine just before his plane engaged the carrier's arresting gear. As Captain Kraus pointed out, this requirement was keeping BuAer and industry from developing very high-powered aircraft with supercharging and high wing loadings.

What was needed as the basis of an adequate carrier-based interceptor was supercharging (for high-altitude performance) and high wing loading—which meant a heavier twin-engine plane that *landed with its engines still turning over*. As Kraus put it, "The use of power in deck landings permits the twin-engined design to develop its inherent superiority in performance." Moreover, "it does not follow that the operating units would not be willing to adopt a different landing technique in exchange for outstanding results in performance." As Kraus wrote, "The consistent use of power in landing is believed to be a reasonable development."[28]

But if the heavier, twin-engine aircraft (fighters or bombers) were to land with power on in order to give their pilots more control, the whole concept of the deck park forward on the flight deck would have to be reconsidered. As noted above, a plane that missed the arresting-gear wires would be stopped by the wires that formed a barrier across the flight deck and shielded aircraft that had already landed. But if a relatively large plane, landing with its engines running, hit the deck at a speed greater than sixty-five miles per hour and bounced over the arresting-gear wires stretched across the deck, it might hurdle over the barrier as well and pile into the planes parked forward. Kraus was well aware of this possible danger, and as a result he recommended that "experiments in deck landing with existing twin-engined aircraft regardless of their military suitability are indicated, if only for prudence."[29]

Here was a clue to the future of carrier operations: larger, heavier, more powerful planes landing at higher speeds with their engines still running. Kraus did not favor this option in 1937. He wanted an aircraft like the F8F Bearcat that Grumman developed in 1944—a lightweight but high-powered single-engine plane with a rapid rate of climb, a powerful armament, and a relatively low landing speed. But industry had yet to produce the sort of engine that could power such a plane, and there is no evidence that senior officers took Kraus's memorandum for what it was—a vision of a very different future for carrier operations.

Instead, BuAer kept after the concept of a small, light plane with high speed and enough endurance to serve as a defensive fighter. NACA's Director of Aeronautical Research supported the effort, saying in April 1940 that "a fighter-type airplane can be designed, using a radial air-cooled engine, which will weigh between 4,000 and 5,000 pounds and will have a speed of 400 miles per hour."[30] BuAer's Plans and Engineering divisions had been studying the feasibility of such a design, and they summed up their analyses in a July 1940 memorandum to BuAer chief Towers.[31] As the memorandum pointed out, the key to high performance in an interceptor was the engine, and the most powerful of the recent engine designs—pushing two thousand horsepower—were heavy and consumed a lot of fuel. To get a lighter, smaller plane, the Navy would have to either find a way to get great power from a dramatically lighter engine or accept significantly reduced endurance from a plane that carried less fuel. In addition, the interceptor would need a heavy armament, and the machine guns and their ammunition would add to the plane's weight. In short, the combat requirements of high speed, rapid rate of climb, firepower, and endurance led logically to a larger, heavier airplane like the XF4U-1—and even beyond it to heavier twin-engine designs. To make matters worse, these powerful aircraft would have to land (with engine power off) at relatively high speeds—at least 75 mph.

The design of the airplane was beginning to tax the physical capabilities of existing and planned carriers and their equipment. In July 1940, the heads of BuAer's Plans and Engineering divisions knew what they wanted: "a further extension in range and power of our striking force, involving basic ranges of 1,500 rather than one thousand miles with fuel for a minimum of 2,250 miles in all types, and more effective and powerful offensive weapons." They also believed that "advances in power plants and aerodynamics" would allow them to attain the goal of "providing a homogeneous carrier force which can strike a heavier total blow at a greater distance."[32] They did not discuss the operational and technological implications of their efforts to develop improved airplanes for long-range attacks. Yet this was just the kind of question that the General Board had assessed and reassessed all through the 1930s. BuAer's division heads—focused as they were on aircraft performance—did not see operational and technological trade-offs as the challenges they would soon become.

Notes

1. For a history of the Naval Aircraft Factory, see William F. Trimble, *Wings for the Navy: A History of the Naval Aircraft Factory, 1917–1956* (Annapolis, Md.: Naval Institute Press, 1990).

2. See Bureau of Navigation, *Navy Directory*, 1 January 1937 (Washington, D.C.: U.S. Government Printing Office, 1937), pp. 234–35.

3. See Charles M. Melhorn, *Two-Block Fox: The Rise of the Aircraft Carrier, 1911–1929* (Annapolis, Md.: Naval Institute Press, 1974).

4. Robert J. Cressman, *USS Ranger: The Navy's First Flattop from Keel to Mast, 1934–1946* (Washington, D.C.: Brassey's, 2003).

5. Data on aircraft are from Gordon Swanborough and Peter M. Bowers, *United States Navy Aircraft since 1911* (Annapolis, Md.: Naval Institute Press, 1976); and Ray Wagner, *American Combat Planes*, 3rd ed. (New York: Doubleday, 1982). The design

competitions are described in "Naval Aviation Confidential Bulletin," no. 3-49 (July 1949), pp. 15–17, in the collection of the Naval Aviation History Office, Washington Navy Yard, Washington, D.C.

6. Edward H. Heinemann and Rosario Rausa, *Ed Heinemann, Combat Aircraft Designer* (Annapolis, Md.: Naval Institute Press, 1980), p. 44. Heinemann noted that incremental improvements to the BT-1 suggested by BuAer's Lt. Cdr. Walter S. Diehl helped Douglas engineers turn the BT-1 into the more effective SBD-1.

7. Swanborough and Bowers, *United States Navy Aircraft since 1911,* pp. 165–66, 213–16.

8. See the *Navy Directory,* 1 April 1941. Also see Clark G. Reynolds, *Admiral John H. Towers: The Struggle for Naval Air Supremacy* (Annapolis, Md.: Naval Institute Press, 1991), p. 597 note 56.

9. George A. Spangenberg, "Oral History," 31 August 1997, *George Spangenberg Oral History,* 2010, www.georgespangenberg.com, p. 30.

10. Roy Grossnick, *United States Naval Aviation, 1910–1995,* 4th ed. (Washington, D.C.: Naval Historical Center, 1997), app. 4, "Aircraft on Hand, 1920–1965," p. 448.

11. Ibid., app. 10, "Aviation Personnel on Active Duty," p. 593.

12. Reynolds, *Admiral John H. Towers,* pp. 294, 356.

13. Ibid., p. 301.

14. David Zimmerman, *Top Secret Exchange: The Tizard Mission and the Scientific War* (Montreal: McGill–Queen's University Press and Alan Sutton, 1996), pp. 147, 192.

15. Reynolds, *Admiral John H. Towers,* p. 382.

16. Grossnick, *United States Naval Aviation,* apps. 4 and 10.

17. Commander VF Squadron Five-B, letter to Chief of the Bureau of Aeronautics, via Commander Officer, U.S.S. Lexington, and Commander Aircraft, Battle Force, subject "Employment of the Two-Seater Fighter Airplane in Carrier Operations," Fleet Problem XVI, 22 May 1935, A4-3/VF/VF5B/CV, para. 11.

18. Ibid., para. 15.

19. Commander Aircraft, Battle Force, letter to Commander in Chief, U.S. Fleet, subject "Fighting Airplanes—Value to the Fleet," 4 April 1936, A4-3/11-Mn/FF2-3, para. 5.

20. Ibid., para. 10(a).

21. Ibid., para. 13, p. 13.

22. Commander-in-Chief, United States Fleet, letter to Chief of Naval Operations, via Chief of the Bureau of Aeronautics, subject "Fighting Airplanes—Value to Fleet," file no. F/2491, 9 May 1936, para. 10.

23. Mitscher's comment was handwritten at the bottom of a typed "comment" on the commander in chief's recommendation.

24. Plans, memorandum to Engineering, via Chief of the Bureau of Aeronautics, subject "Two-engine VF, request for design study," file Aer-PL-3-KMN, 30 October 1936.

25. Chief of BuAer, memorandum to Assistant Chief, subject "Experimental Plane Program for 1938," ABC-GB, 12 February 1937.

26. Aer-Pr-3-CW/BA (VF), 18 March 1937, subject "Class VF Airplanes—Request for Competitive Designs and Proposals."

27. Material, memorandum to Chief of Bureau, via Plans and Assistant Chief of Bureau, subject "Comments on Twin-Engined Fighter," Aer-M-1-KP, 23 July 1937.

28. Ibid., paras. 7 and 8, p. 3.

29. Ibid., para. 12.

30. National Advisory Committee for Aeronautics, letter to Chief of the Bureau of Aeronautics, subject "Design study of high-speed fighter-type airplane using a radial air-cooled engine," National 5212, 30 April 1940.

31. Plans and Engineering, memorandum to Chief of the Bureau of Aeronautics, subject "Experimental Fighter Procurement," Aer-E-2-VML, 27 July 1940.

32. Ibid., "Conclusion," pp. 27–28.

BuAer in World War II

During World War II, the Bureau of Aeronautics tried to accelerate its peacetime process of development. This effort largely failed. In peacetime, the transition from an attack-aircraft design competition to the first operational aircraft took about three years. Unfortunately for the Navy and BuAer, this schedule could not be compressed, because the fleet's wartime requirements shifted dramatically while the aircraft industry was trying to produce new prototypes and thousands of approved aircraft models. For example, BuAer ordered prototypes of the Curtiss XBTC-2, an attack aircraft capable of carrying a large torpedo 1,200 miles, in December 1943. But as the August 1944 *Naval Aviation Confidential Bulletin* pointed out, "changes in requirements and progress in equipment and materials during the two-and-one-half year period of development . . . made the airplane obsolete in many respects."[1]

This turn of events should not have surprised anyone in BuAer. One reason the development of the XBTC-2 was delayed was that BuAer directed Curtiss in the summer of 1942 to put a surface-search radar into the XBTC-1 and XBTC-2 so that the planes could more easily find enemy targets. This had been a "lesson learned" from the battles of the Coral Sea and Midway. Unfortunately, early models of such radars were relatively large and heavy, and placing them on the prototypes added so much time to the planes' development and testing schedules that the XBTC-1 was canceled in 1943 and the XBTC-2 was dropped from the Navy's aviation program after the end of World War II.[2]

Moreover, there was a conflict between quantity (getting enough airplanes for the war) and quality (getting airplanes that were good enough to hold their own with anything that the enemy put up). As a consequence, the manufacturers adopted a strategy of research and design that emphasized integrating improved components into production aircraft. This strategy had two important implications. First, it fostered the accumulation of improvements over short time periods, by which each new aircraft model maintained a rough parity or increased its advantage against enemy aircraft. Second, the strategy complemented the ability of U.S. industrial engineers to crank out a great many planes and trainers for newly recruited pilots. Demands for improved aircraft were met quickly; mass production mattered more than revolutionary design. Curtiss, for example, instead of investing its engineering talent and its capital in ventures like the XSB3C-1, worked on refining and improving the SB2C Helldiver—developing and manufacturing almost a thousand SB2C-1s, over 1,100 SB2C-3s, more than two thousand SB2C-4s, and over nine hundred SB2C-5s.[3] Similarly, Grumman poured talent, time, and money into its TBF/TBM Avenger, producing TBF-2s and TBF-3s with more powerful engines and various modified Avengers for photo reconnaissance and radar search and warning.[4]

In short, developing brand-new aircraft was more risky than upgrading existing models. The large amount of information that flowed into organizations like BuAer from the fighting forces overwhelmed the procedures that had been used to collect, analyze, integrate, and transmit information that designers needed to create new airplanes. As Navy historian Lee M. Pearson pointed out in 1951, "so various were the sources [of information] that it is impossible to trace the flow of information [into BuAer]. The official reports of task forces and CinCPac [Commander in Chief, Pacific], the action reports of the squadrons, special reports, and interviews with officers upon their return from the war theaters were among the chief sources."[5] BuAer civilian engineers and their aviator colleagues faced a dilemma. On the one hand, they did their best to assess what was happening in combat and use their assessments to improve developing and in-production aircraft. On the other hand, once they nailed down a set of required or desired specifications, they "fixed" what historian Pearson rightly called "the direction of development" for at least eighteen months—no matter what was happening in combat or promised to come out of laboratory research.[6]

An indicator of this problem is BuAer's effort during the war to prompt industry to develop large, very-long-range, single-seat attack aircraft. In 1943, the bureau asked Curtiss, Kaiser-Fleetwing, and Martin to build the planned successors to the SB2C Helldiver. The characteristics of the three prototypes are listed in table 2-1, along with comparative characteristics for the in-production SB2C.[7]

TABLE 2-1
Characteristics of Aircraft to Replace the SB2C

CHARACTERISTICS	CURTISS SB2C-1C	CURTISS XBTC-2	KAISER-FLEETWING XBTK-1	MARTIN XBTM-1
Design gross weight in lbs.	14,720	17,910	12,728	19,000
Designed range in miles	1,100 with 1,000-lb. bomb	1,200 with torpedo	1,200 with torpedo	1,200 with torpedo
Prototype date	1940	1946	1945	1944

With the exception of the Kaiser-Fleetwing XBTK-1, the single-seat successors to the multiseat SB2C Helldiver were larger and heavier than the original. The XBTK-1 was intended for use on escort carriers, and so its design reversed the trend toward larger, single-seat carrier aircraft that could carry either bombs or torpedoes.[8]

BuAer's 1943 requests to industry were a wartime improvisation.[9] BuAer, acting on what civilian engineer George Spangenberg termed "invaluable" information from the fleet—from combat—was trying to provide the operating forces with planes that could range farther and faster and carry more ordnance.[10] But the 1943 initiative was based on assessment of 1942 operations—that is, on carrier operations that preceded the deployment of the SB2C Helldiver as the mainstay of carrier dive-bomber squadrons. The peacetime cycle of design competitions, prototype testing, deployment, and assessment of experience could not be followed during the war, and BuAer in 1943 was in the unenviable position of trying to develop a successor to a dive-bomber (the SB2C Helldiver) that had not even been deployed. As Spangenberg recalled, "most of the procurement rules got suspended."[11]

Very important were informal contacts between BuAer personnel and industry engineers. These contacts were facilitated by the intelligence and technical experience of the people on both sides of the relationship. Both Spangenberg and Douglas designer Edward Heinemann, for example, noted in their respective memoirs the creativity of Cdr. (later Capt.) Walter S. Diehl, who was the senior aerodynamicist in BuAer in 1941 and the author of a pioneering study entitled *Engineering Aerodynamics*.[12] Spangenberg also held Heinemann in high regard. As he said in his oral history, "Heinemann's real strength was a good understanding of the entire airplane. He did a superb job of trying to find out what the Navy needed and trying to give them what they needed and he also had a superb engineering organization."[13] On his part, Spangenberg aided Douglas by helping Heinemann's assistant, Leo Devlin, learn how Heinemann and his colleagues—acting as the Navy's agents—could gain major benefits from a comprehensive aircraft weight reduction and control program.[14]

Informal contacts and conversations between government and industry engineers did not, however, completely displace the formal processes of acquisition. BuAer engineers and Navy pilots fresh from operations kept control of the way that performance requirements were drawn up, and the engineers working in industry had to design and build to specifications and standards set by the BuAer staff. One exception to this was the development by Boeing of the XF8B-1. As Spangenberg remembered, "The F8B was started with an unsolicited proposal from Boeing," whose chief engineer, Wellwood E. Beall, had decided that he and his colleagues could produce a better long-range fighter design if they were free of the Navy's normally mandatory specifications and standards.

"Boeing set the configuration," according to Spangenberg, but the plane was, in his words, "inferior as a naval carrier airplane."[15]

A more recent study of this airplane's history takes a different view—that the Navy actually encouraged Boeing in the firm's effort and that "Boeing generally made a good faith effort to meet the requirements of a specification that was, in fact, unsound."[16] Our point is that this particular design was the product of an extemporized development process accepted by BuAer officials because the routine peacetime process was inadequate for wartime needs. As Edward Heinemann notes in his memoir, he and his counterparts in industry therefore worked under intense "pressures of competition, reinforced by the demands of war and, in no little way, patriotic overzealousness."[17]

BuAer aggressively pursued ever larger and heavier aircraft both before and during the war. This trend also extended to fighters, as table 2-2 shows.[18]

TABLE 2-2
BuAer's Fighter Aircraft Characteristics, 1936–43

AIRCRAFT	INITIAL CONTRACT	GROSS WEIGHT (LBS.)	RANGE (STATUTE MI.)
Grumman F4F Wildcat	1936	8,000 for the F4F-4	770
Grumman XF5F-1 Skyrocket	1938	10,000 for prototype	780
Vought XF5U-1 Flying Flapjack	1939	16,700 for nonflying prototype	700
Vought F4U Corsair	1938	12,000 for F4U-1D	1,000
Grumman F6F Hellcat	1941	13,000 for F6F-5	945
Grumman F7F Tigercat	1941	25,700	1,200
Boeing XF8B-1	1943	20,500	2,780
Grumman F8F-1 Bearcat	1943	9,400	1,100

The trend is clear: with the exception of the F8F-1 Bearcat, the fighters got heavier and larger, and their range grew. The Grumman F7F Tigercat was a twin-engine airplane, and the Boeing XF8B-1, though designed as a long-range fighter, was seen by BuAer as a fighter-bomber. The F8F-1 Bearcat was a deck-launched interceptor, designed to get into the air quickly and climb to high altitude before enemy attack aircraft could overwhelm a carrier's limited defensive combat air patrol.

The growth in size and weight of Navy carrier aircraft is even more apparent when the various Navy heavy fighters and bombers are compared with land-based Army bombers deployed in combat in 1942. Table 2-3 compares the Army's A-20A and B-25 bombers with the larger Navy prototype and production carrier fighters and bombers.[19]

TABLE 2-3
Comparison of Navy Aircraft with Army 1942 Models

AIRCRAFT	YEAR PROTOTYPE COMPLETED	DESIGNED GROSS WEIGHT (IN LBS.)	RANGE (IN MI.) WITH ORDNANCE (IN LBS.)
A-20A Havoc	1939	19,750	525 with 2,400
B-25 Mitchell	1940	26,208	1,300 with 3,000
SB2C-1C Helldiver	1940	14,720	1,110 with 1,000
TBF-1 Avenger	1940	13,667	1,215 with 2,000
F7F Tigercat	1943	25,720	1,200 with 2,000
XBTC-2	1946	17,910	1,245 with 2,000
XBTM-1	1944	19,000	1,200 with 2,000
BTD-1	1945	18,140	1,480 with 2,000
XF8B-1	1944	20,700	1,070 with 2,000

Navy aircraft developed during the war became rough equivalents of the early-war Army models. They grew progressively larger and heavier and carried very impressive ordnance loads. Indeed, they even began to outgrow the ability of the CV 9 (*Essex*)–class carriers to launch and recover them safely and efficiently.

Events in 1942 suggested to BuAer's leaders that even larger carrier aircraft were required, and so the bureau officially asked Grumman to develop a twin-engine torpedo bomber for use from carriers.[20] This was the XTB2F-1, which only in 1944 was assembled as an engineering mock-up so that Grumman and BuAer engineers could get an accurate estimate of the plane's weight and dimensions. If built, it would have had a loaded weight of about forty-five thousand pounds and a range of approximately three thousand miles (although sources differ on the XTB2F-1's estimated range). Its wingspan would have been slightly greater than that of the B-25 (seventy-four feet versus sixty-seven feet seven inches) and its length about the same (fifty-two feet). With a height of just over twenty-one feet, it could not have fit into the hangar deck of a carrier of the CV 9 class, and its estimated weight was too great for that carrier's flight deck, elevators, and arresting gear.[21] But it could carry four two-thousand-pound bombs or two torpedoes. That is, it had almost three times the range of the B-25 Mitchell and over twice the ordnance load. Put another way, it was a carrier-based bomber with *operational* (versus tactical) range and firepower.

This emphasis on operational range and firepower can be traced to the Doolittle Raid from carrier *Hornet* in April 1942, but later wartime experience reinforced the desire to develop a long-range carrier strike aircraft that could tap the operational mobility that the U.S. carrier forces developed in 1944 through the use of underway refueling and replenishment. In his report on the operations of his carrier task forces off Okinawa in the spring of 1945, for example, Vice Adm. Marc Mitscher noted that his carriers had "operated daily in a 60 mile square area East of Okinawa, less than 350 miles from Kyushu," where they were vulnerable to both air and submarine attack.[22] With longer-range aircraft, his carriers could have maneuvered both to avoid attack and also to surprise Japanese defenders with air attacks that came from ocean areas other than those near Okinawa.

After the war, Mitscher added another argument in favor of large carriers with very-long-range attack aircraft. As he wrote to Adm. DeWitt Ramsey, "The only two times I was really in trouble with the task force occurred in the first and second battles of the Philippine Seas [*sic*], in which battles my forces were dispersed to such an extent that we could not concentrate and it proved a considerable handicap in my future movements. I was impressed with the absolute necessity of *quick* concentration, particularly when operating against so many shore bases."[23] This is an example of what today is referred to as "operational art"—the combining of concepts such as maneuver and firepower and their application through the theater-level use of forces. It was the vision of carriers able to strike enemy targets *from long range* and then move quickly over great distances to recover their long-range aircraft that had inspired U.S. naval aviators for a long time. Only with the combination of modern carriers, long-range aircraft, and underway replenishment was this vision realistic. Unfortunately, as Mitscher knew, the really long-range aircraft were late in coming. The Doolittle Raid, instead of being a harbinger of massed strikes by large, long-range carrier aircraft, remained just a hint of what might be done.

The trend toward ever larger and heavier carrier aircraft was to some degree masked by two developments. The first was the modification of existing designs in response to wartime experience. In late 1944, for example, Grumman proposed to BuAer that the firm modify the existing TBF Avenger into a single-seat attack aircraft, the XTB3F-1. BuAer had originally suggested to Grumman that the large F7F Tigercat fighter be converted into a torpedo bomber. Grumman's response was to emphasize the potential of the proven Avenger. BuAer accepted that argument, and the XTB3F-1 became the AF Guardian after World War II. The second—and very important—development was the use of carrier fighters as bombers. The F4U-4 Corsair, for example, could carry a maximum of two 1,000-pound bombs, though it usually flew with no more than one. In effect, the Corsair did double duty as both high-performance fighter and attack and ground-support plane. It filled a role that, in 1942, BuAer had thought could be filled only by new bomber designs.[24]

There were other consequences of wartime development. One rarely mentioned was the provision of new catapults for the fleet, light, and escort carriers by the Naval Aircraft Factory's Ship Experimental Unit. The factory's "engineering department had responsibility for the design and manufacture" of catapults (including those for cruisers and battleships), but the Ship Experimental Unit actually tested and installed them.[25] During the war, engineers at the Naval Aircraft Factory "continued to look for alternatives to the hydraulic-pneumatic catapults [then in use], which were heavy and had complicated cable-and-sheave systems requiring careful adjustment and constant maintenance."[26] Of the two primary but tentative alternatives to existing catapults, one was driven by electricity and one was built around the concept of a "slotted cylinder."

In December 1944, BuAer directed the catapult developers to begin work on a small slotted-cylinder catapult to launch target drones. This work was to pay major dividends *after* the war, when "existing hydraulic catapults had reached the limits of their capacity."[27] But the point to keep in mind is the reservoir of experience that engineers at the Naval Aircraft Factory and its experimental station built up during their years of work on aircraft catapults. A partial list of their efforts—covering only the flush-deck catapults for aircraft carriers and the slotted-cylinder type used for launching target drones—is given in table 2-4.[28]

BuAer had also encouraged the Naval Aircraft Factory to develop large catapults mounted on barges that could launch heavily loaded seaplanes. In 1942, for example, the factory had produced the Type XH, Mark III, a hydro-pneumatic device that could accelerate a sixty-thousand-pound aircraft to 120 mph over a 248-foot track.[29] But the catapult weighed nine hundred thousand pounds—450 tons—and so the engineers at the factory searched for a far less bulky aid to takeoffs. What they came up with was JATO (jet-assisted takeoff), involving disposable chemical accelerators or rockets attached to the airplanes. The success of the JATO units eliminated the need for a large

TABLE 2-4
Catapults Developed by the Naval Aircraft Factory, 1936–45

CATAPULT TYPE	YEARS	LENGTH (IN FT.)	CAPACITY (LBS. PER MPH)	WEIGHT (LBS.)
Hydro-pneumatic, Type H, Mark II	1936–37	55	7,000 at 70	50,000
Hydro-pneumatic, Type H, Mark II, Mod. I	1942–45	73	11,000 at 70	65,000
Hydro-pneumatic, Type H, Mark IVB	1942–45	96.6	18,000 at 90	233,000
Slotted cylinder XAT, Mark II	1945	33	300 at 70	5,855

and extremely heavy catapult. JATO units would be very useful after the war, especially with early jet aircraft.

There is one additional consequence of wartime aircraft and related equipment development that we must mention: the effects on people responsible for doing the work. As Lee Pearson pointed out in 1951, the orderly process of prewar design competitions, prototype development, and prototype testing was drastically modified because of the pressure to produce thousands of aircraft and because of the desire of the fleet and BuAer to make best use of improved aircraft design and technology and the lessons learned by combat pilots.[30]

These twin pressures often shaped the careers of relatively inexperienced young officers. Pearson cites the experiences of BuAER's Lt. Cdr. Joseph N. Murphy, who had started in BuAer's Engineering Division as a lieutenant and was selected to head scout-bomber design at the end of 1941 or the beginning of 1942. Pearson argues that Murphy personally began the process of analysis that shifted BuAer from a focus on slower, two-man, unescorted dive-bombers and torpedo planes to one on single-seat escorted attack aircraft that could carry heavy bomb loads from the CV 9s.[31] Pearson points to a January 1942 conference of officers from BuAer's Plans and Engineering divisions as the point at which BuAer personnel reached a consensus about the future of attack aircraft mission requirements. That consensus led to larger, heavier, single-seat attack aircraft that could launch torpedoes as well as drop bombs. Indirectly, the January decision, endorsed by Rear Admiral Towers in February 1942, led to the postwar Douglas AD-1 Skyraider and the Martin AM-1 Mauler.

BuAer carried its prewar organization into the initial months of World War II. When Lieutenant Commander Murphy was making his case for a fast, single-place attack plane in late December 1941, the head of the Experiments and Developments Section in BuAer's Engineering Division was Cdr. Leslie C. Stevens. The head of the Engineering Division was Capt. J. E. Ostrander. Ostrander, Stevens, and Murphy had to coordinate their work on a new attack-aircraft concept with the Plans Division, the Operating Requirements Branch of the Plans Division, and with their own Engineering Division colleagues who were specialists in aircraft engines and aircraft structures.[32] As Pearson points out, this coordination took place through face-to-face conferences within BuAer.

But such conferences placed a lot of responsibility on the shoulders of rather young officers and their civilian colleagues. The aforementioned Joseph N. Murphy, for example, was a lieutenant in April 1941, a lieutenant commander by February 1942, a full commander by late November 1942, and a captain by war's end. Such rapid promotion was common in World War II, but it came *despite* a lack of participation in multiple design competitions. The cycle of competitions—from prototype selection to tests of prototype aircraft, to full-scale production, and then to evaluation of operational experience—was designed to deliver to the fleet tested and *proven* aircraft. The pace of wartime decision making, with a series of conferences serving as an arena of negotiation among representatives of BuAer's branches, forced compromises with the prewar pattern of identifying requirements, soliciting potential solutions from industry, and then carefully testing prototype aircraft. The documentation of the process of developing new aircraft was often so ad hoc, hurried, and informal that even Pearson, the official historian, had problems tracing the course of events. Perhaps it is amazing that the process "worked" at all.

In his memoir, Edward Heinemann describes an incident that could probably stand for many of the hurried and contentious interactions between BuAer officials and their industry counterparts during the war. In late 1943, Douglas wanted to capture the contract to build the successor to the SBD Dauntless and the SB2C Helldiver. Douglas engineers, led by Heinemann, developed what became the BTD Destroyer. But there were two other competitors, Martin (with the XBTM) and Kaiser-Fleetwing (with the XBTK). In June 1944, all three competitors sent their design teams to meet with senior BuAer officials, including the assistant bureau chief Rear Adm. Lawrence B. Richardson and William Z. Frisbie, George Spangenberg's boss. When Heinemann's team got its chance, it argued that the Destroyer was best, but "as the hours droned on it seemed as if we were going around in endless circles without resolving the issue."

Heinemann therefore boldly decided to scrap the BTD Destroyer and ask Rear Admiral Richardson and his staff to accept something new. He asked for thirty days' grace while his team came up with a producible design; the admiral gave the Douglas team one night. Heinemann first grabbed a phone and convinced Donald Douglas to go along. Then he and his team went to work. The next day they presented their design concept to the BuAer officials, and soon they were told they could take the funds slated for further BTD development and apply them to their new design concept, the BT2D, which became the XBT2D-1, which in its turn became the very successful postwar AD-1 Skyraider.[33]

Heinemann's story deliberately portrays himself, his design team, and others at Douglas in a positive—even heroic—light, and we are sure that at least some of his competitors had similar experiences. But his description of the atmosphere of wartime competition, development, and decision making is revealing. BuAer's traditional (since its founding in 1921) approach to development had been to foster both design and production competition within the small but talented aircraft industry. BuAer had also directed its private suppliers to develop their designs around specific engines. BuAer policy was to invest in engine development as a means of pulling aircraft design along.

Engines were the critical factor—the engine was the driver of overall aircraft performance, and more powerful engines gave designers an incentive to come up with larger aircraft that could carry heavier loads over greater distances. Despite the near chaos that resulted from BuAer's efforts to meet the challenges of mass production, mass training, and support for a massive naval air force, the basic approach to stimulating industry turned out to be sound *for the purposes of World War II.*

But the war also led to a new engine concept—the jet engine—and harnessing it for Navy carrier operations proved to be a major challenge for the officers and civilians in BuAer who had "won their spurs" by directing wartime quantity production of mostly proven engine and airframe technologies. In doing that, BuAer personnel had developed a mental "tool kit" different from that needed to foster radically new technologies and operational concepts. They had successfully adapted their organization and its procedures to wartime demands and therefore saw no need later to create a new organization or new processes and relationships to mature the many innovations produced by scientists and engineers during the war years.

Notes

1. Naval Aviation History Office, "Naval Aviation Confidential Bulletin," no. 8-44, p. 46.
2. Lee M. Pearson, "Development of the Attack Concept," "Naval Aviation Confidential Bulletin," no. 2-51 (August 1951), p. 8.
3. Gordon Swanborough and Peter M. Bowers, *United States Navy Aircraft since 1911* (Annapolis, Md.: Naval Institute Press, 1976), p. 151. As Swanborough and Bowers note, two factories in Canada produced almost 1,200 additional Helldivers for U.S. Navy and U.S. Marine Corps use.
4. Ibid., p. 214. The Eastern Aircraft subsidiary of General Motors produced over seven thousand Avengers in one configuration or another. Total production of this aircraft was almost ten thousand units.
5. Pearson, "Development of the Attack Concept," p. 12.
6. Ibid.
7. Aircraft data are from Ray Wagner, *American Combat Planes*, 3rd ed. (New York: Doubleday, 1982), pp. 366–67.
8. Pearson, "Development of the Attack Concept," p. 14.
9. George A. Spangenberg, "Oral History," 31 August 1997, *George Spangenberg Oral History,* 2010, www.georgespangenberg.com, p. 42.
10. Ibid., p. 48.
11. Ibid., p. 50.
12. Ibid., p. 54; Edward H. Heinemann and Rosario Rausa, *Ed Heinemann, Combat Aircraft Designer* (Annapolis, Md.: Naval Institute Press, 1980), p. 44.
13. Spangenberg, "Oral History," p. 61.
14. Ibid., p. 65.
15. Ibid., pp. 85–86.
16. Jared A. Zichek, *The Boeing XF8B-1 Fighter: Last of the Line* (Atglen, Pa.: Schiffer, 2007), p. 44.
17. Heinemann and Rausa, *Ed Heinemann, Combat Aircraft Designer*, p. 97.
18. Fighter data from Lloyd S. Jones, *U.S. Naval Fighters* (Fallbrook, Calif.: Aero, 1977), and Zichek, *Boeing XF8B-1 Fighter.*
19. Aircraft data are from Wagner, *American Combat Planes;* Swanborough and Bowers,

United States Navy Aircraft since 1911; and Zichek, *Boeing XF8B-1 Fighter.*

20. Pearson, "Development of the Attack Concept," p. 6.
21. Ibid., p. 15. However, Pearson also notes that a carrier could launch so few of these large planes that, even given their impressive ordnance loads (the XTB2F-1 was designed to carry two two-thousand-pound torpedoes), it still made sense for a carrier to use smaller dive- and torpedo bombers.
22. Theodore Taylor, *The Magnificent Mitscher* (New York: W. W. Norton, 1954), p. 299.
23. Ibid., p. 328.
24. Pearson, "Development of the Attack Concept," p. 11.
25. William F. Trimble, *Wings for the Navy: A History of the Naval Aircraft Factory, 1917–1956* (Annapolis, Md.: Naval Institute Press, 1990), p. 288.
26. Ibid., p. 290.
27. Ibid., p. 318.
28. Ibid., p. 338, app. 2.
29. Ibid.
30. Historical Section, DCNO (Air), "Aviation Procurement, 1939–1945, Part I," *United States Naval Administration in World War II,* vol. 18, First Draft Narrative, 1946, in the Naval Aviation History Office, Washington Navy Yard, Washington, D.C.
31. Pearson, "Development of the Attack Concept," pp. 4–5.
32. "BuAer Telephone Directory & Correspondence Designations, 24 Feb. 1942," in box 254, "Aviation Command 1941–52," Naval Aviation History Office, Washington Navy Yard, Washington, D.C.
33. Heinemann and Rausa, *Ed Heinemann, Combat Aircraft Designer,* pp. 104–105.

The Potential of the Big Bomber

The previous chapter focused on BuAer's wartime efforts to work with industry to develop and field larger and heavier attack aircraft. This chapter will continue that story, but with a focus on Navy efforts to deliver significant amounts of ordnance on enemy targets at ranges not thought possible in 1939. The date to begin with is 16 April 1942, when USS *Hornet* launched sixteen Army B-25 medium bombers that attacked Tokyo. The spectacular Doolittle Raid raised U.S. morale at a particularly bleak time in the war. It also inspired the naval officers who watched the bombers take off. The carrier's commanding officer, Capt. Marc Mitscher, and Cdr. Apollo Soucek, *Hornet*'s air officer, saw the potential for carriers to strike land targets from great distances, achieving surprise and avoiding enemy counterattack. The ability of *Hornet* to launch the B-25s also caught the attention of the Pacific Fleet commander (or CINCPAC), Adm. Chester Nimitz.[1]

This combination of a carrier and large, long-range bombers posed a major threat to land targets. Early in World War II carriers were perceived as powerful but vulnerable. The flight decks of U.S. carriers were not armored—could *not* be effectively armored, given the tonnage restrictions that had been imposed on their designs by treaty—and in early 1942 fighters could still not be directed efficiently enough by their own carriers to protect them from air attack. The vulnerability of carriers, plus the limited range and bomb loads of existing attack aircraft, kept carriers from posing the same threat to land targets as heavy land-based bombers like the B-17. By using B-25s, however, *Hornet* showed that a limitation on carriers as a threat to land targets could be overcome by increasing the size of attack aircraft.

Hornet's raid also showed the value of operational surprise—that is, strikes from very long range. Such strikes, mounted from outside the enemy's warning network (that is, before the days of effective wide-area radar surveillance), were far more effective than those launched from close offshore. This *operational* surprise would enhance the capacity of the few attack aircraft a single carrier could launch. As we pointed out in the previous chapter, this desire for long range led BuAer to award a contract to Grumman to develop the twin-engine XTB2F-1. Before even a mock-up of that plane could be constructed, however, U.S. carriers had developed techniques, through trial and error, for attacking Japanese land targets in the islands of the South Pacific. Did this mean that the future of "heavy attack" from carriers would not require new planes like the XTB2F-1, just improved versions of such existing models of aircraft as the SB2C Helldiver or the TBF Avenger?

Pilots and engineers could rely only on experience as a guide. For example, in 1942 Captain Mitscher was almost certainly aware of the role of strategic bombing as it was understood by U.S. war planners of the time. At least since 1929 Navy and Army planners had wrestled with the question of how to end a war against Japan. The Navy could offer blockade, which should be effective against an island country wholly dependent on imports for almost all raw materials. However, there was always the possibility that the Japanese would try to hold out, gambling that the United States would lack the patience to enforce a lengthy siege.[2] Invasion was never taken seriously, because the Navy's planners doubted that the United States could or would raise an army sufficiently large to overrun Japan. However, they thought that Japanese cities, which were largely made of wood and paper, would burn easily and hence would make good targets. In fact, the United States had tried late in 1941 to build up a strategic bomber force in the Philippines specifically as a deterrent against Japan (there are reports of an attempt to leak an exaggerated version of the bomber force's strength on the eve of Pearl Harbor, specifically to head off any Japanese attack on the Philippines). Typically war plans envisaged an endgame in which Army bombers would be transported to captured islands near Japan from which they could conduct an air offensive.

Watching the B-25s take off from *Hornet,* Mitscher probably realized that the carrier offered an alternative to land-based bombers. By the time of the raid, BuAer was actively working to provide a shipboard bomber (initially the Douglas XTB2D-1, then the Grumman XTB2F-1) with an ordnance load at least equivalent to one of Doolittle's B-25s. We cannot locate records of BuAer involvement in the planning of the Doolittle Raid, but BuAer officers would have been involved in certifying that the B-25s could indeed take off from a carrier. A few days before the raid, as we noted in the previous chapter, Grumman was asked informally to design a twin-engine carrier bomber, later designated TB2F. Its design specifications suggest that it was far more a "level bomber" (that is, intended to drop ordnance in level flight) than a torpedo plane; it was about the size of a B-25. The bomber would have been too large to stow below decks, and it seems to have been conceived for "special operations." It was also too delicate to catapult.

BuAer decided to kill the project in April 1944 before moving beyond the mock-up stage and committing the government to spend substantial sums. It decided to do so because the Japanese had in the meantime developed radar, thereby denying any carrier aircraft the chance to achieve complete surprise. Bombers would need fighter escorts to penetrate alerted enemy air defenses, but the available carrier fighters lacked the necessary range. One of the BuAer officers at the mock-up conference for the XTB2F-1 objected that the airplane would still be useful for special missions, but he was apparently overruled.

That was not the end of this particular effort to put larger bombers on carriers. At the beginning of March 1944, BuAer proposed converting a PBJ-1, which was the Navy's version of North American's B-25 Mitchell twin-engine bomber, for carrier landings and takeoffs.[3] By the end of April, North American was converting a PBJ-1H (Bureau Number 35277) for arrested landings and catapult takeoffs. Once suitably modified, the plane was to be delivered to the Naval Air Material Center and tested on land to determine its minimum carrier-landing approach speed, how late in its approach it could safely be given a "wave off," and how pilots should engage a carrier's arresting gear.[4] On 30 October 1944, the Chief of Naval Operations requested that a PBJ-1B and an F7F-1 Tigercat be tested aboard the carrier *Shangri-La* (CV 38) in November, and on 10 November Rear Adm. DeWitt C. Ramsey, BuAer's chief, directed the captain of *Shangri-La* to devote a day to completing at least five catapult launchings and arrested landings of the modified PBJ-1H. As Ramsey noted, "Tests of the subject airplanes should be conducted without other airplanes on the flight deck and possibly with barriers down because of expected unsuitability of the barriers installed for stopping twin engine tricycle [i.e., with nose wheel and two main wheels] planes."[5]

Also tested in this way was an Army-type P-51 Mustang fighter. According to the confidential report of the trials, the B-25 was used to test the carrier-landing qualities of a tricycle aircraft like the F7F Tigercat fighter, then being pushed toward production. The P-51 was tested because it was a modern fighter with a liquid-cooled engine, hence presumably different from the air-cooled types the Navy then used. Neither explanation is entirely credible. The Navy already had a prototype F7F for carrier trials (indeed, it flew trials in the same series as the B-25 and the P-51), and it was unlikely that the B-25 had very similar landing characteristics. The P-51 was then being considered for use as a naval fighter, but it was soon dropped in favor of a jet that its manufacturer, North American, was then developing.

At the time, however, the P-51 was the best U.S. escort fighter and hence the potential answer to the problem that had, at least in theory, killed the big Grumman bomber. It is difficult not to imagine that at some point in 1944 the use of carrier-based B-25s escorted by P-51s had been seriously considered. It had probably been dropped well before the *Shangri-La* tests, and it had presumably been developed at a higher level of classification. Its significance for this account is that it suggests continuing U.S. naval interest in long-range carrier attack.

As we argued in the previous chapter, the crosscutting pressures generated by changing operational requirements, advances in research and development, and the need for large numbers of aircraft for combat and training disrupted the BuAer three-year aircraft-development cycle. Heinemann's memoir illustrates this point. In 1943, Capt. Leslie C. Stevens, who had been head of the Experiments and Developments Section of BuAer's Engineering Division before being promoted and sent to the Pacific, returned from the war theater, called Heinemann, and arranged a meeting in San Diego between Navy and Douglas personnel to discuss the need for a new torpedo bomber.[6] The concept they developed was the large (eighteen thousand pounds empty, wingspan seventy feet, length forty-six feet) Skypirate, which was tested in 1945. Stevens was, according to Heinemann, "covering all bets, because the forecast need for a new torpedo bomber was indeed genuine when he talked with us in San Diego."[7]

However, as we have already pointed out, in June 1944 Heinemann decided to abandon the conventional separation of attack aircraft into torpedo planes and dive-bombers and to develop a plane that would carry its ordnance externally, have one pilot and no gunners, and carry a heavy bomb or torpedo load. BuAer's senior officers and civilians, *including Captain Stevens,* agreed with this approach. BuAer approved Douglas Aircraft's mock-up of the new aircraft (the BT2D) at the end of the summer of 1944. In the meantime, in an effort to improve the responsiveness of industry designers, BuAer had offered to send "representatives to the Pacific combat area in order to gain first-hand knowledge of flight operations," and Heinemann was the first to go.[8]

Heinemann spent about two weeks watching carrier operations, interviewing pilots and senior officers, and capturing his observations in a diary. Some of his particular observations affected the detailed design of the BT2D, but what mattered more was that experienced attack pilots agreed that carriers needed just two types of aircraft, "the best possible fighter without compromising it with bomb loads, and a dive bomber that [had] secondary capabilities of dropping torpedoes and working as a scout."[9] Heinemann also gleaned insights from Rear Adm. Arthur W. Radford and Capt. Frederick M. Trapnell. The latter had been a test pilot at Naval Air Station Anacostia in 1941 and the first Navy pilot to test the experimental XP-59A Bell Airacomet—the first U.S.-made military jet plane.[10] Heinemann also interviewed the Royal Navy's observer on *Ticonderoga*, Cdr. F. H. E. Hopkins.[11]

Heinemann's memoir lists a number of detail modifications to the BT2D design that were inspired by his interviews with Navy pilots, including eliminating the nose wheel, dramatically reducing the empty weight of the plane (to enable it to carry more ordnance), changing the design of the wings (to improve low-speed landing performance), and designing a cockpit that could withstand "forty-G crash-landing impacts."[12] Heinemann and his design engineers sometimes disagreed with the specifications that BuAer's design personnel wanted them to meet, but Heinemann's contact with members of BuAer and officers flying in the fleet gave him an almost unique ability to, as he put it, "get on the phone to the proper official and solicit action."[13] Heinemann argues in his memoir that it was the hard work of Douglas's engineers, coupled with the rapid back-and-forth negotiations between them and their counterparts in BuAer, that allowed Douglas to take the BT2D design from paper to first test flight in just nine months.[14] George Spangenberg in BuAer had a slightly different view—that the pressure of competition had taught designers like Heinemann the importance of disciplines like weight control.[15]

To read Heinemann's memoir, one would think that BuAer was focused almost exclusively on *manned*-aircraft design and production. However, that was not the case. In 1936, Lt. Cdr. Delmar S. Fahrney of BuAer began development at the Naval Aircraft Factory in Philadelphia of a radio-controlled pilotless aircraft for use as a target in antiaircraft exercises.[16] The success of that work gave Fahrney's vision of a force of remote-controlled "drones" (as he had named them) credibility, and the growing reliability of television equipment suggested that drones might be used to attack targets while the planes controlling them cruised beyond the range of antiaircraft guns. Successful tests in April 1942 led Fahrney's BuAer superiors to authorize the production of two hundred drones, but the low speed (150 mph) of the first units "made for reduced enthusiasm; the drone did not appear to many aviators to be a serious combat weapon, capable of overcoming enemy defenses."[17] Though drones attacked Japanese targets in July and then in September 1944, the drone squadrons that had been formed at the end of 1943 were disbanded.

But drones weren't the only new weapons developed by BuAer during the war. In 1940, Fahrney, by now a captain, suggested that a carrier fighter such as the F6F Hellcat could tow an armed glider that it could direct—using radio—against stationary targets. Development work at the Naval Aircraft Factory began in 1941. The idea seemed to have merit. A three-thousand-pound glider could carry four thousand pounds of explosive, dramatically augmenting a carrier's strike capacity. As in the case of the drones, however, the glider bomb (christened GLOMB) was judged too vulnerable to antiaircraft fire, and the program was canceled in 1945.[18]

BuAer also developed two powered missiles, Gorgon and Gargoyle. The latter "was inspired by the success of German guided missiles" used against Allied warships in the Mediterranean in 1943.[19] Four hundred were ordered in 1944. It seemed to offer a dramatic improvement in capability: "Gargoyle cost only $8900, and it required only a 35 lb. radio aboard its [launching] airplane; its wing span was only 8 ft. 6 in. It could penetrate any existing armored deck, and was considered immune to antiaircraft fire in view of its high diving speed."[20] Unfortunately for its developers, it was not launched successfully until July 1946, and production was canceled a year later.

The Navy's Bureau of Ordnance also entered the guided-weapons field in World War II. In 1940, the newly established National Defense Research Committee (NDRC) began collaborating with BuOrd on the development of reliable, powerful rocket motors that could accelerate bombs to speeds that would allow warheads to penetrate thick concrete structures.[21] That same year, the NDRC funded projects that explored missile-control techniques and the potential of television guidance for powered missiles and gliders.[22] Out of this research came Bat, an active-radar-homing glider launched by patrol planes against moving targets, and Pelican, an antisubmarine glider guided from the aircraft that carried and launched it. Bat was "the only US Navy air-to-surface missile to enter combat, although Pelican . . . came close."[23] BuOrd also worked on missiles to carry torpedoes, missiles to attack submarines, and Dove, a bomb guided to its target by an infrared seeker.[24]

The BuAer and BuOrd guided-weapons programs were significant. As the Secretary of the Navy pointed out in his annual report for fiscal year 1946, "At the beginning of the fiscal year on 1 July 1945, the Bureau of Aeronautics was supervising contracts providing for over 61,000 combat and tactical airplanes and more than 14,000 'drones' and 'glombs,' known as 'missiles' and 'pilotless aircraft.'"[25] That is, fully 18.6 percent of all the Navy's combat "flying machines" on order were unmanned. Crash programs of research and development—programs made possible only by wartime spending—had produced the beginnings of a guided-weapons revolution, but it would take decades for that revolution to mature.

In the meantime, wartime production of carriers, pilots, and carrier aircraft had generated a powerful naval air force. In October 1944, Navy strategic planners had produced a draft plan, HOTFOOT, for a carrier-based strategic bombing offensive against Japan. By this time there were so many fleet carriers that even their relatively small bombers (Avengers and Helldivers) offered substantial net firepower. Navy planners argued that once the endgame had been reached, the carriers should be used for direct attacks, because there would no longer be many amphibious operations to support and because the Japanese fleet would probably be immobilized by the increasingly effective submarine blockade. In January 1945 Admiral Halsey's Fifth Fleet raided Tokyo, in effect testing the HOTFOOT concept. Although accounts of this raid suggest that it was less than successful, HOTFOOT survived (as HOTFOOT III), the final version estimating that carriers could deliver about half the weight of bombs that Twentieth Air Force B-29s were delivering. To make HOTFOOT more effective, the planners suggested reversing the trend, adopted to deal with kamikazes, of increasing carrier fighter strength at the expense of attack aircraft.

By the spring of 1945 the end of the Pacific War was in sight, and that April the Navy convened a high-level committee to discuss the character of the next aircraft carrier.[26] By this time planners had some hard estimates of the performance of various guided weapons; these weapons could greatly increase the effectiveness of the limited number of aircraft a carrier could launch. In the Atlantic, the Germans were deploying new U-boats that could probably overcome existing kinds of defenses. The sole counter to such craft might well be attacks at the source, either by mining approach routes to the open sea or by destroying boats in their pens. The latter was difficult, because the pens were heavily protected by concrete. However, the British had demonstrated very heavy bombs capable of accelerating to supersonic speeds and penetrating such havens. The Army was developing bomb-guidance systems to steer such weapons right onto the pen roofs. In a future war, it could hardly be guaranteed that land-based heavy bombers would be in position to make such attacks—or, for that matter, that they would not be so busy with other tasks that they could not be used that way. Carriers striking at fixed targets might be a vital mode of fighting the next naval war.

Although the new carrier committee did not report formally until January 1946, by the early fall of 1945 BuAer was arguing that the lessons of the European war included a clear requirement for a deep-strike, carrier-based bomber capable of delivering eight to twelve thousand pounds of bombs. The reference to Europe suggests a connection with the U-boat problem (we can find no copy of a relevant study of the European war). Of course, by the fall of 1945 it was also clear that only a large aircraft could deliver a nuclear bomb, and the Navy was rejecting the Air Force's attempt to secure a nuclear monopoly.

However, it appears that the BuAer proposal was not primarily for nuclear delivery. That made sense at the time. It seemed that there would never be many nuclear bombs and that World War III, if it came, would be fought largely with conventional weapons. The post-1945 U.S. Navy was struggling with the question of how to use sea power against a land empire—the probable new enemy, the Soviet Union. The most obvious use of sea power would be to maintain sea lines of communication with forces in forward areas, such as Western Europe, and to the U.S. Navy that meant countering the new generation of submarines.

This conclusion, that the future lay with a large carrier bomber, was by no means accepted widely. On 30 August 1945, Fleet Adm. Ernest J. King, the Navy's commander in chief, had convened a series of Pacific Fleet panels to lay out the war's lessons in such areas as ship and aircraft characteristics, ordnance, radar, and radio (plus sonar). The report on ship and aircraft characteristics, submitted in October, made no mention of a heavy carrier bomber. It was concerned with amalgamating the dive- and torpedo-bomber types, preferably into a new single-seat bomber. This was a call for a medium attack bomber like the new BT2D-1 (later the AD-1) Douglas Skyraider. CINCPAC was skeptical of the practicability of this proposal, due to failed attempts to develop a multipurpose carrier bomber over the previous twenty-five years. There was even some hope that all carrier aircraft functions might be amalgamated into a single airplane, such as the new Grumman F7F twin-engine fighter. Noticeably lacking in the report was interest in jet aircraft.

This report, which might be read as a rather direct extrapolation of the aircraft that had won the carrier war in the Pacific, contrasted dramatically with the accompanying report on submarines, which pointed toward the postwar submarine revolution. The surviving texts of submarine officers' responses to a questionnaire for inclusion in the Pacific Fleet report show considerable knowledge of what was happening in Europe, as German submarine technology was revealed. The aircraft questionnaires seem not to have survived, but in any case the aircraft discussion shows little or no concern with recent European developments or, indeed, with the possibility of delivering atomic bombs from carriers (a very important theme a year later). It suggests that Vice Adm. Alfred E. Montgomery, commander of Navy air forces in the Pacific at the end of World War II, was right when he noted with some concern that the lessons learned in the great carrier battles against Japan were most likely "only applicable to *this war,* will soon be obsolete and if absorbed will focus the naval mind to a point [2 September 1945] which will soon be in the past and therefore misleading."[27]

Notes

1. Captain Mitscher noted in his report to Admiral Nimitz that "the take-off could be made easily when properly executed" and that it took fifty-nine minutes to launch all sixteen B-25s. Commanding Officer, USS *Hornet,* memorandum to Commander in Chief, U.S. Pacific Fleet, subject "Report of Action, April 18, 1942, with notable events prior and subsequent thereto"; Action Report, Commander in Chief, Pacific Fleet (ser. 01338, 4 May 1942), microfilm 385, part 1, reel 2, "U.S. Navy Action & Operational Reports from World War II, Pacific Theater," part 1, Naval War College Library, Newport,

R.I. The same microfilm contains the letter from Admiral Nimitz to Admiral King in Washington in which the former notes that *Hornet* carried its own seventy-two aircraft in addition to the sixteen B-25s.

2. An interesting discussion of this is James B. Wood, *Japanese Military Strategy in the Pacific War: Was Defeat Inevitable?* (New York: Rowman & Littlefield, 2007).

3. BuAer, memorandum to Bureau of Aeronautics Representative, El Segundo, subject "Model PBJ-1H airplane—conversion for arrested landings and catapulting," Aer-F-342-JST, file VPBJ-1/F13-5, C-09661 (14 April 1944), in PBJ-1 (North American) Mitchell F 41 file.

4. BuAer, memorandum to CO NAMC, subject "Arrested landing and Catapult tests of converted Model PBJ-1H airplane BuNo. 35277," Aer-F-342-JST, file VPBJ-1/F13-5, C-10529 (22 April 1944), in PBJ-1 (North American) Mitchell F 41 file.

5. BuAer, memorandum to CO USS *Shangri-La,* subject "Brief Carrier operation tests of Model F7F-1 and PBJ-1B airplanes," Aer-F-342-JST, file VPBJ-1/F13-5, C-30771 (10 November 1944), in PBJ-1 (North American) Mitchell F 41 file.

6. Edward H. Heinemann and Rosario Rausa, *Ed Heinemann, Combat Aircraft Designer* (Annapolis, Md.: Naval Institute Press, 1980), p. 108. See also "BuAer Telephone Directory & Correspondence Designations, 24 Feb. 1942," in box 254, "Aviation Command 1941–52," Naval Aviation History Office, Washington Navy Yard, Washington, D.C. The phone books show both personnel and organizational changes.

7. Heinemann and Rausa, *Ed Heinemann, Combat Aircraft Designer,* p. 109.

8. Ibid., p. 110.

9. Ibid., p. 116.

10. Ibid., pp. 115, 117. See also *Navy Directory,* 1 April 1941, for then–lieutenant commander Trapnell's duty station.

11. Heinemann and Rausa, *Ed Heinemann, Combat Aircraft Designer,* p. 118.

12. Ibid., p. 129.

13. Ibid., p. 131.

14. Ibid., p. 132.

15. George A. Spangenberg, "Oral History," 31 August 1997, *George Spangenberg Oral History,* 2010, www.georgespangenberg.com, p. 59.

16. Norman Friedman, *U.S. Naval Weapons* (Annapolis, Md.: Naval Institute Press, 1982), p. 215.

17. Ibid., p. 216.

18. Ibid., p. 201.

19. Ibid.

20. Ibid., p. 202.

21. Buford Rowland and William Boyd, *U.S. Navy Bureau of Ordnance in World War II* (Washington, D.C.: U.S. Navy Dept., Bureau of Ordnance, 1953), p. 294.

22. Ibid., p. 341.

23. Friedman, *U.S. Naval Weapons,* p. 202.

24. Ibid., pp. 202–203.

25. U.S. Navy Dept., *Annual Report of the Secretary of the Navy for the Fiscal Year 1946* (Washington, D.C.: U.S. Government Printing Office, 1947), p. 15.

26. Theodore Taylor, *The Magnificent Mitscher* (New York: W. W. Norton, 1954), p. 319.

27. Clark G. Reynolds, *The Fast Carriers* (Annapolis, Md.: Naval Institute Press, 1992), p. 383.

Royal Navy Wartime Experience and Analysis

Until at least 1936, the Royal Navy did not try to interest the British Air Ministry in the development of high-performance fighters for its aircraft carriers, because the RN's air officers did not think that an effective combat air patrol could be mounted around a carrier. By the time approaching bombers could be sighted and identified, it would be too late. Consequently, the RN carriers that followed *Ark Royal,* which was laid down in 1935, had armored flight decks so that they could absorb punishment and still operate attack aircraft. The advent of shipboard air-search radar in the first year of World War II, however, changed the situation, and the RN procured Royal Air Force (RAF) and U.S. Navy fighters and experimented with the central control of fighter defenses.

The RN also did not expect *before World War II* to have to operate its carriers against waves of high-performance land-based bombers—as it would be forced to do first in Norway in 1940 and then, in 1941, in the Mediterranean. The RN's decision to construct carriers with armored flight decks restricted the number of aircraft such carriers could operate, so it chose to emphasize strike aircraft over fighters. The RN projected the logic of its own decisions about carrier-based strike aircraft upon the Imperial Japanese Navy (IJN). Accordingly, it was surprised by the IJN's very effective carrier-based attacks in the Pacific and the Bay of Bengal in the spring of 1942.

The leaders of the RN responded to the challenges to the Fleet Air Arm posed by operations against the Germans in the Mediterranean and the Japanese in the Indian Ocean by creating the Future Building Committee (FBC), chaired by the Deputy First Sea Lord, in July 1942. The FBC was "the only organization within the Admiralty charged with the overall review of British naval requirements," and its deliberations supported those of the Joint (i.e., Royal Air Force/Royal Navy) Technical Committee.[1] At the end of 1942, the Joint Technical Committee had accepted the idea that future strike aircraft would be significantly heavier, and it recommended that all future carrier aircraft therefore be designed to use rocket-assisted takeoff equipment. The committee also approved an increased carrier-landing speed for all aircraft.[2] In February 1943, the FBC specified that "carrier interceptor fighters should be the equals (in performance) of their land counterparts," which implied significant increases in the size and weight of carrier fighters.³ In March 1943, the Aircraft Design Subcommittee of the FBC was split off to become a distinct organization—the Naval Aircraft Design Committee. This committee was an "early proponent of the catapult as the primary means of launching aircraft" from carriers.⁴

Also in 1943, the RN's famous test pilot Eric Brown successfully landed a combat-loaded, twin-engine Sea Mosquito fighter on a carrier, and the Future Building Committee recommended that the Mosquito design be modified to create a long-range carrier fighter equipped with radar.⁵ The resulting aircraft, christened Sea Hornet, first flew in April 1945.⁶ In September 1944 the First Sea Lord, Adm. Andrew B. Cunningham, asked the chief of the RAF's Air Staff to provide the RN with Mosquitoes modified for use on carriers. Admiral Cunningham was thinking in early 1945 about long-range attacks from RN carriers against Japanese bases like Singapore.⁷ The Admiralty asked for two hundred Sea Mosquitoes "for delivery in 1945 and 250 to follow in 1946."⁸

That same month (September 1944), the Naval Aircraft Design Committee recommended to the Ministry of Aircraft Production (MAP) that it develop a jet interceptor for use from carriers. The members of the committee were aware that "such a fighter would demand catapult-only launching and that no other aircraft could be within thirty feet of it when its engine opened up to full power," but they felt that the better air-to-air performance of the jet would more than compensate for the problems created by operating it from existing and planned carriers.⁹ By late 1944, the MAP had stopped work on new piston-engine designs and was focused on jet turbines and turboprops.¹⁰ In December 1944, the Naval Aircraft Design Committee "proposed that future naval aircraft be designed without undercarriages, to land on soft (flexible) decks," and in February 1945 the Royal Aircraft Establishment (RAE) at Farnborough "concluded that any future high-performance naval fighter would have to be a pure jet, and that requirements for takeoff, military load, and landing speed would have to be modified."¹¹

Things were moving fast. By 7 June 1945, the Naval Aircraft Department of the RAE had developed a "Proposed Programme of Experimental Work" for determining whether a carrier could operate jets without undercarriages. The "target for flying trials under seagoing conditions" was May 1946.¹² This project was sent forward to the MAP with an endorsement by the director of the RAE two days later.¹³ On 4 July, engineer Lewis Boddington, who headed the Naval Aircraft Department at RAE, completed a paper entitled "Assisted Take-off for Future Naval Aircraft," which he presented on

17 July to the Naval Aircraft Research Subcommittee of the Naval Aircraft Design Committee. He put his main point right up front: "The large increase in take-off speed which will result from the developments in the aircraft and its power plant, and the resulting necessity to remove the present free-deck take-off restrictions will demand assisted take-off under all conditions."[14]

Boddington's paper laid out many of the *engineering* problems entailed by operating jets from carriers, especially the need for catapult launchings that would not be so violent as to damage an aircraft's structure and the need safely to recover planes landing with their engines running. He argued, first, that "future aircraft will have no undercarriage and will land on flexible decks," and, second, that "the solution of the problem giving the best handling and deck operating conditions will be a landing deck immediately under which will be the take-off deck. Ranged aircraft for take-off will not obstruct any landing operations."[15] By 12 July, the deputy director of RAE's Panel on Flexible Landing Decks had reviewed the feasibility of an approach technique for a carrier with an (as yet only conceptual) flexible deck and had decided to recommend trials of actual landings using jet aircraft. (See chapter 7 for the "flexible deck" idea.)

On 18 September 1945, Boddington presented a second paper for the Naval Aircraft Research Subcommittee, "Landing of Future Naval Aircraft." As he observed, "The object of this note is to briefly present the problems of landing on a carrier deck in the future and discuss the effects on the equipment and carrier design." His argument was that the development of jet aircraft "will result in a new approach technique ending in flight parallel to the deck and engaging the mechanical arresting gear under 'flying' conditions."[16] His paper provided the conceptual justification for the angled flight deck. As he noted, "To cover for the baulked landing, the jet engine will be running at 90% full revs. . . . Non-engagement of the wire will allow the pilot to take-off [*sic*] again depending on the deck arrangements (barriers, parks, etc.) and the carrier design."[17] To allow a plane that had missed the arresting gear to get back in the air safely, the flexible deck that Boddington advocated would have to be located away from the deck park. His solution—already proposed—was to have "separate landing and take-off decks."[18]

Boddington also understood that jet aircraft would require more powerful catapults.[19] In Britain, catapult development was shared between the Royal Aircraft Establishment at Farnborough and the Engineer-in-Chief Department of the Royal Navy. About 1943 Farnborough began experimenting with a new kind of catapult (Type K) using a flywheel to store energy.[20] In 1946, the catapult engineers supervised by Boddington also explored the potential of gas turbines as power sources for carrier catapults.[21]

As the Allied armies had surged across northern France in the fall of 1944, they had encountered the fixed sites built by the Germans to launch V-1 missiles against

London. The missile's pulse-jet engine could not function until it reached a set speed, about 150 mph. Thus the catapults built by the Germans were not too different from what a streamlined jet, with a similar takeoff speed, might require. Unlike the explosive-driven catapults then in use in the U.S. Navy for launching scout planes from cruisers and battleships, the German catapult applied its force directly to the airplane. It was a tube with a slot running along its upper side. A reaction in the tube pushed a piston along it, and the piston was hooked through the slot to the airplane. In the German case, the reaction was the decomposition of concentrated ("high-test") hydrogen peroxide, which the British called HTP. This was one of several German applications of HTP, others being as an oxidant in the Me-163 rocket fighter and as an oxidant in the Walter closed-cycle U-boat. In each case, HTP showed lethal properties that more or less disqualified it if any alternative could be found.

The British report on the V-1 catapult was written by C. C. Mitchell, at that time a Royal Navy reservist but in peacetime a catapult designer in an Edinburgh engineering firm that produced what the RN referred to as "accelerators" for use on carriers. He had patented a slotted-tube catapult, which he called a "popgun" catapult, in 1938, but the RN had not adopted it. After the war, while working for Brown Brothers (also in Edinburgh), he realized that steam from a ship's propulsion plant could substitute for the dangerous HTP. He formally proposed such a catapult (it is not clear exactly when) when trials of the Type K showed that the weight of existing hydro-pneumatic catapults was growing faster than their capacity to launch aircraft at high speeds. After 1947 the British formally chose the slotted-tube steam catapult as the sole direction for future development. By 1950, the prototype, christened BXS.1, was ready for testing on HMS *Perseus,* a war-built light carrier now used for experiments.[22]

The Royal Navy used low-temperature, low-pressure steam on all of its existing carriers, as well as those under construction. Low steam pressure made it easier to build a gasket that would hold the steam inside a slotted-cylinder catapult as the steam drove the piston—attached to the airplane—forward. However, low steam temperature and pressure made for poor efficiency in ship propulsion. The U.S. Navy used much higher steam temperature and pressure in its carriers' boilers, which made them more efficient thermodynamically and therefore increased the carriers' endurance—a valuable capability in the Pacific War against Japan. Wartime contact with the U.S. Navy convinced the British to develop a new generation of high-pressure steam plants for their late-war and postwar fleets.

Because Mitchell's catapult was adapted to the conditions of earlier British ships, it was by no means obvious that steam was the appropriate choice if new British carriers using higher steam pressures were built. Similarly, American observers of British catapult development knew that it was by no means obvious that a catapult adapted to British steam systems would succeed on board an American carrier. Wartime U.S. Navy boilers operated at about three times the temperature and twice the pressure of British plants, and by 1950 the U.S. Navy was contemplating doubling the pressure used during wartime, to 1,200 pounds per square inch.

British wartime analysis produced the conceptual foundation for the modern aircraft carrier operating high-performance jet aircraft. Because jets accelerated slowly, jet aircraft would need assistance at takeoff. Because jets landed at higher speeds and needed to do so with their turbines turning over at close to maximum revolutions per minute, the axial deck—with the deck park forward, shielded by a barrier—had to be modified. In effect, the Royal Navy had defined the "problem set" by the end of the summer of 1945. From that point forward, attention focused on possible solutions.

The choice of the steam catapult coincided with the beginning of design work on carrier modernization. As originally envisaged, modernization would have combined a steam catapult, new heavier-duty arresting gear, and a U.S.-style deck-edge elevator, the latter to provide an easier flow of aircraft between hangar deck and flight deck. For the British, the new elevator—the one major American-inspired element of modernization—was by far the most expensive part of the project. It was incompatible with the enclosed, protected hangars that had formed the cores of the existing British fleet carriers. To install the U.S.-style elevator the British had to remove the carrier's flight deck and tear open its hangar deck. That they were willing to do so suggests the extent to which they considered the U.S. wartime experience, rather than their own, the key to the future.

In effect, the Royal Navy ended World War II with a policy of developing jet aircraft to replace propeller-driven types; experimenting with the flexible and angled flexible deck; and placing steam catapults in its new and modernized aircraft carriers. A lack of funds limited the speed with which these innovations could be developed, tested, and installed. However, incremental development of new equipment and techniques, rather than concurrent development, allowed RN engineers and aviators to identify problems and potential "dead ends" before large sums had been appropriated or spent.

A classic "dead end" they encountered was the "carpet," or flexible, flight deck, which was tested successfully at sea on the carrier *Warrior* in the fall and winter of 1948–49.[23] The combination of the flexible deck and jet fighters without landing gear appeared successful, but it had a major flaw. As Rear Adm. Dennis R. F. Cambell, RN, who is closely identified with the origin of the angled deck for carriers, put it years later,

> It soon became obvious that there was a world of difference between one-off trials [of the flexible flight deck proposed by Lewis Boddington] and practical front-line operation. Two major points

needed to be resolved—how were aircraft with no wheels to be dealt with ashore? . . . The one other big problem was how to ensure that speed of operation wasn't to be sacrificed by imposing some elaborate mechanical substitute for the previous easy routine of just taxying [sic] forward into the deck parks; and the vulnerability of the whole scheme was surely obvious.[24]

Moreover, it took a very skilled pilot to put his aircraft down on the "carpet" safely. For example, in the first test of the flexible rubber deck at Farnborough at the end of December 1947, RAE's test pilot, Eric Brown, crashed his aircraft. Brown was fortunate to survive, and his description of what happened is vivid:

> After crossing the arrester wire the plane continued to swing nose-down towards the deck and plunged into it with such violence that the nose completely vanished and penetrated right down to the bottom layer. . . . Then it was thrown harshly up again in a nose-up attitude. I opened it up to full power and was climbing away safely when I realized that the stick was jammed solid, with the elevators keeping the plane in a nose-up attitude. I throttled back gently and she settled on to the grass ahead of the deck. The crash split the cockpit all round me.[25]

This initial accident, however, was followed by many successful attempts, once formal tests began again at Farnborough in March 1948. Brown says in his memoir *(Wings on My Sleeve)* that he made forty successful landings on the flexible deck at Farnborough in the spring and summer of 1948.[26] By November of that year, the light carrier HMS *Warrior* had been fitted with a full-scale flexible deck, and Brown landed a small jet fighter (a Vampire) on it. As his memoirs have it, "The plane's belly scraped the wire, the hook caught. The arrester wire and the deck had been deliberately set hard and the chock was uncomfortable, though only for a split second."[27] Not all his landings were as successful, but Brown nevertheless came away from the trials confident that the system would work. He noted in his official report, "It may even be that future swept-back and delta plan form aircraft will be forced to adopt this method of landing on carriers, since all calculations point to serious wheeled landing problems on such aircraft."[28]

Films of Brown landing his aircraft on the flexible deck were shown to staff in the U.S. Navy's Bureau of Aeronautics when Lewis Boddington and two colleagues visited the United States in March 1949. The British team members spent most of their time at the naval aviation test center at Patuxent River, Maryland, the Naval Aircraft Factory in Philadelphia, and five aircraft manufacturing firms—Grumman, McDonnell, Chance Vought, Douglas, and North American. In his report of the trip, Boddington noted that "discussions were at all times free and open" and that "in general, similar methods of solving difficulties [were] in progress in both countries."[29] Facilitating this exchange of ideas was Capt. Frederick Trapnell, who had commanded an escort carrier in World War II and was in March 1949 the chief test pilot at Patuxent River.

The discussions among the technical specialists went into great detail and covered such topics as carrier-landing approach techniques, the coordination problems associated with high-speed approaches, the gravitational forces imposed on airplane structures by arrested landings and catapulted takeoffs, safe and functional barriers to shield the already-recovered aircraft in the deck park from those still landing, the problems associated with getting a jet to an adequate airspeed at the end of its catapult run, and the difficulties of moving increasingly heavy aircraft around on a carrier's flight deck. Boddington and his colleagues observed that it was evident to officers in BuAer that "the direct application of present requirements and methods for catapulting and arresting is not satisfactory," *especially for large (hundred-thousand-pound) aircraft.*[30] This need to place very large aircraft on U.S. carriers was based on the formal requirement to develop nuclear-capable bombers. It drew the Americans away from the British, though the two navies otherwise shared the same basic problems that stemmed from the innovations—jet aircraft, radar, and missiles—produced during World War II.

The parallels between the two navies in the immediate postwar period are striking. Because of their wartime experiences, both naval air arms wanted larger, heavier, and longer-range aircraft for their carriers. Both had officers and engineers who believed that it was possible to develop ways to launch and recover high-performance jet aircraft on carriers. Although, as Boddington observed, American engineers in aircraft firms and military and civilian officials were working on similar problems, it was the British who first grasped all the problems entailed in adapting existing carriers to jet aircraft. Their initial solution to this set of problems—the flexible landing deck—did not survive careful scrutiny, but the idea of the slightly offset flexible deck led to the angled deck, and it was the angled deck that opened the way for the large modern carrier.

Notes

1. Norman Friedman, *British Carrier Aviation: The Evolution of the Ships and Their Aircraft* (London: Conway Maritime, 1988), p. 245.
2. Ibid.
3. Ibid., p. 276.
4. Ibid., p. 272.
5. Brown's test of the prototype Sea Mosquito on HMS *Indefatigable* is described and illustrated by photographs on pages 64–65 of Brown's *Wings on My Sleeve* (London: Orion Books–Phoenix, 2007).
6. Ibid., pp. 275–76.
7. Michael Simpson, ed., *The Cunningham Papers* (London: Ashgate and the Navy Records Society, 2006), vol. 2, pp. 324–25.
8. Friedman, *British Carrier Aviation*, p. 280.
9. Ibid., p. 272.
10. Ibid., p. 283.
11. Ibid., pp. 272, 285. See also Brown, *Wings on My Sleeve*, p. 91.
12. "Operation of Undercarriage-less Aircraft: Proposed Programme of Experimental Work," 7 June 1945 (Naval/2001-4/LB/43), in AVIA 13/654 Ministry of Aviation file, Public Records Office [hereafter PRO], esp. p. 5.
13. Director of RAE, memorandum to the Secretary, Ministry of Aircraft Production, subject "Operation of Undercarriage-less Aircraft," 9 June 1945, Naval/2001-4/LB/43, in AVIA 13/654.

14. Lewis Boddington, "Assisted Take-off for Future Naval Aircraft," 4 July 1945, in AVIA 13/654, p. 1.
15. Ibid., pp. 2–3.
16. Lewis Boddington, "Landing of Future Naval Aircraft," Copy no. 30, 12 September 1945, in AVIA 13/654, p. 1.
17. Ibid.
18. Ibid., p. 4.
19. Boddington, "Assisted Take-off for Future Naval Aircraft," pp. 2–3.
20. Geoffrey Cooper, *Farnborough and the Fleet Air Arm* (Hersham, Surrey, U.K.: Midland, 2008), pp. 99–101.
21. Ibid., pp. 101–102.
22. Ibid., p. 281.
23. Ibid., p. 198.
24. Rear Adm. Dennis R. F. Cambell, RN, "The Angled Deck Story (DRFC's Own Account)," *Rear Admiral Dennis Royle Farquharson Cambell, C.B., D.S.C.*, March 2008, www.denniscambell.org.uk, pp. 2–3.
25. Brown, *Wings on My Sleeve*, pp. 177–78.
26. Ibid., p. 179.
27. Ibid., p. 188.
28. Ibid., p. 190.
29. Lewis Boddington, R. R. Duddy, and F. Holroyd, "Report on a Visit to U.S.A. to Discuss the Operation of Aircraft from Aircraft Carriers, March 1949," Tech Note N.A. 197, Aero. 2004, in AVIA 6/16021 Ministry of Aviation file, PRO, p. 5.
30. Ibid., p. 33.

Adopting Jet Engines

Jet engines were the first British innovation the Bureau of Aeronautics adopted. This was a clear case of deliberate technology transfer, and it sparked a revolution in aircraft-engine technology in the United States. But the story of what happened *after* the initial transfer is important and interesting, if only because it called into question BuAer's policy of funding engine development separately from airframe development. BuAer's practice had been to finance new engines and then furnish them to the aircraft makers, such as Grumman, Douglas, Curtiss, and Vought. However, the engineering challenges that faced the developers of jet turbine engines, combined with BuAer's policy of relying on one or two main engine suppliers, almost derailed the modernization of the Navy's carrier air forces in the late 1940s and early 1950s.[1]

Why the Europeans Developed Effective Turbojets First

In the years before World War II, in the United States, the National Advisory Committee on Aeronautics, a federal research and development organization, was an important source of innovations for the Navy, Army, and the various aircraft manufacturers. Formed in 1929, NACA had developed a cowling that significantly improved the efficiency of radial piston engines, which would otherwise have suffered badly from the drag generated by their large frontal area. NACA also devised standard airfoil (wing) sections, much as the British Royal Aircraft Establishment at Farnborough did.

NACA formed a committee to encourage the development of turbojet engines after the British revealed the existence of Frank Whittle's design in the fall of 1940. Why then, and not earlier? There are four basic reasons. First, prior to Army general Henry H. "Hap" Arnold's chance introduction to the Whittle engine in early 1941, there was no American military demand for jet propulsion. Propeller driven aircraft performed acceptably, piston engines were reliable, and the commercial aircraft manufacturers knew how to design airplanes around them. In addition, the existence of a great number of World War I–surplus "Liberty" engines—many never used—for sale at a fraction of the cost of newer types of power plants stifled research. (For example, it was only in

1934 that the U.S. Army was able to halt the use of Liberty engines in Army aircraft. That was because Representative Fiorello H. La Guardia, a World War I veteran and student of military aviation, inserted a rider into the appropriations act directing the Army to do so.)[2] These factors led to a "lock-in" of piston engines in civilian and military aircraft and created insurmountable obstacles for those who wanted to study and develop alternative power plants.[3] Aircraft engine performance was investigated in terms of existing speed ranges; most American power-plant engineers accepted propeller-driven aircraft as a given.[4]

Second, reliance on piston engines was reinforced by studies suggesting that jet propulsion of aircraft was an unrealistic goal. It was not that American engineers were unaware of the concept of the turbojet. In 1919, years before anyone demonstrated a practical turbojet, European and American engineers had proposed using them as aircraft engines.[5] French and British experimental work in the field was published in the early 1920s, and in 1922 the U.S. Bureau of Standards investigated the turbojet as a means of aircraft propulsion. Two years later, Edgar Buckingham, the Bureau of Standards propulsion investigator, concluded that jet propulsion would be impractical for either civilian or military purposes. He argued that the top speed of a jet-powered aircraft would be only 250 miles per hour, fuel consumption would be four times higher than in a piston engine with equivalent horsepower, and that the turbojet would be more complicated than a piston engine.[6]

Thereafter proposals for jet aircraft cropped up persistently in the United States, but subsequent studies completed at the Bureau of Standards and NACA confirmed Buckingham's 1924 conclusions that low speeds and high fuel consumption made jet engines impractical. By the mid-1930s, however, some researchers in the aircraft design community were beginning to question the likelihood of continued progress in propeller-driven aircraft technology. In 1934, NACA researcher John Stack reported a practical limit to speeds achievable by propeller-driven aircraft. A different power plant would have to be employed if aircraft were to fly near or faster than the speed of sound.[7]

Meanwhile, several U.S. manufacturers had embraced the turbine engine as a means to supply pressurized air to railroad diesel engines. In July 1935, for example, the American Locomotive Company (ALCO) was granted a license by a Swiss syndicate to manufacture superchargers for ALCO's diesels.[8] Building reliable turbines as superchargers posed many design and metallurgical problems for railroad-engine builders, but manufacturers kept investing in their development because their use promised to lower engine operating costs while dramatically boosting the amount of power that a diesel of given weight could provide.[9] There was little or no understanding within the railroad or aviation engine industries that the blast of hot air from a gas turbine engine would in itself provide the forward force needed to propel an airplane.

The turbo-supercharger is interesting technologically because it is just a step away from a turbojet, at least in its configuration. In a turbo-supercharger, exhaust gas from the engine spins a turbine. The turbine in turn is connected to a compressor, the output of which enters the engine. In *The Jet Pioneers,* Glyn Jones describes in some detail the work of General Electric's (GE's) supercharger developer, Dr. Sanford A. Moss. Moss may have been the first person to build a successful gas turbine—in 1903, for his PhD degree at Cornell University. Moss's turbine was driven by the combustion of pressurized air. After receiving his degree, Moss joined a group at GE building low-pressure centrifugal compressors—one of the other two elements, after the turbine, of a successful gas turbine or jet engine (the third element is a combustion chamber). When the United States entered World War I, Moss and his GE associates were asked to develop an engine booster for high-flying aircraft, and Moss chose to work on the turbo-supercharger. It was tested successfully on Pikes Peak in June 1918.[10]

Jones suggests that the Army Air Corps barely kept Moss's project alive after World War I. The Army's desire to field very-high-flying bombers revived the project after 1935, and prototype turbo-superchargers fitted to the engines of an Army bomber in 1937 enabled the plane to fly at thirty-seven thousand feet. GE was mass-producing turbo-superchargers by 1940, having overcome problems of turbine-blade reliability, but Moss himself never took the next step to turn his invention into a jet turbine.

The experience of Douglas Aircraft engineer Vladimir Pavlecka further illustrates the difficulties that faced engineers who wanted to develop turbojet engines for aircraft. According to Glyn Jones, in 1933 Pavlecka proposed using a gas turbine to drive a propeller.[11] Pavlecka was an experienced engineer; he had produced the design for the pressurized cabin for the commercial version of the DC-4. His superiors at Douglas Aircraft forwarded his proposal to Pratt & Whitney, which sent it on to MIT, whose staff concluded that it would be too heavy for use in aircraft. Pavlecka later joined Northrop, which split from Douglas in 1939, and apparently wrote up a proposal for using public funds to develop what became known as a turboprop engine. He sent that proposal to the Navy's Bureau of Aeronautics and to the Army in 1940. Jones concludes that the Navy rejected Pavlecka's proposal because its wooden carrier flight decks could not withstand the heat of a jet's exhaust. The Army also rejected the proposal, though Jones believes that Pavlecka's proposal to the Army may have supported those who favored initial development of the Lockheed L-1000 axial-flow jet engine, first begun in 1940.

Third, no official in NACA or the military championed the need to build research facilities and fund a team of researchers that could amass a body of knowledge about jet propulsion and supersonic flight. There was no appreciation among these officials and officers of the impact of what they did not know on their evaluations of what could be. In Europe, scientists and engineers who investigated alternatives to propeller-driven aircraft gathered in 1935 at the Fifth Volta Congress on High Speed Flight, the first international conference devoted to the science of supersonic flight. Sponsored by the Italian Academy of Sciences and held in Rome, the Volta Congress brought together the world's preeminent aerodynamicists, including the Hungarian-American Theodore von Kármán. He was impressed with the reported research results on high-speed flight and concerned about the lack of theoretical work in the United States. American engineers produced first-rate empirical data regarding the design of subsonic aircraft and piston-engine aircraft, but it was German or German-educated scientists who led the theoretical investigations of high-speed and turbocompressor phenomena. In terms of quality of theoretical research on high-speed flight, the British were slightly behind the Germans, and the Americans lagged badly.[12]

Not only were the Europeans doing the best theoretical research, they were building the research tools to maintain their research lead. While attending the conference, von Kármán visited the Italian research center at Guidonia and saw an Italian 2,500 mph wind tunnel that was used to investigate supersonic phenomena. Upon his return to the United States, von Kármán attempted to persuade Army Air Corps leaders to build a supersonic wind tunnel, but they rejected his idea, arguing that it would be too expensive, even assuming that any funds at all could be found to construct it. Von Kármán urged NACA to build such a wind tunnel, but George W. Lewis, NACA's executive director, turned him down. Lewis's argument was that there was no need to build a wind tunnel capable of speeds greater than the existing NACA 650 mph tunnel, because propellers rapidly lost efficiency at speeds greater than 600 mph. Lewis did not critically examine his own assumption that aircraft would always be driven by engines powering propellers.[13]

Fourth, neither U.S. aircraft firms, the Army, nor the Navy closely followed European advances in aeronautics and aerodynamics. Prohibitions in the Neutrality Acts of 1935, 1936, and 1937, especially the 1937 law, prevented U.S. firms from dealing with any belligerent nation except on a "cash and carry" basis. Even those interactions were blocked by Congress in 1939, when it limited professional contacts between American civilian aeronautical engineers working for the major manufacturers, such as Douglas, Grumman, and Curtiss, and their counterparts overseas.

Moreover, by 1939, the United States had the biggest airline network in the world, and its largest airplane manufacturers (Boeing, Douglas, and Martin) produced the largest and most advanced airliners. Given this record of achievement, the Army and Navy had no reason to imagine that foreign aircraft innovations might revolutionize military aviation in ways that American designers did not themselves foresee. That view was probably reinforced by intense French and British attempts to buy U.S. combat aircraft from 1938 onward.

In 1938, prompted by a report written by a Navy officer who had seen gas turbines in Europe, the National Academy of Sciences set up a committee on jet propulsion.[14] The following year, according to BuAer's *Ten-Year R&D History,* the Navy—mindful of developments overseas—asked the National Academy of Sciences to evaluate gas turbines for marine propulsion. It later added a request that they be evaluated for aircraft propulsion. The academy's report, which was printed in the Bureau of Ships' *Technical Bulletin* in January 1941, judged gas turbines far too heavy for aircraft use—sustaining the view of NACA regarding gas-turbine technology. Theodore von Kármán, now a member of the Navy's board of engineers charged to review the applicability of gas turbines to flight, later denied that he had attended the meetings on the subject or had read the report and regretted affixing his signature to it.[15]

BuAer's *Ten-Year R&D History* reports that the Army and Navy jointly funded a Northrop turboprop project for a 2,500 hp engine, signing a contract to that effect on 30 June 1941, *despite* the pessimistic assessments of both the National Academy and NACA. William Green and Roy Cross note that Northrop made its proposal in March 1939, calling its engine "the Turbodyne." It was not a successful design.[16]

In a turbojet, the piston engine between compressor and turbine is replaced by a combustion chamber, and compression ratio and outlet temperature are considerably higher. Instead of helping a piston engine turn a propeller, the jet engine uses its exhaust to push the airplane ahead. In 1939, General Electric was the dominant U.S. turbocharger manufacturer. Though at that date GE had not yet developed methods for mass-producing reliable turbine blades and for overcoming the disruptive effects of turbine stall inside its superchargers, the firm was an obvious candidate to build a U.S. jet engine, once the government had decided to enter this field.[17]

The Hunt for an Effective Jet Engine Begins

In sending the Tizard Mission to the United States in the fall of 1940, Prime Minister Winston Churchill decided to present the Americans, who he expected would eventually enter the war, with the fruits of advanced British research. The best-known example was the magnetron, which made short-wave (centimetric) radar possible. However, the mission also brought an account of jet propulsion, which was then under development. In its official postwar history, the General Electric Company argues that it was the first U.S. firm to develop a jet turbine—in response to a request from General Arnold, as commander of Army Air Forces, in the summer of 1941. But Green and Cross, in their *The Jet Aircraft of the World,* suggest that Lockheed had already decided to develop a jet engine by that time. Lockheed christened its jet engine L-1000, and the firm hoped to interest the Army Air Forces in a fighter (L-133) powered by its new engine. Its reasoning paralleled that which had produced the first German engine: a young German engineer, Hans von Ohain, sold the idea to the Heinkel aircraft company, which produced first a test airplane (the He-176) and then a prototype fighter (He-280). Lockheed was not nearly so lucky. Its engine never worked well, and the Army showed no interest in its futuristic fighter.

By early 1941, two events paved the way for the mass production of jet engines. First, the Whittle engine—using centrifugal flow—was nearing the flight-test stage, the prototype engine having run long enough to show that it had the necessary endurance to power a combat aircraft. Second, the Lend-Lease bill, which ended the restrictions of the 1939 Neutrality Act, came into effect in March, implying that the United States would produce the weapons the British needed to fight the war. A further implication for the British was that new technology should be shared. That included the new jet engine, although it is not clear to what extent it was described to the Americans in detail.

Accounts of what happened next vary. On 25 February 1941 General Arnold, then still Deputy Army Chief of Staff for Air, asked Dr. Vannevar Bush, who headed the new National Defense Research Committee, to form a jet-propulsion group. In March a NACA committee was formed, headed by Professor William F. Durand, who had taught Dr. Sanford A. Moss, the developer of U.S. turbochargers, at Cornell. Durand was also a founding member of NACA. His special committee included representatives of the Army, the Navy (BuAer), the Bureau of Standards (in effect, the government's physical research laboratory), Johns Hopkins University, MIT, and the three major U.S. turbine makers (Allis-Chalmers, GE, and Westinghouse). General Arnold specifically barred American piston-engine makers, on the ground that jet development would distract them from the urgently needed production of masses of piston engines optimized to fight the coming war.

By the end of June 1941, all three U.S. turbine companies had responded to secret requests from the Army and Navy that they examine the Whittle engine and simultaneously develop their own concepts.[18] Contracts were let in July, and soon GE was working on the world's first turboprop engine. According to the BuAer *Ten-Year R&D*

History, all three companies proposed axial-flow engines. Westinghouse proposed both a simple turbojet and a ramjet. GE proposed the already mentioned turboprop. Allis-Chalmers proposed a ducted fan (turbofan). Contracts were negotiated in the fall of 1941.[19] The Navy decided to back the Westinghouse and Allis-Chalmers projects; the Army backed GE, whose engine was called the TG-100.[20]

Allis-Chalmers was asked by the Navy to submit a detailed proposal in November 1941 and Westinghouse that December. Allis-Chalmers received an eighteen-month development contract in January 1942, but at the end of that time its design was dropped as less promising than existing engines. Westinghouse received its first contract on 8 December 1941, for a nineteen-inch-diameter engine (called the Type 19). In 1942 it became clear that its thrust could be increased considerably by increasing its inlet temperature; the resulting Type 19A was the first Navy turbojet. Because it was conceived as a booster, it had none of the usual engine accessories (e.g., a generator). However, a modified version, the 19B, was equipped with auxiliaries (mounted on the outside) so that it could be used as either a booster or a main power plant. This change was embodied in a May 1943 contract. Aircraft were first designed around the 19B engine in the summer of 1943.[21] A further improved 19XB offered an increase of thrust to 1,680 pounds (1944), up from 1,360 pounds in the 19A and 1,200 in the original 19. By way of comparison, GE's I-16 produced 1,600 pounds of thrust (see below).

Once the design was well under way, BuAer became interested in the possibility of clustering smaller engines in place of one or two large ones. Presumably the expected advantage was that an airplane could gain range by cruising on part of its power plant (later a selling point for the F2H Banshee, which could shut down one of its two engines on combat air patrol). The result was a 9.5-inch-diameter engine (Type 9.5, or J32), the main application of which was in the Gorgon missile. It was conceived as having half the diameter of the 19-series engine, with a quarter of the thrust (because the mass flow through the engine, which determines thrust, is proportional to the area of the air intake).

By 1944 BuAer was interested in gaining more power, so it let a contract to Westinghouse for a three-thousand-pound-thrust engine. That required about 1.32 times the diameter (twenty-five inches); improvements in efficiency made it possible for Westinghouse to offer the desired power in a twenty-four-inch package, the resulting engine being called the Type 24. The BuAer history associates this engine with the Ryan FR-1 hybrid-power fighter. The twenty-four-inch engine was later redesignated J34 (a scaled-up redesign, offering 4,500 pounds of thrust, was the J46).

General Arnold had visited England in 1941. He was shown the prototype E28/39 aircraft and was much impressed by British progress. Arnold selected GE as the lead

American company to cooperate with the British, because it already had considerable experience in centrifugal compressors and supercharger turbines. Details were provided to two American engineers in London on 22 July 1941, and in September an agreement was made to provide the United States with full details of the British engines, subject only to secrecy. GE was given plans of the British Whittle (centrifugal-flow) engine, and ultimately it also received an example. The company used the term "Type I supercharger" for this project, so its early engines were numbered in an *I* series (e.g., I-16, I-40). The I-40—the designation presumably indicates a goal of four thousand pounds of thrust—powered the first American-production jet fighter, the P-80 (later F-80) Shooting Star. Production of these engines was licensed to Allison in 1944, and the engines were given *J* designations (the I-16 became the J31 and the I-40 the J33). Allison later took over J33 development, ultimately increasing its thrust to 6,350 pounds. Allison also took over development of GE's axial-flow J35, which was the precursor to the successful J47.

The Durand committee divided up the development and production effort, the Army supporting the GE centrifugal-flow engines derived from the British prototypes and the Navy supporting axial-flow engines. However, the BuAer R&D history (late 1945) suggests limited Navy interest in jet propulsion, on the ground that it was suited only to a short-range interceptor, which was hardly what the Navy was after—it wanted long-endurance aircraft, to occupy combat air patrol stations. In his history of early Navy jet fighters, Tommy Thomason notes that the FH-1, the first operational jet fighter, "had twice the internal fuel capacity of the contemporary F8F-1 [Bearcat]." But "the jet had only 60 to 70 percent of the endurance of the piston engine fighter, even though it carried twice the fuel."[22] This lack of endurance is why the Navy initially preferred mixed piston-jet aircraft like the Ryan Fireball (FR-1) to all-jet aircraft like the Phantom (FD-1). However, the BuAer fighter correspondence files associate the Fireball with a special requirement—an escort-carrier fighter, as an alternative to the Bearcat, proposed before that aircraft—rather than with a general-purpose fleet-carrier fighter. The Navy did contract with Curtiss for a mixed-power heavy fighter (F15C), but this airplane was soon discarded. Grumman design files of this period show crude sketches of both all-jet and mixed-power aircraft, but the company offered only an all-jet fighter for the 1944 competition, apparently the first in wartime fighter design.[23]

The Hunt for an Effective Jet Engine Intensifies

We should discuss the difference between the two types of jet engine, because the choices made in 1941 had important implications. A centrifugal compressor is simpler than an axial one, because it has only one or two stages (the latter uses two such compressors back to back). Centrifugal compressors were incorporated in the superchargers of the

1930s. Such a compressor is short but requires considerable diameter; the way to increase mass flow, hence thrust, is to increase diameter. Flow can also be increased by making the compressor run faster, but ultimately the output of such an engine is limited by its diameter. The engine also loses some power because the air flowing through it must, in effect, turn a corner. However, until jet engines approached seven thousand pounds of thrust, centrifugal flow was quite attractive.

The British and the Germans used centrifugal flow for their first jet engines, but the Germans soon turned to the theoretically much more attractive axial-flow configuration. In the axial-flow design, the air moves straight through the engine. Each stage of the compressor (i.e., each ring of blades) adds a degree of compression, so that the net effect of the compressor depends on how many stages it uses—as well as, of course, on its diameter. Ultimately the axial configuration is more efficient and much easier to scale up. Once engines were producing more than 7,000 to 7,500 pounds of thrust, axial flow became universal.

The dominant theme in early British development was centrifugal flow, although there was early interest in axial-flow engines. Inventor Frank Whittle sold the jet idea to the Royal Air Force and subsisted for years on very limited public funding for it plus considerable privately raised money. Only about 1939 did the British government begin funding Whittle on anything like a sufficient scale. Once the war began, the government enforced cooperation among possible producers, almost all of which developed variations of Whittle's basic themes.[24] Thus, when Americans bought British engines, though from different manufacturers, they were really buying much the same device in different sizes.

GE began by copying Whittle's W1 engine, and it then adapted a de Havilland engine (the Goblin) to power the prototype of the first major U.S. jet fighter, the P-80 Shooting Star. Meanwhile Rolls-Royce developed a series of engines with "river" names: Derwent, Nene, Tay. Once GE had successfully copied the Goblin (as the I-40), it became interested in a more powerful engine (four thousand pounds of thrust). In response the British designed the Rolls-Royce Nene, more powerful (five-thousand-pound thrust) and lighter than the new GE engine, even though at that time the Air Ministry did not envisage a fighter requiring that much power. This development proved fortunate for BuAer, because it made possible a single-engine fighter at a time when it seemed that the bureau's engines would not suffice except in pairs.

The Durand committee was intended to coordinate U.S. research (and, probably, to avoid wasteful duplication), but it was in a position very different from that of the British gas-turbine committee: it did not have a central R&D organization (like the Royal Aircraft Establishment) the fruits of which could be distributed to manufacturers.

Instead, American companies were encouraged and funded to do their own developmental work, *as they had been in the 1930s*. BuAer's practice was to foster engine improvements and then offer the newly produced engines to the airframe manufacturers, like Grumman, Douglas, and Curtiss. Axial flow was virgin territory, of which the British were not supplying any prototypes. It says a great deal for Westinghouse that its first axial-flow engine (J30) was running successfully at the end of 1943.

Indeed, BuAer's success in fostering an entirely domestic jet engine in the face of improved air-cooled piston engines (like the Pratt & Whitney 3,500 hp R-4360) and opposition from its own engine specialists is surprising. The main problem with all early jet aircraft, whether they had centrifugal-flow or axial-flow engines, was that they lacked endurance because of high rates of fuel consumption.[25] The cycle of aircraft operations from carriers was:

- Launch a strike or patrols
- Move any aircraft still on deck forward, so that returning aircraft would have a space in which to land
- Recover the aircraft coming back from their flights
- Move the aircraft parked forward back aft so that the carrier could begin launching aircraft again.

As Thomason pointed out, "the relatively limited endurance of jets forced this cycle to become significantly shorter and less flexible." This imposed "a much stricter operating timetable on flight operations than had previously been the case."[26]

Moreover, jet engines were slow to accelerate. According to Thomason, "The Pratt & Whitney R-2800 piston engine powering the Grumman F8F Bearcat would develop about 7,000 pounds of thrust with a 13-foot diameter propeller at . . . takeoff power. The total thrust in the first jets was less than half that, even when the engines were new, and old was measured in tens of hours."[27] This relatively low power and the inability to accelerate and decelerate quickly made taking off and landing in the early jets a very different—and more hazardous—proposition than it had been in even heavy, powerful piston-engine aircraft like the F4U Corsair. Is it any wonder that officers in BuAer's Powerplant Division had doubts about turbojets and preferred turboprop engines?[28] As longtime BuAer engineer George A. Spangenberg observed in his oral history, "The Navy had a very real problem in attempting to get into the jet age."[29]

The Westinghouse engine (J34) seems to have been specified for the Navy jet fighter (specifically, night fighter) competition in 1944, though Spangenberg notes that Grumman "surprised everyone by submitting a four engine arrangement with [Westinghouse] J30 engines."[30] It is intriguing that sketches in Grumman files appear to show designs built around *centrifugal-flow* engines. The implication would seem to be that the facts of jet engines were disclosed to all major U.S. manufacturers but that BuAer had no interest in using the engine that the Army was then adopting for its first fighters (the P-59A Airacomet and then the P-80). The use of the phrase "all-American" (as opposed to British-conceived) in a BuAer *Confidential Bulletin* account of the first jet fighters suggests a sense that the U.S. alternative was inherently better.

The Grumman sketches may be explained by the 1943 visit of British engineers who described the new British Halford H-1 engine (the de Havilland Goblin); it was to be built starting in 1945 as the J36 centrifugal-flow jet engine under license in the United States by Allis-Chalmers.[31] Producing 2,700 pounds of thrust, the J36 was an alternative to the General Electric I-40 installed in the Army's P-80. It was also considered for use in the Curtiss F15C. In Britain, de Havilland installed the H-1 Goblin in its Vampire fighter. The H-1/J36 was superseded by GE's improved I-40 (J33).

BuAer sponsored two Westinghouse engines, designated according to their diameters, nineteen or twenty-four inches. Two nineteen-inch engines powered the first Navy jet fighter, the McDonnell FD-1 (later FH-1) Phantom. Single twenty-four-inch engines were used in the 1944 competition, the winners being the North American Fury (FJ-1) and the Vought Pirate (F6U). Apparently the FD-1 was considered no more than a feasibility experiment; BuAer's official position was that it would not be a particularly good carrier fighter, but it was produced in some numbers so that pilots could gain experience with jet-propelled aircraft.[32] At least some of these aircraft went to the Marines, even though these jets could not possibly operate from the escort carriers the Marines were then using.

Additional fighter orders in 1945 used multiple twenty-four-inch engines, as did the 1946 interceptor, the Vought F7U Cutlass (two engines). All of these engines were limited to about four thousand pounds of thrust. As seen at the time, the next step was for Westinghouse to scale up the engine to about 7,500 pounds of thrust, the result being designated the J40 (Westinghouse Type 40, for its forty-inch diameter). It was slated to power the F3H Demon, which the Navy hoped (unfortunately incorrectly) would provide performance equivalent to that of the new land-based fighters. The failure of this engine apparently killed Westinghouse as a jet engine builder. As Thomason put it, "After successfully developing very capable jet engines literally from scratch in the early 1940s, Westinghouse lost its touch."[33] Spangenberg, who by 1946 was the assistant director of BuAer's design review office, agreed: the J40 was "one of the big powerplant busts that the Navy had."[34] Douglas's Ed Heinemann, who designed the F4D Skyray, apparently suspected that the new engine might fail. He gave the plane's structure sufficient diameter to take an alternative, which proved necessary—the airplane used the new J57 (a Pratt & Whitney axial-flow turbojet). The F3H was redesigned to take a new Allison J71.

GE, the primary competitor to Westinghouse, developed its own axial-flow engines, first the J35 and then a production version, the J47, which powered such Air Force classics as the F-86 Saberjet and the B-47 Stratojet. These engines do not seem to have held much attraction for the Navy, and it is not certain why. It is possible that Air Force orders consumed all of GE's productive capacity. All general BuAer program documents refer to the steady progression of Westinghouse axial-flow engines; it is not clear that BuAer was even interested in any other manufacturer in the period immediately after World War II. However, immediately after World War II there was no engine more powerful than the twenty-four-inch type (originally called the 24C). At some point in 1946 the British Nene (which was produced under license by Pratt & Whitney) was added to the list of engines that companies could offer in their proposals.

It also seems that BuAer suddenly realized that the fighters it had chosen in 1944 could not match current land-based types. It had chosen Grumman to build a four-engine night fighter, or intruder, the F9F, in a 1945 jet-night-fighter contest (the other aircraft chosen was the twin-engine Douglas F3D Skyknight). Late in 1945 BuAer canceled the F9F-1 but left the contract alive. Grumman designed a single-engine day fighter powered by the Nene engine, offering it in August 1946. It is not clear to what extent Grumman had been encouraged officially or unofficially to develop such a design.[35] It was more powerful than the 1944 fighters but much less sophisticated aerodynamically than the interceptors of the 1946 competition. In retrospect it seems to have been conceived as an interim fighter, but that is not clear from records now available.

The interesting point here is that BuAer seems to have found in the British centrifugal-flow engines a useful alternative to the Westinghouse axial-flow ones. It seems to have been BuAer's decision, because at least one company offered a 1946 interceptor powered by a Nene in June 1946, before Grumman offered the proposal for what became the F9F-2 Panther. The Grumman airplane, in turn, had a fuselage big enough to accommodate a centrifugal-flow engine and thus became a candidate for any follow-on British engine. Pratt & Whitney became the U.S. producer of the Nene, collaborating with the British manufacturer, Rolls-Royce, on the next type, the Tay (U.S. J48). Note that none of the other BuAer projects could accommodate such bulky engines; the bureau clearly saw the British engines as a stopgap until better axial-flow turbojets came along. Again, as during the war, it had no particular reason to consider British technology superior to American. It is perhaps interesting that the BuAer *Confidential Bulletin,* which included a section on engines in every issue, devoted no attention to

British engines in the years immediately after World War II, though the bulletin did contain articles on Soviet and even Swedish developments.

It mattered that engines like the J40 worked, because they were frequently buried in fighters' fuselages. Altering a fighter design to accept an alternative engine with a different diameter was not trivial, because the airplane's aerodynamics would change quite drastically, as would its weight balance. Any such drastic change equated to substantial delay in an aircraft's scheduled development.

Some background on the diffusion of engineering knowledge about jet turbines from the Royal Navy to the U.S. Navy may also be relevant. In 1945 the United States clearly led the world both in carrier aircraft and in carrier operating techniques. Contact with the Royal Navy had not revealed areas of British equality, let alone superiority, with the sole exception of the armored flight deck—which the U.S. Navy adopted in its last World War II carriers. The Royal Navy had purchased large numbers of American-supplied Lend-Lease aircraft, but it was not in the position of approaching U.S. industry hat in hand, desperate for whatever could be provided. C. R. Fairey, head of the experienced aircraft design and production firm of the same name, spent the years 1941–45 as the head of the British Air Commission in Washington, and he supervised the growth of the commission from a liaison office to a thousand-person staff, many of whose members were resident in U.S. aircraft firms.[36] British industry had produced many outstanding aircraft just before and during World War II. As we showed in *American & British Aircraft Carrier Development, 1919–1941,* the problem for the RN was that it had not correctly anticipated the campaigns its carrier force would have to carry out and hence had asked the British Air Ministry for what might be termed "the wrong planes." In addition, the RN never could devote the tremendous manpower and industrial resources to carrier aviation that the USN did during the war; the gap between the sizes and resources of the two carrier forces was dramatically in favor of the latter.[37]

In 1945 the victorious Allies scrambled to seize German technology.[38] For example, the multivolume *Ten-Year R&D History* of BuAer R&D, produced in about November 1945, consistently included sections on German developments alongside those describing BuAer's. German advances in engine and aircraft design were a powerful stimulus to aircraft designers in Britain, the Soviet Union, and the United States. Cdr. Alfred B. Metsger, who had a graduate degree from MIT and became BuAer's chief fighter "class desk" officer in October 1945, after serving as air group commander on carrier *Saratoga,* quickly grasped the importance of both the jet turbine engine and the swept-wing aircraft designs prototyped by the Germans during the war. Spangenberg recalled years later Metsger's strong and persistent advocacy of "pure" jets over the "mixed" type like the Ryan FR-1 Fireball and turboprop designs.[39] Spangenberg also notes that

Metsger was opposed by colleagues such as Capt. Selden B. Spangler, who headed the power-plant design branch within BuAer.[40] Spangler was well aware of the limitations of the early jet engines and did not want to gamble on what he saw as an uncertain future. Westinghouse's trouble with the J40 seemed to show that scaling up the power of axial-thrust jet engines would not be as straightforward as the aircraft (as opposed to the engine) designers expected. Spangenberg points out that tests with a P-80 fighter flying simulated combat against a Navy F8F Bearcat "educated a lot of the people" in the advantages of the jet fighter.[41] Still, the concerns about the future of axial-flow jet engines would continue. As Thomason recognized in his study of carrier fighter development, all the major jet engine manufacturers had difficulty during and immediately after World War II producing reliable, high-output turbine engines.[42]

Notes

1. Tommy H. Thomason, *U.S. Naval Air Superiority: Development of Shipborne Jet Fighters, 1943–1962* (North Branch, Minn.: Specialty, 2007).

2. Robert Schlaifer, *Development of Aircraft Engines* (Boston: Graduate School of Business Administration, Harvard University, 1950), p. 160. Also I. B. Holley, Jr., "Jet Lag in the Army Air Corps," in *Military Planning in the Twentieth Century,* ed. Harry R. Borowski (Washington, D.C.: U.S. Government Printing Office, 1986), p. 133.

3. For application of the economists' concept of "lock-in" to innovation in military innovation, see Mark D. Mandeles, *The Development of the B-52 and Jet Propulsion: A Case Study in Organizational Innovation* (Maxwell Air Force Base, Ala.: Air Univ. Press, 1998), chap. 3. See also Paul A. David, "Clio and the Economics of QWERTY," *American Economic Review* 75 (May 1985).

4. Schlaifer, *Development of Aircraft Engines,* p. 445.

5. Ibid., p. 440.

6. Holley, "Jet Lag in the Army Air Corps," pp. 124–25.

7. Ibid., pp. 125–26.

8. J. Parker Lamb, *Evolution of the American Diesel Locomotive* (Bloomington: Indiana Univ. Press, 2007), p. 60.

9. Ibid., pp. 125–26.

10. Moss's first turbo-supercharger was far more efficient than any gear-driven supercharger, because it was not shaft driven. A brief description of Moss's work is in John Anderson Miller, *Men and Volts at War: The Story of General Electric in World War II* (New York: McGraw-Hill, 1947), pp. 72–74.

11. Glyn Jones, *The Jet Pioneers: The Birth of Jet-Powered Flight* (London: Methuen, 1989), pp. 184–85.

12. Theodore von Kármán with Lee Edson, *The Wind and Beyond* (Boston: Little, Brown, 1967), pp. 216–23; Edward W. Constant II, *The Origins of the Turbojet Revolution* (Baltimore: Johns Hopkins Univ. Press, 1980), pp. 154–56.

13. Constant, *Origins of the Turbojet Revolution,* pp. 156–59; Holley, "Jet Lag in the Army Air Corps," p. 126; Alex Roland, *Model Research* (Washington, D.C.: National Aeronautics and Space Administration, 1985), vol. 1, pp. 186–87.

14. Roland, *Model Research,* p. 188.

15. Von Kármán with Edson, *Wind and Beyond,* p. 225.

16. William Green and Roy Cross, *The Jet Aircraft of the World* (New York: Hanover House, 1956), p. 20.

17. Ibid., pp. 73–74.

18. Ibid., pp. 77–80.

19. Note that by 1941 it was possible for the military services to negotiate cost contracts with industry. The prior restrictions on negotiated contracts in favor of "sealed bids" had been partly removed by Congress. For details, see Irving B. Holley, *Buying Aircraft: Materiel Procurement for the Army Air Forces* (Washington, D.C.: Office of the Chief of Military History, U.S. Army, 1964), and Robert H. Connery, *The Navy and the Industrial Mobilization in World War II* (Princeton, N.J.: Princeton Univ. Press, 1951).

20. U.S. Navy Dept., *Ten-Year History and Program of Future Research and Development of Aircraft Power Plants* (Washington, D.C.: Bureau of Aeronautics, 1945) [hereafter BuAer, *Ten-Year History*], vol. 4, pp. 154–59.

21. The aircraft designed around the Westinghouse 19B (or J30) were the McDonnell FD (Phantom), the Ryan FR-1 (Fireball), and an Army flying-wing fighter (P-79). The 19B was also considered as a booster for the Douglas BTD-1 (Destroyer) and as the main power plant for a missile canceled in 1944. Pratt & Whitney later received a production contract for the 19B engine, designated J30.

22. Thomason, *U.S. Naval Air Superiority*, p. 13.

23. Grumman has always said publicly that the Bearcat was a private venture conceived by the firm rather than a response to a BuAer initiative, but that may not have been quite true. As Thomason notes, Grumman was a "preferred BuAer supplier," and so exchanges between BuAer and company personnel were frequent during the war and often difficult to document. See ibid., p. 57.

24. Note that this meant the British did not pursue mixed piston-and-jet-powered aircraft like the Ryan FR-1.

25. Thomason, *U.S. Naval Air Superiority*, pp. 12–13.

26. Ibid., p. 13.

27. Ibid., p. 11. Thomason drew on BuAer engineer George A. Spangenberg's 1997 "Oral History," 31 August 1997, *George Spangenberg Oral History*, 2010, www.georgespangenberg.com, for this information; see p. 67.

28. Thomason, *U.S. Naval Air Superiority*, p. 30.

29. Spangenberg, "Oral History," p. 66.

30. Ibid., p. 93.

31. BuAer, *Ten-Year History*.

32. In his memoir, retired vice admiral Donald Engen notes that the small number of early-postwar jets available for training kept many pilots—even veteran pilots—from gaining the air time necessary to fly them with skill. Donald D. Engen, *Wings and Warriors: My Life as a Naval Aviator* (Washington, D.C.: Smithsonian Institution Press, 1997), p. 88.

33. Thomason, *U.S. Naval Air Superiority*, p. 91. Thomason mentions labor problems within Westinghouse on p. 57 but does not elaborate.

34. Spangenberg, "Oral History," p. 100.

35. In his oral history Spangenberg notes only the change in the Grumman contract.

36. H. A. Taylor, *Fairey Aircraft since 1915* (Annapolis, Md.: Naval Institute Press, 1974), pp. 24–25.

37. Geoffrey Till, in his *Air Power and the Royal Navy, 1914–1945* (London: Jane's, 1979), makes this point—that by 1945 the USN's carrier force was decidedly and dramatically larger than the RN's and that this had a psychological effect. See pp. 109–10.

38. Eric Brown describes his adventures in Germany at war's end in his delightful *Wings on My Sleeve* (London: Orion Books–Phoenix, 2007), chaps. 9, 10.

39. Spangenberg, "Oral History," p. 102.

40. Ibid.

41. Ibid., p. 103.

42. Thomason, *U.S. Naval Air Superiority*, p. 95.

CHAPTER SIX

British and American Prospects after the War

> *It was the best of times, it was the worst of times, . . . it was the spring of hope, it was the winter of despair, we had everything before us, we had nothing before us.*
>
> CHARLES DICKENS, *A TALE OF TWO CITIES*

At the conclusion of World War II, the U.S. Navy contracted "dramatically, the number of naval personnel alone dropping from over 3 million to less than 1 million by June 1946. The Bureau of Ships canceled over $1 billion in wartime shipbuilding contracts, over 7,000 vessels were declared war surplus, and 2,000 more were mothballed."[1] The immediate postwar demobilization was followed by a longer-term decline: "The Navy reduced aviation forces 80 percent to a total of 10,232 pilots, 56,767 aviation ratings, and 20 aircraft carriers of all classes by the end of 1949."[2]

Making matters even worse was the war-produced "bulge" of qualified younger naval aviators, who now faced the prospect of slow promotion. As aviator Donald Engen recalled, "In the late 1940s and early 1950s, many of the more senior naval aviators had two or more opportunities for aviation commands while all officers were virtually frozen in their current ranks until the personnel turmoil associated with the end of the war could be dealt with."[3] In many U.S. Navy squadrons, as Adm. James L. Holloway III would recall, "morale was at rock bottom and discipline was nonexistent."[4]

For the Royal Navy, the years after World War II were, from the financial point of view, even more catastrophic. As naval historian Michael Isenberg notes, "At the time of Pearl Harbor, Great Britain had mounted a navy of 363 combat ships and 300,000 men, and the Americans had 339 combatants and 353,000 men—the two fleets were at rough parity. . . . Ten years after Pearl, the bell had tolled: Korea and anticommunism had swollen America's Navy from its immediate postwar doldrums to 958 combatants and 705,000 men. . . . The Royal Navy had only 175 combatants and 150,000 men."[5]

The cause of the RN's severe decline was simple: "The British were bankrupt, with overseas debts fifteen times their reserves of gold and foreign currency. Their export trade [in 1946] was one-third the level of that in 1939, and their visible exports could finance only 10 percent of their overseas requirements."[6] The government of the United States had not helped matters when it abruptly cut off Lend-Lease aid to Britain within a month of the end of World War II in the Pacific.

Both postwar navies—the USN and the RN—had suffered in financial and personnel terms, but the U.S. economy had not suffered the way that the British had. Indeed, the American economy had actually grown in real terms during the war. This economic growth meant that the U.S. Navy had more actual and potential financial resources available to it.

Moreover, aviation within the U.S. Navy had strengthened *institutionally,* as a result of its wartime performance. As Vincent Davis documented in his 1962 study of the Navy's postwar leadership, naval aviators came out of World War II with the strong support of the Navy's civilian leaders. In May 1944, in testimony to a congressional committee studying postwar defense organization, Assistant Secretary of the Navy for Air Artemus Gates argued that "it must be clear to all by now that the naval air force has proved to be the most important member of the Navy team."[7] A year later, Navy secretary James Forrestal described to a Senate subcommittee a true transformation in naval warfare:

> One of the major purposes of the fast carriers' interdiction strikes in advance of an invasion is to knock out or pin down Japanese land-based air power all around our target. These battles of our carrier-based air power against Japanese land-based air power now comprise one of the great struggles going on in the Pacific. It really points up the question, Can sea air power cope with land-based air power? I think the answer is obvious in the fact we are coping with it and we have beaten it.[8]

Forrestal backed up his endorsement of this new concept of naval aviation's mission with action to shift the center of gravity of the Navy from surface ships to aviation. As the young aviator Donald Engen saw firsthand, there were immediate benefits for the more senior naval aviators: "In the first major postwar promotion of Regular Navy line captains to flag rank, fourteen out of the total of eighteen were aviators."[9] In fiscal year 1941, only 12 percent of unrestricted line officers were aviators. In fiscal year 1947, the proportion had nearly tripled, to 34 percent.[10] Funding for the Navy fell dramatically, and a huge number of trained personnel left the service, but aviation was significantly stronger *within the Navy* than it had been before the war.

But what about U.S. Navy aviators' perception of the Royal Navy's carrier force? It was negative; most Fleet Air Arm aircraft by 1944 were U.S. designs, because many British designs had not been successful. U.S. Navy aviators attributed the lack of effective British carrier aircraft to the two-decades-long control over all British military aircraft development by the Royal Air Force. The U.S. Navy's aviators argued that their wartime successes had stemmed from the control their own air arm had exercised over development, procurement, and training. They did not support the campaign by the Army Air Forces or, later, the U.S. Air Force to incorporate all fixed-wing military aviation into one service.[11]

Cooperation between American and British scientists and engineers had been close since April 1941, when the British government had set up a special office in Washington to facilitate the exchange of technical information.[12] Moreover, the U.S. Navy had been allowed to place liaison officers on RN carriers in the Mediterranean in the winter of 1940–41, with positive consequences for the USN, and the carrier forces of the two navies had traded information and insights when they had the opportunity during the war.[13]

As Vincent Davis, Jeffrey Barlow, and other researchers have noted, U.S. Navy aviation policy after World War II was most influenced by four developments: the advent of nuclear weapons; the beginning of the Cold War; the political and bureaucratic conflict over service roles and missions; and rapid technological change. We add a fifth factor—the administrative changes that drew the policy-making responsibility out of BuAer and placed it in OPNAV and that weakened the General Board. Perception and support by senior officers of innovations in carrier aviation had to occur within this highly charged and changing bureaucratic, technological, and administrative environment.

Memoirists like retired vice admirals Jerry Miller and John T. Hayward have made it very clear that the attempt to show that carriers could launch nuclear strikes and the anxiety and anger that stemmed from the "strategic bomber versus carrier" struggle dominated other issues.[14] As Hayward recalled, "From 1946 on, building the carrier-based big-bomber force [to carry nuclear weapons] evolved along two parallel, interactive lines. One focused on hardware; the other, on hiring and training able people. In both, we were 'pushing the envelope,' as pilots say."[15]

As we have pointed out, the organization of Navy aviation had also changed during the war. The authority and role of the Bureau of Aeronautics had been weakened by the creation of the office of the Deputy Chief of Naval Operations for Air (DCNO [Air]) in August 1943.[16] As Rear Adm. Julius A. Furer put it in his book on wartime Navy administration, "Broadly speaking, naval aviation planning, training of flying personnel, logistics, planning and aviation operations were now responsibilities of DCNO(Air). BuAer was responsible for all that related to the aviation materiel of the Navy, including 'designing, building, fitting out, and repairing Naval and Marine Corps aircraft, accessories, equipment, and devices, connected with aircraft.'"[17]

At first, the separation seemed beneficial. For example, Rear Adm. John S. McCain, who served as BuAer chief from October 1942 to mid-August 1943, shifted from the bureau to the Office of the Chief of Naval Operations as the first DCNO (Air). Capt. Arthur Radford, who had been Director, Training Division, in BuAer, went with McCain to OPNAV, where he headed several review boards that hammered out a comprehensive program of aircraft production, maintenance, and pilot training.[18] Again, what facilitated the development and implementation of policy was the fact that senior officers knew one another well. Complementing this familiarity was the fact that younger officers tended to rotate into and then out of BuAer or OPNAV (and of course into and out of fleet assignments), so that the shared experience gained from time spent in both organizations gave midcareer officers a common understanding of the problems facing naval aviation. But there was also the chance that aviation officers in the postwar Navy would gradually and quietly settle out into two camps—one focused on making policy in OPNAV and the other concentrating on relations with aircraft and engine manufacturers.

The Battle over Service Unification

What Barlow calls "The Fight for Naval Aviation" in the years between the end of World War II and the start of the Korean War in 1950 was just as challenging and a lot more psychologically punishing than the effort to create a nuclear strike force for the Navy. "Unification" in fact covered two issues, and both demanded the time and the energy of the Navy's highest-ranking officers. The first was service unification—the idea that the efficiency and effectiveness of U.S. forces could be improved significantly if all the services were unified under one commander and his staff. The second was the U.S. Air Force argument that it would be more efficient to place all fixed-wing aviation in one service than to spread it among the three military departments (Army, Navy, and Air Force).

The political and bureaucratic struggles over service unification and over service roles and missions have been studied in detail, and we won't review all the relevant research here. But it's important to get at least a flavor of the intensity of these past disputes. In December 1947, for example, Adm. Chester Nimitz, retiring as Chief of Naval Operations (CNO), argued, "It is improbable that bomber fleets will be capable, for several years to come[,] of making two-way trips between continents . . . with heavy loads of bombs. . . . In the event of war . . . , if we are to project our power against vital areas of an enemy across the ocean before beachheads on enemy territory are captured, it must be by air-sea power."[19] Gen. Carl A. Spaatz, the first Chief of Staff of the new Air Force, promptly fired back: "If the Navy is trying to spend hundreds of millions of dollars building aircraft carriers of a hundred thousand tons to move thirty-six bombers somewhere close to the hostile shores to deliver devastating attacks, it shows an utter lack of realization of what the hell strategic air and what air power is."[20]

Vice Adm. Arthur Radford, an aviator who was also the new Vice Chief of Naval Operations, well knew the challenge that he and other Navy leaders faced. As he told the CNO in August 1947, "The most serious mistake that we can make in the Navy at this time is to assume that everything insofar as naval aviation is concerned is alright.... It will take bold and aggressive leadership after careful advance planning to combat the Air Force arguments and drive."[21]

This dramatic confrontation between the Navy and the Air Force would scar the feelings of personnel in both services and consume much precious time and attention. The effort expended on both sides of the battle is a classic example of a high "opportunity cost." Senior aviation officers in the U.S. Navy were unavoidably preoccupied by their urgent efforts to beat back the Air Force arguments for "unification" (in both senses) and by their equally intense—and ultimately successful—campaign to create a carrier-based nuclear striking force.

For example, why didn't the U.S. Navy pioneer the concept of the angled flight deck for carriers once it realized that jet aircraft would land on carriers at higher speeds than had World War II piston-engine planes? Part of the answer has to do with the different ways that the U.S. Navy and the Royal Navy planned to use aircraft carriers after World War II. As a retired USN aviator, Rear Adm. Paul T. Gillcrist, put it in his memoir, the Royal Navy's postwar carrier concept emphasized using fighters to protect convoys from air attack, "whereas the U.S. Navy emphasized strike and air defense operations." These differing postwar operational concepts led to different operating tempos for the carriers of the two navies. The British used "a measured round-the-clock type of operation." By contrast, U.S. carriers had to produce surges of sorties for major strike operations, which meant that they wanted plenty of deck space to line up sizable numbers of attack aircraft prior to strike missions.[22]

A Grumman F9F Panther jet lands on *Essex* (CV 9). The athwartship barrier is up, but from the pilot's view he's landing into a deck full of aircraft.

Naval War College

British carriers did not have to generate the volume of sorties that U.S. carriers accepted as normal.

These operational differences meant that the RN could accept an angled deck with a four-degree offset, while the USN could not. As Gillcrist noted, "When an eight-degree angled deck was examined, however, much less deck area forward of the landing area had to be given up, and the obvious operational benefits of the angled deck became much more attractive."²³ Adm. James S. Russell, then a captain in the Office of the Chief of Naval Operations, also "wasn't completely sold on" the angled deck until he "realized its great virtue in handling jets, with which we'd had all sorts of trouble."²⁴ (See appendix B.)

Immediate Postwar Carrier Concepts

At the end of 1944, Vice Adm. Marc Mitscher, the most successful carrier-force commander in the Pacific in World War II, advocated the creation of an informal board to recommend a new carrier design to DCNO (Air).²⁵ In effect, he wanted an organization that would function much as the General Board had in the interwar years. As one would expect of Mitscher, he had been evaluating the performance of both his carriers and the aircraft flying from them. His call for a careful assessment of combat experience was echoed in May 1945 by Commander, Air Force, Pacific, the "type commander" of Navy air forces in the Pacific, who wrote to the Chief of Naval Operations to press for the modification of the *Essex*-class carriers still under construction. Specifically, he wanted the centerline aircraft elevators in the *Essex* class replaced with deck-edge elevators.²⁶ In this he was thinking in tune with BuAer, which in the same month had returned to earlier studies of the possibility of launching and recovering large, long-range bombers from new and existing carriers.²⁷

What every pilot feared—missing the arresting gear and vaulting over the barrier. The F2H-1 is headed for two Skyraiders parked at the forward end of the flight deck of USS *Coral Sea* (CV 43). The flight deck crew members are running for their lives.

U.S. Navy, courtesy of Captain Charles T. Creekman, Jr., USN (Ret.)

The F2H-1 has collided with the two Skyraiders; it will push both overboard and then go overboard itself. The driver of the jeep tractor on the centerline is miraculously alive.

U.S. Navy, courtesy of Captain Charles T. Creekman, Jr., USN (Ret.)

Nearing completion were three large (over forty-five-thousand-ton displacement) armored-deck carriers whose design had been based on earlier experience with carrier-versus-carrier combat at Midway in June 1942. These ships would be the first U.S. carriers constructed with armored flight decks. They would also have large aircraft complements—over a hundred planes. The question was whether they would satisfy both the "lessons learned" by Mitscher *and* the demands placed on any carrier by the new and promising jet aircraft.

To come up with some answers, Capt. W. T. Raisseur, who had commanded an escort carrier in World War II and had become head of the Aviation Military Characteristics office in DCNO (Air) in early 1945, conducted a thorough analysis of war experience and complemented it by consideration of the impact of newer, heavier aircraft on carrier design. As his notional aircraft he chose the F7F twin-engine fighter and the proposed BT3D turboprop attack plane.[28] Raisseur's analysis considered the carrier air group (fifty-four F7Fs and thirty-six BT3Ds) and the carrier as a single system. What did that system have to do? It had to generate sorties. To generate enough sorties in a given period of time, it had to be able to launch aircraft from several catapults simultaneously. Those aircraft would need deck space on which to wait their turns at the ship's catapults. The need for deck space would require the carrier's designers to place the aircraft elevators at the edges of the flight deck, and one of the aft catapults would have to be canted to port.[29]

The special board Mitscher wanted within OPNAV, reporting to DCNO (Air), to consider any new carrier designs was in place by June 1945, and Captain Raisseur submitted his analysis to it at the end of that month. Early in July the members of the board endorsed his analysis and his concept of a carrier that had "a radically redesigned flight deck and a new mode of operations."[30] Captain Raisseur's basic ideas—

especially that a carrier could not be designed in isolation from a concept of what aircraft it would carry and how they would be operated—would influence all future carrier designs.

In parallel with the work being done in DCNO (Air), engineers at BuAer's Naval Air Development Center in Johnsville, Pennsylvania, were developing characteristics for carrier aircraft that would be powered by turboprop engines and therefore have longer range and heavier bomb loads. Their studies led the chief of BuAer, then Rear Adm. H. B. Sallada, to propose to the Chief of Naval Operations in December 1945 that the Navy procure carrier-based bombers capable of carrying significantly larger bombs. As Sallada pointed out, "Analysis of bombing results in Germany has revealed that lethal damage to many targets required 12,000 lb bombs." As a result, BuAer sought to discover "what extension of range and of bomb size in carrier-based aircraft can be attained through technological advances in the foreseeable future." BuAer's assessment was that "a definite program be initiated to extend greatly the limiting ranges and bomb sizes of carrier-based aviation."[31] Sallada also proposed that "serious consideration . . . immediately be given to the development of an additional type" of carrier "that will accommodate aircraft of about 100,000 lbs with a 2000 mile radius."[32]

Sallada's recommendations that BuAer pursue the development of larger, heavier aircraft with significantly greater bomb loads and that a new carrier be constructed to launch and recover these planes were endorsed by the Chief of Naval Operations at the end of December. Sallada's initiative was also supported by Vice Admiral Mitscher, by then DCNO (Air), in January 1946, as well as by the informal board that Mitscher had helped create. In February the Vice Chief of Naval Operations, Adm. DeWitt Ramsey, an aviator, ordered the Bureau of Ships to begin studies of a new carrier design.[33] As Norman Friedman has discovered, BuShips developed a new design, called "C-2," in April 1946 and placed its preliminary characteristics before the Ship Characteristics Board, which reported to the Deputy CNO for Logistics (DCNO [Logistics]) that June.[34]

But in fact there were two new carrier designs under consideration. The C-2, based on wartime experience, was an alternative to the new *Midway* type. A second concept carrier (CVB-X) was developed specifically for the very-long-range and very large attack aircraft that would be able to carry heavy nuclear weapons like the implosion plutonium bomb dropped on Nagasaki in August 1945. This second carrier concept, which eventually became the design of the ill-fated *United States*, was also submitted to the Ship Characteristics Board as a potential entry in the fiscal year 1948 ship-construction budget.[35] It is in this second design that the "threads" of the heavy aircraft, the carrier designed to launch it, and the Navy's concept of carriers as nuclear weapons systems come together.

Two AJ-1 Savages on *Hancock* in late November 1955. The plane on the starboard catapult is being launched; that on the port catapult is waiting its turn. Note the early-model jet-blast deflectors.
Navy Department, National Archives

The prospect that the carrier force could fill the nuclear strike mission led the Acting Secretary of the Navy in July 1946 to write President Truman that "the high mobility of the Naval Carrier Task Force combined with its capacity for making successive and continuous strikes in almost any part of the world make this force a most suitable means of waging atomic bomb warfare." The president assented to this approach, and in November 1946 the CNO "directed the DCNO(Logistics) to modify the three CVBs [*Midways*] to permit the operation of AJ Savages carrying atomic bombs."[36] Navy leaders thought, however, that they needed a new carrier, designed from the first to carry both nuclear weapons and aircraft that could deliver them at long range. As Friedman notes, "In a sense the navy could consider the presidential authorization for carriers to project nuclear strikes an authorization for the big strike carrier."[37]

However, the trade-offs between the C-2 and the CVB-X caused problems for the General Board. For example, the aviators wanted a flush (i.e., clear, flat, and unobstructed) flight deck. The ship designers answered that at least a minimal "island" structure was necessary to carry away the exhaust from the carrier's fire rooms and to mount electronic antennas. The effort to resolve this dispute has obscured the fact that carrier operations in World War II *and* BuAer's parallel efforts to work with industry to develop larger, more powerful, and longer-range carrier aircraft led to two new carrier concepts right after the war. We will turn to later developments in the story of what became *United States* after we broaden our view of the problems and promise of World War II technological innovations.

The Larger Revolution in Technology

Aviation wasn't the only area to be changed dramatically by emergency wartime investments in new technology. In 1946, even if one sets aside the implications of nuclear weapons for the Navy and for amphibious warfare, one thing was clear: the fleet that had triumphed in World War II was now largely obsolete. Technological advances during the war had produced many types of radars, improved forms of sonar, streamlined submarines that could stay submerged and run at high speeds by supplying their diesels with air from snorkels, jet aircraft that flew too fast for existing antiaircraft fire-control systems to target, homing torpedoes of several types, missiles, more-sophisticated sea mines, and larger, heavier antisubmarine weapons.

The hundreds of destroyers and destroyer escorts that had fought in World War II were now too small; the light cruisers produced by the dozen after 1940 could not protect existing aircraft carriers from attack by jet aircraft; battleships were no longer necessary; aircraft carriers now in service were not large enough to launch and recover new aircraft like the AJ-1 Savage; and most amphibious ships lacked the speed needed to converge quickly on a beach and unload their cargoes before an enemy equipped with high-speed submarines and jet aircraft could mount an effective defense. The postwar Navy had plenty of active ships and even more in reserve, but most had been designed before the great advances in technology brought on by the heavy investment in research and development during the war and were therefore severely limited in capability.

What to do about this consumed much of the time of the members of the General Board. In an effort to help the secretary and CNO set priorities for investment, the board reviewed the impact of likely future technological developments in a series of classified hearings in 1948 and 1949. In the hearings representatives of the Navy's material bureaus (its acquisition organizations, such as BuAer), OPNAV, the new Office of Naval Research, and the Marine Corps offered their views about the direction of future science and technology and about the implications of that future development for the Navy.

These hearings give us a window on Navy thinking in this period of rapid, even chaotic, technological progress. In one hearing, held to review the planned 1951–60 long-term shipbuilding program, a representative of DCNO (Logistics) argued that future ships should be designed "from the electronics standpoint." That is, they should be built *around* their electronics instead of having the electronics simply placed on board.[38] This had dramatic implications for new ships and for older ships that were modified. For example, more space would be needed for workshops for new electronic systems, as well as living spaces for the technicians who would maintain the new sensors and communications equipment.[39] Recruiting and retaining the technicians would also pose problems: Who would train them? How much would they be paid? Where would they "fit" into a ship's authority structure? And how would the data from the new electronic sensors be analyzed and displayed? These were not trivial issues.

The demand for more electronic equipment would also put its developers on a collision course with the Navy's own naval architects, who were committed to "cleaning up the topside structure of ships." Those who wanted more and larger antennas were at odds with those who wanted less "clutter." This was especially true on carriers, where there was already "insufficient room for proper antennas, both communications and radar."[40] As one senior officer on the team representing the Deputy Chief of Naval Operations for Logistics noted, "We have discovered no new basic techniques in electronics which would lead us to believe that we can obtain greatly improved performance over the radars of World War II without a corresponding increase in the size and weight of radar components."[41]

As this same officer observed, "A forward-looking, imaginative outlook is required which views the ships as a system, really, rather than a combination of systems."[42] The implications of this perspective were dramatic for carriers. For example, larger aircraft with faster approach speeds required a new carrier-controlled approach (CCA) system, but this new system—then still under development—needed "six clear channels of communications" and the antennas to support them.[43] In addition, "foreseeable aerial task groups may require as many as 20 simultaneous transmitting and receiving channels aboard a carrier, which means a critical antenna design problem for the carrier." Moreover, future carriers would have to have, for safe air navigation, "a minimum of two special radars, six simultaneous communication channels and an additional control center which will approximate the present" combat information center.[44] These requirements were pushing up carrier size and displacement and presenting the Navy with a problem—which was, to state it simply, continuing pressure on carrier costs.

A captain from BuShips had more bad news for the members of the board: "Before looking ahead 15 years, let us look back the same number of years and we will find the surprising fact that communications in the Fleet was in a healthier condition than it is today. . . . Formerly a ship carried communication antennas worthy of the name. Today we find metallic spikes called whips feebly probing the ether, and relegated to locations where, surrounded by every known enemy of a radiator or collector, they exemplify the present day expression that everything on our ships radiates except the antennas."[45] The way around this problem was to use the ship's superstructure as an antenna, but that approach again set the electronics engineers against the aviators, who wanted a flush-deck carrier large enough to let them safely land their faster jet aircraft—and of course their nuclear-capable AJ-1 Savages, too.

The board was also reminded that ship designers had to find spots on superstructures for detectors that could alert a crew to the presence of radioactive dust and debris. Radioactive contamination was a particularly vexing problem for carriers, because of their large flight decks and their need to recover more and more expensive and sophisticated aircraft as those planes, low on fuel, returned from missions. Carrier flight decks could be washed down, but building systems to do that into existing and planned carriers would require more money, consume precious space, and push up overall displacement in and atop carrier hulls that were not designed for such loads.

What about cooperation with the British? Their carrier force faced the same basic problem of adopting both new aircraft (jets) and new electronics. Was cooperative development part of the solution to the problems facing both navies? In November 1948, representatives of the Office of Naval Intelligence (ONI) in the Office of the Chief of Naval Operations informed the board that the Royal Navy was studying antiaircraft missiles and was "well advanced in experimentation with a flexible, rubber and pneumatic landing deck for airplanes . . . to permit employment of very high performance, wheelless [sic], jet fighter aircraft."[46] Two years later, in October 1950, the board asked Rear Adm. C. F. Coe, DCNO (Air), about this British idea, and Coe's assistant noted the response of Rear Adm. A. M. Pride, then chief of the Bureau of Aeronautics, that it was "tough enough to operate planes on a carrier without trying to operate them in a mattress."[47] This offhand dismissal of British work would not preclude later trials of the "mattress," as we shall show, but Pride's attitude was that of a man beset by too many problems at the same time—a condition we believe was widespread throughout the senior ranks of the postwar U.S. Navy.

In 1948, the problems the British faced in finding the resources for research, development, and production were clear to staff of ONI. As an ONI officer told the board, "While the United States and Britain led the world at the close of World War II [in radar technology], the British . . . are at present making very little progress, and except in so far as U.S. equipment is made available to them and unless their present policy changes, they may well lag considerably behind the United States and even some other countries by 1960."[48]

Yet BuOrd and BuAer maintained close contact with their counterparts in the Royal Navy. The RN had two officers assigned to BuOrd in Washington, and BuOrd had an officer "attached to the Naval Attache's Office" who was an "ex-officio member of the British Ordnance Board."[49] One goal of this cooperative arrangement was the development of effective close-range air defense for carriers.[50] BuAer too worked closely with the Royal Navy. In fact, the British tried to persuade BuAer to take over funding and management of their flexible flight deck in 1950, but BuAer turned the offer down. As a representative of the DCNO (Air) told the board that October, the pneumatically inflated flexible flight deck "doesn't look like what we need now."[51]

But *something* certainly was needed. As a BuAer officer told the board in November 1948, "the trend in carrier aircraft weight and speed has been upward at an accelerated rate for the past 20 years. Fighters of 1927 were 3,000 lbs., those of 1949 nearly 20,000 lbs., the escort fighter of 1955 will probably be 50,000 lbs. Attack aircraft during the same period have risen in weight from 5000 to 50,000 lbs., and [one likely future] design will be about 100,000." Our tables and charts (see appendix B) show how accurate this linear extrapolation was. This growth in aircraft weight and size required stronger and heavier carrier decks and elevators, higher hangar decks, and, as the BuAer representative noted, "more powerful catapulting and arresting machinery."[52]

Accordingly, BuAer was developing more powerful catapults. But the hydraulic catapults were heavy. One capable of launching a 100,000-pound aircraft at 150 knots "would approach 800 tons." To get around that, BuAer was banking on the "slotted-tube catapult," weighing "only a third as much." It was supposed to be ready in 1952 or 1953. Unlike the existing hydraulic catapults, the slotted-tube type required explosive fuel—"approximately 1000 lbs. of powder, or about 150 lbs. liquid-oxygen gasoline, or nitromethane, per shot." BuAer's representative reassured the board that the slotted-tube catapult had been used successfully by Germany in World War II to launch large missiles. It was not considered exotic technology, though, of course, some of the members of the board knew that rapid-oxidizing catapult fuels did not belong on a carrier likely to be damaged in battle.

Neither did large numbers of jet-assisted takeoff units that had been developed during World War II. But the heavier aircraft would require larger JATO units or several of the smaller, "standard" ones. Standard units weighed two hundred pounds each, and the usual fitting was two per plane per takeoff. As BuAer noted, a large carrier with a hundred aircraft could use upward of six hundred of these units each day, creating "quite an ammunition stowage problem." Making the JATO units larger would not eliminate the risk of storing what were essentially rockets.

Also, of course, the larger aircraft required the development of more powerful arresting-gear units and perhaps even a new barrier, "actuated by spaced powder charges under the wire across the deck."[53] In 1948, BuAer did not see the need for such new devices, as either entailing much technical risk or stressing the process of designing new carriers or modernizing existing ones. Officially, "The Bureau of Aeronautics feels confident that it can produce catapults and arresting gear for the period under discussion which will be adequate for any aircraft it may build, that is, up to [aircraft] sizes permitted by the deck strength and other physical limitations imposed by vessels."[54] BuAer would soon change its tune.

Immediate Postwar Cooperation with the British

Relations between the USN and RN during World War II had been close, especially in technological and scientific areas. That "special relationship" continued after the war, but not quite at the same level. At the end of May 1946, for example, the British assistant naval attaché informed his boss, Adm. Sir Henry Moore, who served in what remained of the wartime Combined Chiefs of Staff, that the U.S. Chief of Naval Operations had made it more difficult for him and other military members of the embassy staff to talk freely with their American counterparts. This did not make sense to the assistant naval attaché, because "access is much easier for American officers in London to technical developments than it is for us over here."[55] When told by his U.S. Navy counterpart that the Bureau of Ships "had given a great deal of information to the Admiralty without receiving much in return," he was quite surprised. As he wrote to Admiral Moore, the American officer had "admitted frankly that in many other directions, the U.S. Navy Department had learned far more from us than they had given in exchange, but added that many officers in the Bureau of Ships were not in the position to appreciate this fact."[56]

Admiral Moore considered this apparent lapse in cooperation so potentially serious that he sent a letter making just that point on 3 July to the Secretary of the Admiralty.[57] The latter promised, in his reply of 15 July, to take the matter up with the RN's Engineer-in-Chief (EIC) and the Director of Naval Construction (DNC). The director replied first, on 27 July 1946. He observed that the then chief of the Bureau of Ships had led the U.S. Navy's technical mission to London even before the United States had entered the war and that "there is no doubt the Americans had at that time much to learn from us in respect of nearly every type of ship. Since then although we have continued to supply them with information it is inevitable they do not find much that is new since all important lessons have been absorbed by them."[58] Moreover, "they are investing staff and money for naval research much more largely than we are and the thought naturally follows why should they, by collaboration, finance the research for the British Navy and incidentally for British Industry."[59] At the same time, he wanted to make sure that Admiral Moore understood that there was still a "channel for the steady flow of information in both directions"—that is, from the RN to the USN and vice versa.[60]

The EIC responded on 12 August, and he supported the points made by DNC. As he pointed out, "It is perfectly true that in the high pressure high temperature field [for steam turbine propulsion] we have received much valuable information from the

Americans." But during the war, the USN "had the benefit of all our war lessons," and "since then they have been given all machinery information and data for which they have asked."[61] Yet he also admitted that "it is the paucity of our research and development facilities and efforts which keeps the U.S. Navy from full collaboration."[62]

Despite obstacles and differences, the exchanges—both of information and of delegations—continued. For example, in November 1948, two members of the Admiralty's Naval Construction Department visited Washington to study the latest developments in carrier construction and the use of catapults and arresting gear on carriers. As the two engineers noted in their trip report, "On every subject dealt with there was a very full and free discussion, and . . . no information was withheld. We obtained a mass of information, drawings and pamphlets, including the only set of plans of C.V.A. 58 [the carrier *United States*] outside America."[63] Their American hosts were indeed candid. They informed their British guests that the *United States* was a "normal" carrier rather than "a specialised carrier designed for a particular objective" and that "future Fleet carriers must be able to operate the largest types of aircraft of increasing 'take-off' and landing speeds." This implied that "we shall reach a stage when all aircraft will have to be catapulted."[64] In addition, the USN officers agreed that "the complete development of AEW [airborne early warning]" was "essential."[65]

The report of this mission to the United States was an excellent review of the U.S. Navy's progress and problems in the field of carrier aviation. The British engineers learned that the USN was developing a slotted-tube catapult—the one described to the General Board by the Bureau of Aeronautics that same year.[66] They also were given the maximum aircraft "takeoff" weights for the existing carriers: sixty-two thousand pounds for *Midway*, fifty-two thousand for *Oriskany*, and twenty-seven thousand for the unmodified ships of the *Essex* class.[67] Information on the loaded AJ-1 Savage was also given them, as were the particulars concerning the modifications to *Oriskany*.[68]

They held detailed discussions with their American counterparts in BuShips and BuAer concerning arresting gear, barriers to capture planes that missed the arresting-gear wires, and catapults. They even spoke with engineers at BuAer's Naval Air Material Center (NAMC) about arresting-gear hooks for aircraft, discovering that NAMC staff members did not agree with the views expressed by BuAer personnel.[69] This was indeed "inside" information. But it was an important issue: Could existing arresting gear—the hooks and the cables they caught—capture the faster-landing and heavier jets without allowing the jets to slide to the left or the right?

Navy officers at the Patuxent Naval Air Station in Maryland showed the British the latest Navy aircraft, including the F9F and the still-experimental F7U-1. As the two Admiralty engineers remarked in their report, "The main particulars of most, if not all of these aircraft, are known to those concerned with Naval aircraft at the Admiralty and Ministry of Supply."[70] What the British did not already have, however, were the landing weights at given speeds for most of these aircraft; as their report noted, "records of many of these landings were handed to us for our information and are now available."[71] From this information they inferred that "the Americans have a much more effective control of the landing speeds of their Naval aircraft than we have for our own Naval aircraft."[72]

This mattered, because aircraft models changed faster than carriers and their equipment, which meant that RN carriers not yet built might find it impossible to take aboard and successfully arrest aircraft then on the drawing boards. It was the by-then-familiar problem of finding safe and efficient ways of throwing jets off carriers and then capturing them as they returned. The Americans were better at it because of their aircraft, not because their catapults and arresting gear were superior. This ability to analyze American developments because the Americans were so forthcoming is just another sign of the continuing and close cooperation between the two navies, especially in the field of naval aviation.

A Pandora's Box of Technology

In the spring of 1947, then–lieutenant commander (later rear admiral) James D. Ramage devoted his Naval War College thesis to the topic "The Atom Bomb and the Fast Carrier Task Force."[73] Ramage could know little enough about nuclear weapons at the time, because of the secrecy that covered the nuclear program, but his argument was clear: with nuclear weapons, Navy carrier task forces could pose a significant threat to targets on land. He argued, "The use of the atomic bomb not only will multiply the destructive force of a carrier air group from forty tons of TNT to the twenty thousand equivalent tons of TNT of the present atomic charge, but will also double the number of fighters . . . that will be used to protect the force. Thus one of the chief weaknesses of the task force, that of defense, is strengthened simultaneously with the multiplication of the offensive power of the force by fifty fold."[74] In short, "The carrier task force therefore is just entering into the outer fringe of its potential. . . . A small or medium carrier based attack plane, heavily escorted, and operating from the movable airfields of the fast carrier task force now has the advantages of destruction formerly held only by fleets of very heavy bombers with the added advantages of extreme mobility."[75]

Ramage, a decorated dive-bomber pilot and squadron leader in World War II, would go on to play a major role in the maturing of Navy carrier nuclear-attack squadrons, and he would rise in rank quickly.[76] For him, the immediate postwar years were "the best of times." For his Royal Navy counterparts, that was not the case. Theirs was "the winter of despair." Hopes of a peacetime force of ten large carriers, seventeen light carriers, and eighteen escort carriers in 1946 were dashed by 1948.[77] Even carriers of the *Malta* class, ordered in 1945 and based on lessons learned during the war, were never built. In 1938, the carrier *Ark Royal* was considered adequate for aircraft in commission and under development. It had two hydraulic catapults that could accelerate its sixty aircraft to a launch speed of fifty-six knots, if they did not exceed a weight of twelve thousand pounds. *Ark Royal*'s arresting gear could stop an eleven-thousand-pound plane landing at forty-five knots within forty feet.[78] The canceled *Malta*s would have operated ninety aircraft each, mounted catapults capable of launching thirty-thousand-pound aircraft at 130 knots, and possessed arresting gear able to stop a twenty-thousand-pound aircraft landing at seventy-five knots.[79]

Our argument is that the innovations picked up by the USN from the RN—the steam catapult, the angled deck, and the mirror landing aid—cannot be appreciated separately from these larger developments, the "threads" that make up the story of postwar carrier aviation and the background to it. There's a "heavy bomber" thread that carried over from World War II, as well as "threads" representing the need of jet aircraft for catapults to get off the deck and for angled decks to get "home" safely, and the debates over service unification, the unification of all aviation forces, and the optimal way to deliver nuclear weapons. There's also a "thread" for financing innovation and another for the range of the innovations themselves. The latter covers a lot of ground—from the introduction of effective jet (and then supersonic) aircraft, to nuclear submarines, cruise and ballistic missiles, and even space satellites. World War II had opened a Pandora's box of technology, and both the USN and the RN struggled to take advantage of all the ideas and inventions that had popped out of that box.

But very quickly after the war it became clear to officers and civilians in both navies that the U.S. Navy had a huge advantage in terms of resources. The disparity in resources, however, did not cut off close and confidential exchanges between the RN and the USN. The two navies had established communication at multiple levels, and the contacts persisted, despite the fact that the futures of the carrier forces in the two navies were beginning to diverge sharply.

Notes

1. Robert W. Love, Jr., *History of the U.S. Navy, 1942–1991* (Harrisburg, Pa.: Stackpole Books, 1992), p. 291.
2. Donald D. Engen, *Wings and Warriors: My Life as a Naval Aviator* (Washington, D.C.: Smithsonian Institution Press, 1997), p. 70.
3. Ibid., p. 77.
4. James L. Holloway III, *Aircraft Carriers at War* (Annapolis, Md.: Naval Institute Press, 2007), p. 15.

5. Michael T. Isenberg, *Shield of the Republic*, vol. 1, *1945–1962* (New York: St. Martin's, 1993), p. 249.

6. Ibid., p. 132.

7. Vincent Davis, *Postwar Defense Policy and the U.S. Navy, 1943–1946* (Chapel Hill: Univ. of North Carolina Press, 1962), p. 124.

8. Ibid., p. 148.

9. Ibid., p. 203.

10. Ibid., p. 127, chart 3.

11. Ibid., p. 148. Also see Jeffrey G. Barlow, *Revolt of the Admirals: The Fight for Naval Aviation, 1945–1950* (Washington, D.C.: Naval Historical Center, 1994), p. 259.

12. Julius A. Furer, *Administration of the Navy Department in World War II* (Washington, D.C.: U.S. Government Printing Office, 1959), p. 797.

13. Thomas C. Hone, Norman Friedman, and Mark D. Mandeles, *American & British Aircraft Carrier Development, 1919–1941* (Annapolis, Md.: Naval Institute Press, 1999), chaps. 5–6; Norman Friedman, *Network-centric Warfare: How Navies Learned to Fight Smarter through Three World Wars* (Annapolis, Md.: Naval Institute Press, 2009), pp. 58–59.

14. Jerry Miller, *Nuclear Weapons and Aircraft Carriers: How the Bomb Saved Naval Aviation* (Washington, D.C.: Smithsonian Institution Press, 2001); John T. Hayward and C. W. Borklund, *Bluejacket Admiral: The Navy Career of Chick Hayward* (Annapolis, Md., and Newport, R.I.: Naval Institute Press and Naval War College Foundation, 2000).

15. Hayward and Borklund, *Bluejacket Admiral*, pp. 166–67.

16. Secretary of the Navy, Op-01-MD, ser. 71802, of 18 August 1943 had created DCNO (Air). Op-01-MD, ser. 71902 (18 August 1943), also from the secretary, had transferred the Planning, Personnel, Training, and Flight divisions to the new office from BuAer, along with the Air Information Branch. See Furer, *Administration of the Navy Department in World War II*, p. 392.

17. Furer, *Administration of the Navy Department in World War II*, p. 393.

18. Ibid., p. 394.

19. Barlow, *Revolt of the Admirals*, p. 54.

20. Ibid., p. 56.

21. Ibid., p. 58.

22. Paul T. Gillcrist, *Feet Wet: Reflections of a Carrier Pilot* (New York: Presidio, 1990), pp. 137–38.

23. Ibid., p. 138.

24. E. T. Wooldridge, ed., *Into the Jet Age: Conflict and Change in Naval Aviation, 1945–1975* (Annapolis, Md.: Naval Institute Press, 1995), p. 56.

25. Norman Friedman, *U.S. Aircraft Carriers: An Illustrated Design History* (Annapolis, Md.: Naval Institute Press, 1983), p. 230.

26. Ibid., p. 227.

27. Ibid., p. 231.

28. Ibid., p. 228.

29. See the drawing in ibid., p. 229.

30. Ibid., p. 204.

31. Ibid., pp. 231–32.

32. Ibid., p. 241.

33. Ibid.

34. Ibid., pp. 237, 244.

35. Ibid., p. 242.

36. Ibid., p. 244.

37. Ibid.

38. General Board of the Navy, hearings [hereafter Hearings], "Shipbuilding Program, FY 1951–1960," 15 November 1948, Microfilm Publication M1493, roll 27, National Archives, p. 659.

39. Ibid., p. 660.

40. Ibid., p. 661.

41. Ibid.

42. Ibid., p. 663.

43. Ibid., p. 665.

44. Ibid., pp. 698–99.

45. Ibid., p. 670.

46. Hearings, "Shipbuilding Program, FY 1951–1960," 19 November 1948, p. 739.

47. Hearings, "Attack Carrier (New Construction)," 24 October 1950, p. 979.

48. Hearings, "Shipbuilding Program, FY 1951–1960," 19 November 1948, p. 755. See also pp. 759, 761.

49. Hearings, "Shipbuilding Program, FY 1951–1960," 24 November 1948, p. 770.

50. Hearings, "Military Characteristics for CV (Project 27A Conversion)," 28 April 1950, p. 452.
51. Hearings, "Attack Carrier (New Construction)," 24 October 1950, p. 979.
52. Hearings, "Shipbuilding Program, FY 1951–1960," 24 November 1948, p. 784.
53. Ibid., p. 785.
54. Ibid., p. 786.
55. Cdr. (E) F. G. Bowring, RN, "Report on Conversation between Commander Bowring, Assistant Naval Attaché and Captain Mumma, U.S.N., of Bureau of Ships," 25 May 1946, folder ADM 1/20/76, Public Records Office [hereafter PRO], pp. 1–2.
56. Ibid., p. 2.
57. Adm. Sir Henry Moore, RN, Offices of the Combined Chiefs of Staff, letter to Secretary of the Admiralty, 3 July 1946 (ref. R.P. 768/46), folder ADM 1/20/76, PRO.
58. Director of Naval Construction, minute, 27 July 1946 (register no. C.W. 46.175), folder ADM 1/20/76, PRO.
59. Ibid.
60. Ibid.
61. Engineer-in-Chief, minute, 12 August 1946, folder ADM 1/20/76, PRO.
62. Ibid.
63. "Report of the visit of Mr. J. L. Bartlett & Mr. D. W. Smithers to the U.S.A., November 1948," Naval Construction Department (Admiralty, Bath), folder ADM 281/109, PRO, p. 4.
64. Ibid., p. 6.
65. Ibid., p. 8.
66. Ibid., p. 14.
67. Ibid., p. 22.
68. Ibid., pp. 23–24.
69. Ibid., p. 43.
70. Ibid., p. 46.
71. Ibid., p. 48.
72. Ibid., p. 50.
73. James D. Ramage, "The Atom Bomb and the Fast Carrier Task Force" (junior thesis, Naval War College, May 1947), record group 13, Naval War College Naval Historical Collection.
74. Ibid., p. 10.
75. Ibid., p. 11.
76. James D. Ramage, "Taking A-Bombs to Sea," *Naval History* 9, no. 1 (January/February 1995), pp. 29–34.
77. Richard Hill, "British Naval Thinking in the Nuclear Age," in *The Development of British Naval Thinking*, ed. Geoffrey Till (London: Routledge, 2006), p. 174.
78. David Hobbs, "Naval Aviation, 1930–2000," in *The Royal Navy, 1930–2000: Innovation and Defence*, ed. Richard Harding (London: Frank Cass, 2005), p. 73.
79. Ibid., p. 80.

The Flexdeck

The story of the flexible deck, or what some in Britain called the "carpet deck," is interesting, because it was an ingenious but failed innovation that helped move Royal Navy aviators toward the angled-deck concept. The idea that led to the flexible deck was simple enough—to improve the flying performance of jet aircraft by eliminating their landing gear. An aircraft would be recovered back aboard the carrier by flying it softly into an inflated mattress and catching an arresting-gear wire. Then a winch would pull the plane onto a small dolly, from which the plane would be transferred to a catapult and then, rearmed and refueled, launched for its next flight.

The idea seemed elementary, and it was conceptually attractive, particularly given the high fuel-use rates and resulting low endurance of early jet engines. In the early jets, designers were under great pressure to hold down the weight of the aircraft's structure in order to increase aircraft endurance, and the weight of aircraft undercarriages could be traded for more fuel or ordnance.

The idea was well along in Britain by the early spring of 1945. Official records show that the Royal Navy's offices of the Director of Naval Construction and the Engineer-in-Charge had already developed various concepts of what was then called a "sprung deck" for use in existing carriers. The Royal Aircraft Establishment had already tried out some of these ideas "in model form" and was ready to move ahead with full-scale trials.[1] The Royal Navy and the RAE sought the support of the Naval Aircraft Subcommittee of the Aeronautical Research Committee of the Ministry of Aircraft Production, which would have to fund the trials.

On 18 April 1945, MAP officials sponsored a meeting attended by Royal Navy, Air Ministry, and RAE representatives. Representing the RN's EIC was Cdr. Colin C. Mitchell, who—as we've already noted—held patents for the steam catapult. One of the RAE's representatives was Lewis Boddington, who years later shared credit for coming up with the concept of the angled flight deck.[2]

The head of MAP's delegation opened the meeting by stating that MAP had decided to apply the concept of jet aircraft operating without landing gear to the RAF as well as to the RN. As he put it, "This aspect, then, must be kept in the minds of people concerned with the Naval Application."[3] As we shall show, this insistence on the joint (RAF and RN) application of the concept was to have a strong influence on future decisions.

The RN representatives did not challenge this statement of policy by their MAP counterparts. The RN was aware that the approach was contingent on successful trials; if the idea didn't work, it wouldn't matter that it had been initially proposed for both the RAF and the RN. Rear Adm. M. S. Slattery, the Chief of Naval Research (CNR), noted that "the first approach is to try to find a scheme which could be incorporated in existing carriers.... Such a scheme would be an interim measure which, if used with existing jet designs with their undercarriages removed, would teach us a lot and show the way to the solution of the complete problem."[4] The admiral also asserted that "complete mechanization" of carrier landings and takeoffs was "the ultimate aim" of the informal consortium (composed of engineers from the Admiralty, the RAE, and the private firms Vickers and Westland's) that had been considering the idea.[5] Finally, Rear Admiral Slattery proposed two key measures of effectiveness that needed to be applied to any development effort: "landing and take-off times at least comparable with those at present[,] . . . 20 seconds and 30 seconds respectively."[6] Like the MAP decision that any new concept would have to apply to both the RAF and the RN, this metric would turn out to have a decisive influence on the assessment of the proposal to operate jet aircraft without undercarriages.

Mr. J. L. Bartlett, speaking for the Admiralty's DNC, noted several possible structural alternatives. One was a "thin metal or steel deck in hinged panels supported by a large number of low pressure shock absorbing air cylinders."[7] Another was a kind of air mattress, which had the virtue of being able to absorb the impact of a landing jet without damaging the aircraft's structure. The key point that Bartlett made was that it would take time, talent, and funds to narrow the alternatives down to the one that should be pursued. The RAE did not then have satisfactory concepts for either the "sprung deck" or the means by which aircraft would be taken from this deck and prepared for launching.[8]

Commander Mitchell, the catapult specialist, noted to his colleagues that the RAE had already determined that aircraft-carrier catapults would have to be upgraded if the "sprung deck" were to be developed. As he observed, "the accelerators" on the RN's existing carriers were "capable of about 100 knots (including wind over the deck) and new construction . . . aimed at a maximum speed of 110 knots (with wind over the deck)." But the RAE's engineers had determined that jets without undercarriages would require a catapult that could accelerate them to 125 knots; therefore, work on the "sprung deck" would also entail improvements in catapult technology.[9]

The April 1945 meeting appears to have been the first interaction between technical specialists and senior decision makers that focused on the interrelationships among the new concepts of the steam catapult, the angled deck, and what came to be called the "flexible deck," or "flexdeck." Because the MAP controlled overall wartime aircraft production, the RN had to persuade it to fund further development of concepts such as the "sprung deck." The MAP supported the RAF and the RN's air arm, insisting on a program that would benefit both services. The RN, unlike the RAF, had "targets," or metrics, for "undercarriage-less" jets operating from existing and future carriers, because the RN practiced, as a matter of operational doctrine, rapid takeoffs and landings from its carriers.

The stage was set for development and testing. According to Eric Brown, work began in the summer of 1947 on a "carpet deck" at the RAE's facility at Farnborough.[10] Once the prototype—"composed of five layers of vulcanized rubber, above three layers of NFS hoses, inflated at varying low pressures"—was completed, it was subjected to a series of tests, one of which was to have a Vampire jet manned by Brown dropped on it from various heights by a crane.[11] By the middle of December of that year, the flexible deck was ready for trials at RAE. Once the weather conditions were right, Brown was ready to land his Vampire on it.

A Fleet Air Arm Vampire on the "flexible rubber carpet" at RAE Farnborough. Note the air-filled "sausages" that support the flexible rubber deck.

Fleet Air Arm Museum

Though Brown had successfully practiced approaching the flexible deck, his initial landing was a failure. A ramp was positioned at the forward end of the flexible deck so that the tailhook of an aircraft approaching just above the ground would slide up the ramp before engaging the arresting gear, suspended just above the flexible deck itself.

Unfortunately, there was also a ridge where the ramp met the deck, and Brown's tailhook "caught in the ridge and was flung up against the fuselage, and the tail booms of the Vampire hit the ridge."[12] The tailhook lodged in its housing—something that should have been impossible—and Brown's Vampire "pitched nose-down towards the deck," scraped over the arresting-gear wire, dug right down into the rubber hoses, and then "was thrown harshly up again in a nose-up attitude."[13] Brown's Vampire couldn't accelerate enough to get back into the air, crashing into the ground forward of the flexible deck. Brown was not hurt, though the "crash split the cockpit all round me."[14]

As Brown noted in his autobiography, "We had full camera coverage of the accident" and "found that my approach speed had been a little lower than normal but should have been safe enough"—yet it wasn't. Further tests revealed the problem: "In the approach speed range which we had been using any increase in engine power caused a change in airflow behaviour around the wing-root air intakes which aggravated rather than improved the lift."[15] It took ten weeks to fix that and other problems, and Brown made a "perfect" landing on the flexible deck on 17 March 1948. The program was still not out of the woods, but Brown and others successfully conducted sea trials of the flexible deck from May to November 1948.[16] At the same time, engineers at the RAE assessed the advantages of "undercarriage-less aircraft" as significant: "With constant endurance the present weight of armament can be doubled."[17]

But there was still the MAP requirement that the new system be applicable to the needs of the RAF, and that became a sticking point. By the end of September 1950, the RAF had decided that "the complications of catapults and mats" were "operationally unacceptable" for both Fighter Command and the force of long-range bombers.[18] There indeed were advantages in performance for aircraft without landing gear, but those advantages did not outweigh the operational "costs." As Group Captain S. R. Ubee put it in a memo on 27 September, "I do not think we can contemplate any system that ties fighter aircraft down to particular airfields."[19] By the end of October, the RAF's position was clear: "The Air Staff would be glad to see a demonstration of the complete cycle of take-off, landing, ground-handling, refuelling and re-arming, and preparation for take-off of a fighter type aircraft, without the use of an undercarriage."[20]

British firms (Vickers and Supermarine) still supported the concept of the flexible deck—even for land-based aircraft—but the RAF would not endorse the program unless and until it could see a clear demonstration of its operational success *on land*, and with numbers of aircraft, and it was not likely to see that, given the program's fiscal constraints. But the RN stayed with the program, despite the fact that test results could not meet the standards for landing and takeoff intervals of twenty and thirty seconds, respectively, set in 1945. A 1953 report of trials with three Vampire aircraft landing in

This photo from Farnborough shows how the jet without an undercarriage would be moved off the rubber deck and onto a trolley.
Fleet Air Arm Museum

rapid succession noted that the shortest landing interval was forty-four seconds, though suggesting that the interval could be reduced to twenty-four seconds—still just a bit short.[21]

In the meantime, however, the concept of the flexible deck had caught the attention of both the U.S. Air Force and the U.S. Navy. In November 1952, the classified *Naval Aviation Bulletin* reported that officers from BuAer had witnessed a demonstration of landings on the flexible deck at Farnborough and had "unanimously recommend[ed] that a comprehensive flexible-deck development program be begun in the US, preferably in collaboration with the Air Force and the British Royal Navy."[22] A year later, Lt. Cdr. Donald Engen, then detailed to RAE Farnborough to test the RN's visual-glide-slope development program, was directed to try out Farnborough's 60-by-144-foot flexible deck.

Engen expected to repeat the method pioneered by Brown in 1948. He would approach the flexible deck in a modified Vampire (known as a Sea Vampire) at 105 knots with the tailhook about eighteen inches above the ground. The hook would catch in the arresting gear, the plane would plop down on the flexible deck, and then the plane would be towed off the flexible deck to where a crane would lift it so that the pilot could lower the landing gear and taxi away. Engen's first landing went more or less as he had hoped: "The arrestment of the forward motion of the airplane was not unlike a normal carrier landing. The cushioning of the rubber bolsters was gentle enough, but I was thrown around in the cockpit even though I was wearing a seat belt and shoulder strap."[23]

But his fifth try went awry. As the tailhook caught, Engen "allowed the Sea Vampire to climb very slightly. With upward movement . . . , the Sea Vampire flew out until the wire stopped it in midair, and I was thrown back down into the flex deck, which then . . . threw the Sea Vampire back into the air in a series of bounces." The effect of this bouncing on Engen was severe: "My body had literally flailed about the cockpit. . . . I felt like a wet rag, with the pain bringing sweat to my forehead."[24] But this experience did not cause Engen to turn thumbs-down on the flexible deck.

The USAF and USN proceeded with their tests. The Air Force was apparently concerned that a surprise attack by Soviet aircraft on its bases in Europe would fatally cripple the tactical fighter-bomber force assigned to support U.S. ground forces stationed there. One way to avoid being caught by surprise was to have fighter-bombers that could take to the air immediately on warning, and the USAF planned to mount combat-loaded F-84G Thunderjets on mobile launchers designed for the large Matador cruise missile. But these attack aircraft would be more effective if they were stripped of their landing gear, and so the USAF examined the flexible-deck concept as a means to recover such "zero-length launch" planes.

The USAF's version of the RN's flexible deck was four hundred feet long, but the extra length (as compared to what the RN was using) did not protect the pilot of the first test flight from severe injury. The engineering problem faced by the project team had been to find a way to retract the F-84G's flaps, which would be down during the aircraft's approach, once the plane's tailhook had caught. The engineers had feared that bringing the plane down on the rubber deck with its flaps extended might ruin the deck, and so they had installed a system to pull the flaps up into the wings as soon as the plane caught the arresting wire. Unfortunately, on the first attempt this system worked even though the plane *didn't* catch the wire, with the result that the F-84G bounced twice on the mat and then crashed heavily beyond it. Though a second attempt to land an F-84G on the mat was successful in December 1954, the pilot was violently thrown around in the cockpit and badly injured. The USAF then abandoned testing.[25]

The Navy, proceeding in parallel with the Air Force, first sent two pilots to Farnborough to gain experience landing on the flexible deck there. BuAer also had Grumman modify two F9F7 Cougar swept-wing jets for tests planned for early 1955. Both aircraft retained their landing gear, but both were also equipped with powerful Pratt & Whitney J-48 engines.[26] In an effort to protect its own test pilots and those of the Navy from injuries of the kind suffered by their Air Force counterparts, Grumman developed "a rigid torso harness, a formfit helmet with wraparound jaw protector, and a device for rigidly connecting the helmet to the harness."[27] Though this apparatus successfully protected the spines of the two test pilots who made the initial landings at Patuxent River, one, Lt. John Moore, USN, made the following observation: "It was calculated that with the harness on and the life jacket inflated (in the event of a water landing), the buoyancy was slightly negative. . . . [I]n the event of a ditching and following the pilot's safe egress from the airplane, he had but to remove the life jacket, remove the parachute, remove the protective harness, reinstall the life jacket and inflate it. It was expected that this could be accomplished while the pilot was standing on the bottom of Chesapeake Bay."[28] Such sarcasm aside, Moore made a number of successful landings on the 80-by-570-foot flexible deck.

Like the British flexible deck, the one constructed for use at Patuxent River was composed of air-filled rubber "sausages," or bags, that were eighty feet long and thirty inches in diameter. The bags were stretched across the deck's base and topped by "rubberized fabric mats" that held them in place. The Navy's flexible deck, again like its counterpart in Farnborough, had a front ramp (also composed of air-filled bags) and a single arresting-gear wire. "To provide a slippery surface for landings, a compound of silicon and water was applied to the deck surface by crewmen with swabs."[29]

The first flexdeck landing took place on 18 February 1955, at a speed of 135 knots. The last landing took place on 4 August 1955, and "the whole project was terminated 13 March 1956."[30] One reason for ending the program was the danger that landing on the flexible deck posed to even the best pilots. Lieutenant Moore, after landing successfully a number of times, pushed the envelope just a bit too far in an effort to find out how the flexdeck would handle a heavily loaded airplane. He deliberately caught the arresting-gear wire at the maximum height above the deck, but he also "let the right wing drop slightly after hook engagement so that deck contact was made with a bank angle of about five degrees right wing down." His plane immediately dove into the deck, pitched back up, rolled to the left, hit the deck again, and rolled to the right. As Moore recalled, "The rolling and pitching continued until the Cougar came to a halt, which seemed like about four days. It was a wild ride. Black rubber deck marks were found on the upper surface of the right wing."[31]

We have quoted from the reports of U.S. Navy pilots who tested the flexdeck, such as Engen and Moore, because their reports sounded the death knell of this once-promising innovation. As Moore recalled later, "Pilot skills demanded for successful landings . . . were stretched close to practical limits and . . . the possibilities of successfully deploying a squadron of higher performance sweptwing jets on a Flexdeck aircraft carrier by our Navy had to be considered unfeasible."[32]

Yet the RN's famous test pilot Eric Brown had not felt that way after his tests of the flexible deck on HMS *Warrior* in 1948. In his official report, he argued that

> the principle of flexible deck landing for undercarriageless aircraft is fundamentally sound. . . . The experiment is probably ahead of its time in that it apparently does not offer much gain to the conventional type of jet aircraft in service at the moment, but it should offer a lot to an aircraft specifically designed for flexible-deck operation, provided that arrester gear development can keep pace with increasing approach speeds. . . . It may even be that future swept-back and delta planform aircraft will

be forced to adopt this method of landing on carriers, since all calculations point to serious wheeled landing problems on such aircraft.[33]

In his memoirs, Brown admitted that going over to the flexdeck would have meant acquisition of a very different fleet of carrier aircraft, along with the wholesale reconstruction of numerous airfields—to say nothing of changes to existing and planned aircraft carriers. He well knew that the British government could not afford all that.

But assessments of the flexdeck operational trials stimulated work on a major, lasting innovation—the angled deck. To quote Eric Brown once more:

> After the successful flexible deck ship trials on HMS *Warrior*, a meeting was held [in August 1951] at the Ministry of Aviation to discuss issues that had been highlighted, one of which was how to land and catapult aircraft as a simultaneous operation in view of the fact that no crash barrier was envisaged for the flexible deck.
>
> During the meeting . . . , Captain Dennis Cambell was in the chair, and during discussion, made pencil sketches on a pad in front of him without really appreciating the practical significance of his doodling ideas. At the meeting was Lewis Boddington, the Head of Naval Aircraft Department at RAE, and his quick mind saw the potential in the sketch proposals for normal carrier operations. Back at Farnborough he produced a design for ten degrees angled deck to be suitable for a carrier such as *Ark Royal*.[34]

Cambell's notes of the meeting, written on 9 August, state that "there was no prospect . . . of a one-type carrier for undercarriageless aircraft only." The attendees had to come up with a design that would handle aircraft with wheels and those without. Moreover, they agreed on two other requirements—that the "aircraft stowage and operating capacity of the carrier must not be reduced" and that there would be no "fundamentally different approach technique" with the new carrier design.[35] As Cambell recalled later, he had decided to withhold "my angled idea until it had become clear to all that the paramount need in accepting the rubber mat idea was to retain the deck park. When it was coming to be seen that no simple solution was in the offing, I presented a large sketch . . . showing the mat and the four arresting wires offset 10 degrees to port." Though, to quote Cambell, "the meeting's reaction" to his proposal "was a mixture of apathy and mild derision," engineer Lewis Boddington took the idea with him back to his office at RAE Farnborough.[36] As we showed in chapter 4, Boddington was one of the conceptual pioneers in the Royal Navy's efforts to adapt carriers to jet aircraft. On 28 August 1951, Boddington wrote to both Cambell at the Ministry of Supply and J. L. Bartlett at the Admiralty with a proposal to offset future carrier landing decks by eight degrees.[37]

Though most contemporary naval aviators have no knowledge of the flexible deck or of the role it played in the development of the angled deck, the story of the flexdeck is important because it shows that the U.S. Navy was willing to follow the RN's lead despite the fact that the USN had more financial resources and its own research organizations. The USN's decision reflects the uncertainty that surrounded tactical aircraft operations in the early Cold War years. To overcome that uncertainty, the USAF and the USN decided to spend research and development funds to "buy" knowledge, realizing that it was cheaper in the long run to try out new ideas by investing in prototypes than to make a commitment to an expensive program that might not pan out. This willingness—even eagerness—to experiment is a key to innovation.[38]

But the issue that most concerns us is the constant desire of senior officials to reap the benefits of innovations without paying the concomitant costs, and among the most important of these costs are the time, energy, and money invested in innovations that do not work out as anticipated. The flexdeck was one of these, and the lesson of its development and testing is that—as we have said before in other publications—developers will inevitably "waste" resources on what appear to be promising innovations.

Notes

1. "Undercarriage-less Aircraft, Operation from Aircraft Carriers—Development," draft agenda, "Undercarriageless Aircraft—Operation from Aircraft Carriers," attached to a note addressed to the DNC and others, 22 March 1945, folder AIR 2/5785, Public Records Office [hereafter PRO].
2. Minutes of meeting held at MAP on 18 April 1945 (SB61567), folder AIR 2/5785, PRO.
3. Ibid., p. 1.
4. Ibid., p. 2.
5. Ibid., pp. 2–3.
6. Ibid., p. 2.
7. Ibid., p. 3.
8. Ibid., p. 8.
9. Ibid., p. 9.
10. Eric Brown, *Wings on My Sleeve* (London: Orion Books–Phoenix, 2007), p. 169.
11. Ibid.
12. Ibid., p. 177.
13. Ibid.
14. Ibid., p. 178.
15. Ibid.
16. Jan Jacobs, "Follow the Bouncing Cougar: The Flexdeck Program," *Hook* 12, no. 1 (Spring 1984), p. 11. See also Brown, *Wings on My Sleeve*, pp. 187–90.
17. T. V. Somerville and A. L. Courtney, "Advantages in Performance of Undercarriageless Aircraft Operated from a Flexible Deck," Technical Note AERO 1986, February 1949, folder AIR 2/5785, PRO, p. 1.
18. Air Vice Marshal C. B. R. Pelly, memorandum to the Vice Chief of the Air Staff, 25 September 1950, folder AIR 2/5785, PRO.
19. Group Captain S. R. Ubee, Deputy Director of Operational Research, memorandum to the Director of Operational Research, 27 September 1950, folder AIR 2/5785, PRO.
20. Air Vice Marshal C. B. R. Pelly, memorandum to the Ministry of Supply, 24 October 1950, folder AIR 2/5785, PRO.
21. A. W. Hotson, "Rapid Handling Trials of Vampire Aircraft on a Flexible Deck," RAE Technical Note NA 259, "Summary," August 1953, folder AVIA 6/24483, PRO.
22. *Naval Aviation Bulletin* 2-52 (November 1952), p. 2. The bulletins have been declassified and are available from the Naval Aviation History Office, Washington Navy Yard, Washington, D.C.
23. Donald D. Engen, *Wings and Warriors: My Life as a Naval Aviator* (Washington, D.C.: Smithsonian Institution Press, 1997), pp. 151–52.
24. Ibid., p. 152.

25. Jacobs, "Follow the Bouncing Cougar," pp. 11, 14. See also the excerpt from John Moore's "The Wrong Stuff: Flying on the Edge of Disaster" in *From the Flight Deck: An Anthology of the Best Writing on Carrier Warfare,* ed. Peter B. Mersky (Washington, D.C.: Brassey's, 2003), p. 182.

26. Jacobs, "Follow the Bouncing Cougar," p. 14.

27. Ibid., p. 16.

28. Moore, in *From the Flight Deck,* ed. Mersky, p. 186.

29. Jacobs, "Follow the Bouncing Cougar," p. 17.

30. Ibid., p. 19.

31. Moore, in *From the Flight Deck,* ed. Mersky, p. 188.

32. Ibid.

33. Brown, *Wings on My Sleeve,* p. 190.

34. Ibid., p. 191.

35. "Notes of D.N.D.P./D.C.N.R. (A)'s Meeting on 7.8.51 to discuss the Formulation of a Staff Requirement for the operational [*sic*] Version of the Flexible Deck," 9 August 1951, ref. 855/4, p. 1, paras. 2, 5, in Dennis R. F. Cambell folder, collection [coll.] 337, U.S. Navy Operational Archives, Naval History and Heritage Command, Washington Navy Yard, Washington, D.C.

36. Cambell's memoir is "The Angled Deck Story" (no date). The memoir, as well as the drawing to which Cambell refers, is in coll. 337 of the U.S. Navy Operational Archives. The quotations are from page 2.

37. Lewis Boddington, letter to Capt. D. R. F. Cambell, RN, 28 August 1951 (Naval/2055-1/LB/70), coll. 337 of the U.S. Navy Operational Archives.

38. See Mark D. Mandeles, *Military Transformation Past and Present* (Westport, Conn.: Praeger Security International, 2007), pp. 91–93.

Catapults
Choosing an Option under Pressure

After World War II, the USN's catapult developers in the Naval Air Material Center believed that existing hydraulic catapults could be scaled up to cope with jet aircraft. At the same time, they also examined other alternatives, including the steam catapult developed by their British counterparts at the RAE. As it turned out, the USN chose the British alternative; it worked when it was needed. However, that choice apparently did not entirely satisfy the NAMC developers or their colleagues in BuAer, because steam catapults draw their power from a carrier's boilers, and BuAer engineers did not want catapult capacity tied so closely to the efficiency of a ship's steam plant. In 1959, for example, long after the decision had been made to adopt variations of the British steam catapult, BuAer was still studying a new internal-combustion (C14) catapult designed specifically for the nuclear carrier *Enterprise* (CVAN 65).

Introduction

The requirement that carrier aircraft equal the performance of their land-based contemporaries drove postwar Navy jet aircraft development. The new aircraft, as we have shown, were larger and heavier than their piston-engine predecessors. This was especially true of the bombers, such as the AJ-1 Savage and the A3D Skywarrior, which carried nuclear weapons. It was essential to develop catapults that could propel such large aircraft off a carrier's deck. As both American and British engineers began to realize, "the operation of wire ropes and pulleys in hydro-pneumatic . . . systems was reaching its limit."[1] The British, lacking the resources required to pursue multiple catapult concepts, settled early on steam catapult. The Americans, with more resources and confident that incremental improvements to existing technology would be adequate, adopted the British steam alternative once they saw it demonstrated successfully. As they knew, failure to develop more powerful catapults was unacceptable; without a dramatic increase in catapult power, nearly the entire postwar U.S. naval aircraft program faced collapse.

The Problem

It took a few years for the problem to bite. To some extent a carrier could make up for limited catapult performance by running into the wind. This had long been standard practice. For example, the standard U.S. Navy specification sheets for aircraft postulated takeoff runs into a twenty-five-knot wind over the flight deck. The performance of existing catapults could also be enhanced. Thus war-built *Essex*-class carriers successfully operated jet fighters and fighter-bombers off Korea in 1950–53. However, they could not operate aircraft that were already under test, such as the new jet night fighter (F3D Skyknight) and the new swept-wing fighters. For such aircraft BuAer could offer the H8, the ultimate version of its earlier hydraulic catapults, planned for carriers converted specifically for jet operations, beginning with USS *Oriskany* (CV 34). However, H8 could not launch the A-3 Skywarrior, the first of the jet bombers envisaged under BuAer's postwar aircraft development program.

The Navy's catapult developers were at the Naval Aircraft Factory in Philadelphia. A wartime reorganization in the summer of 1943 made the factory and the associated Naval Air Experimental Station subordinate to the Naval Air Material Center. BuAer funded NAMC, and therefore NAMC engineers and test personnel responded to the direction of BuAer. There were specialists in catapults in both organizations, and they were supposed to communicate regularly. But the surviving documentation suggested to us that the NAMC engineers persisted longer than they should have in trying to improve incrementally the Navy's well-understood hydraulic catapults.[2]

Until about 1951, delays in the long-range BuAer catapult program were tolerable, if disappointing. By 1951, however, aircraft like the A3D (later designated A-3) were about to enter production. Fortunately, the British steam catapult became demonstrably mature by the spring of 1951, and senior American naval officers chose to acquire the rights to it a year later. Yet BuAer's catapult developers were dubious about the projected performance of the steam catapult, as we shall show. Until 1950 they had consistently maintained that their efforts to upgrade existing catapult technology were succeeding, and it appears that BuAer's leadership was slow to appreciate just how serious the catapult problem was. The failure to produce a catapult powerful enough for the new jets—especially the A3D—threatened to derail the Navy's argument that its carriers could and should play a strong role in deterring the Soviet Union.

Postwar, BuAer spent most of its money on engines and airframes. In the late 1940s and early 1950s, the most critical problem must have seemed to be the new J40 engine, which BuAer wanted to use in its new generation of high-performance airplanes, both fighters (the F3H Demon and F4D Skyray) and bombers (the A-3). Though it appears as though catapults were taken for granted at the top level of BuAer, it is more likely that these other problems—directly associated with aircraft development—took center stage and absorbed the attention and energy of senior aviation officers.

Background

Although carriers had catapults almost from the beginning, they were little used before World War II. It was simpler and faster for airplanes to *roll* down a carrier's flight deck. Even the heaviest aircraft launched in combat during the war, Doolittle's B-25 bombers, made unassisted rolling takeoffs. During the war, however, catapults came into their own. The deck space available for a rolling takeoff under a plane's own power was limited by the practice of parking aircraft awaiting takeoff on the flight deck. It became clear that a catapult could be traded for open deck space. That was particularly obvious on board small escort carriers, whose catapults enabled them to operate relatively heavy bombers, such as TBF Avengers. By the end of the war it was standard practice for small carriers to launch Army aircraft during amphibious operations, so that the aircraft could arrive ashore ready to operate. Such launches were generally by catapult, and even aircraft as large as the B-25 and P-61 night fighter were adapted to catapult launch.

The unstated but obvious implication was that given a powerful enough catapult, a carrier could launch any airplane whose structure could handle the acceleration involved.[3] Conversely, using strong enough arresting gear, almost any kind of airplane could be recovered. As we noted in chapter 3, in November 1944 the new carrier *Shangri-La* in effect proved this point by launching and recovering the Navy's version of the B-25 medium bomber, by far the heaviest aircraft yet to operate from a carrier.

By that time, BuAer was paying McDonnell to develop jet fighters, though not heavy carrier bombers. Far more than conventional piston aircraft, jets might need catapults to take off at all in the length of a crowded flight deck. Without propellers to create airflow over their wings, they needed higher speeds to generate enough lift. It also seemed that jet engines might accelerate them relatively slowly.

Postwar Developments

Prior to World War II, Navy catapult developers designed two types of catapults: powder-driven devices for accelerating battleship and cruiser floatplanes and hydraulic catapults for carriers. In December 1944, BuAer initiated its postwar catapult program by considering new sources of power. That month it issued a draft specification for a new-generation catapult suited to jets.[4] Like the British, BuAer saw the German-developed slotted-cylinder catapult as a way to achieve the high power it wanted—but only for various missiles then under development.[5] Presumably NAMC personnel became acquainted with this technology when German V-1 launch sites were overrun by Allied forces in the summer of 1944. As we've seen, the German catapults were powered by the steam produced when hydrogen peroxide decomposed in the presence of a catalyst.

Ships had long used hydraulics as a way of transmitting power from their engines for auxiliary purposes. Pumps driven by a ship's engines drove fluids that in turn could push pistons or drive turbines where they were needed. In a carrier catapult, the motion of a piston near the catapult was magnified by wires running over pulleys. A piston movement of a few feet at low speed translated into a much longer stroke at higher speed. The power such a catapult could develop was ultimately limited by the strength of the wire, which could snap under heavy loads. There was also another constraint that applied to catapults—the need to limit the weight of their machinery.

Initially the new catapult program was justified by the trend in aircraft design toward greater weight and speed. Eventually, however, OPNAV's Military Requirements Division, responsible for setting the characteristics of new aircraft, realized that development would stop unless more powerful catapults became available. On 11 January 1946 the Military Requirements Division sent the director of the BuAer Engineering Division a note: aircraft weighing over twenty thousand pounds with takeoff stall speeds over 100 mph could not be catapulted from existing fleet carriers (i.e., of the *Essex* class), even with the usual relative wind of twenty-five knots. What limits would expected catapults impose on future aircraft? Surely the chief of BuAer would want to know.[6]

Aircraft designers certainly wanted to know. In June 1946, for example, Douglas designer Edward Heinemann noted in a letter to BuAer that his firm's two Navy projects—the AD Skyraider attack bomber and the F3D Skyknight fighter—could be launched by an *Essex*-class carrier using a catapult and wind over the deck, but only barely. Heinemann and his staff were then working on the design of a new pilotless aircraft designated "P/A V." This aircraft was expected to weigh fifteen thousand pounds but to stall at a relatively high speed, about 180 mph, which was significantly greater than the stall speed of the XF3D, which was 107 mph (or knots—the source uses just the number). Heinemann was afraid that existing catapults would not be able to accelerate the P/A V enough to get it into the air.[7]

During World War II the U.S. Navy had experimented with large catapults to launch heavy seaplanes, the theory being that in this way the seaplanes could carry more than their usual loads. One such catapult was installed on board a special barge, and in 1941 BuAer was seeking designs for a more powerful follow-on. The latter offered the sort of performance that the bureau sought postwar but in far too large a package. In effect it demonstrated that the hydraulic technology used before and during the war could not now suffice.[8]

BuAer simultaneously supported three primary approaches to the new catapult. One was to push existing hydraulic-catapult technology to the limit. A second was the slotted cylinder. A third was an electric catapult, since a modern warship could generate considerable electric power (the U.S. Navy already had experience with electric rather than hydraulic power in its ships and aircraft). BuAer used both contractors and its own catapult developers at the Naval Aircraft Factory in the Philadelphia Navy Yard. It saw the hydraulic approach as insurance against the failure of new technology.[9]

The hydraulic approach produced the H8 catapult, which entered service on board rebuilt carriers after World War II. It sufficed for first-generation jet fighters, and its limits influenced the design of the first postwar heavy carrier bomber, the AJ-1 Savage. BuAer seems to have realized that the H8 represented the limit imposed by wire strength in the size and weight allowable on a carrier.[10] When BuAer needed more power for the postwar heavy attack carrier, it saw a pair of H8s working together (under the designation H9) as a fallback solution, but that proved so unsatisfactory that it was soon abandoned.

As the bureau encountered problems in catapult development, however, it seems to have relied on the H9 as a form of insurance. Thus the H9 survived longer in BuAer statements to other organizations in the Navy than in reality. The BuAer Confidential Correspondence file in the National Archives mentions that a test installation of the H9 for use at the aircraft flight test center at Patuxent River was ordered in March 1948.[11] In addition, as of January 1949, the Naval Air Material Center—the catapult-developing organization—informed the Navy's Bureau of Ships that the planned carrier *United States* would carry the H9. That same month, however, the chief of BuAer, Rear Admiral Pride, noted in a letter to the head of NAMC that slotted-cylinder catapults would eventually replace the H9.[12] The ultimate hydraulic catapult, H9D, a monster composed of two H9s, was described by BuAer in 1951 as entirely impractical. It was also not powerful enough to launch the A3D heavy attack bomber, which by 1951 was the standard for new catapult requirements.[13]

An electric catapult was proposed by Westinghouse in 1943, and it was pursued for a time as the XE-1 Electropult, a prototype of which was set up at the aircraft test center at Patuxent River. Representatives of BuShips inspected the device on 3 October 1946. The catapult consisted of an electric "shuttle car" riding along a track. The track, 1,495 feet in length, was the fixed element of what amounted to an electric motor. Power was supplied by an aircraft engine driving a direct-current generator, which in turn drove a flywheel alternating-current motor-generator that supplied the necessary burst of launch power. BuShips considered the aircraft engine inadequate as a prime mover and suggested instead either two of the host ship's regular generators, driven by boiler steam, or a separate generator, or a 7,500 hp gas-turbine unit. As installed at Patuxent River, the Electropult could launch only one airplane every five minutes.[14]

A small version of this device was evidently used at NAMC. A similar catapult using a hydraulic clutch was tested in 1944–45, but scaling up the prototype proved difficult. The drawback of electric-drive catapults was the time it took between releasing the energy stored in the flywheel in one launch and building up energy in the flywheel for the next. But the idea seemed worth studying, and work on it continued into the late 1940s.[15] Another contract, for a linear turbine catapult, went to the M. W. Kellogg Company. Work was stopped in December 1948. The catapult was described as promising for guided-missile launching but as requiring too expensive a launch car, which would be difficult to recover after firing.[16]

The slotted cylinder offered the greatest promise, not least for future growth. It was also the simplest type of catapult. Some power source would drive a piston along the cylinder, and a hook would be attached to a shuttle connected to the piston. Until October 1951, BuAer envisaged firing the catapult aft from the bow of a carrier, driving the shuttle attached to the airplane the other way (forward), presumably by a wire passing over a single pulley. It called this "direct drive," because there would be no attempt to amplify mechanically the motion of the piston. But after October 1951, the Naval Aircraft Factory, then designing the C10 powder (explosive driven) catapult, put the explosive chamber aft, so that the shuttle would go in the same direction as the piston.[17] Power was taken off using a projecting tab emerging from the piston through the slot.[18] The larger the cylinder, the more powerful the catapult—apparently almost without limit, though such a catapult would need to be cooled while it was being used, and the slot greatly weakened the cylinder, requiring designers to find a means to use the carrier's structure to support the cylinder.

BuAer's catapult designers were authorized to go ahead with a slotted cylinder, soon designated XC1, in November 1945. The Naval Aircraft Factory submitted its preliminary design study on 26 December 1945. By this time the Navy was vitally interested in surface-to-surface missiles. Like the Germans during the war, it expected to use a catapult to launch them. A missile could be accelerated much more violently than a manned aircraft. BuAer thus developed a second slotted cylinder, XC2, specifically for this purpose, to achieve up to supersonic end speeds—for example, for ramjet-powered surface-to-surface missiles. An XC4 version was intended to launch antiaircraft missiles but was stopped in March 1949 because components required for the envisaged high-acceleration launching were not available. XC6 was designed specifically to launch

Grumman's Rigel (XSSM-6) ramjet surface-to-surface missile. Other slotted cylinders were devised for smaller missiles and for targets. Another slotted-cylinder catapult was built to accelerate aircraft on the ground for crash tests (it was installed at the Patuxent River Naval Air Test Center).

The great question was the source of power. For BuAer, the alternatives seem to have been internal combustion (as in a car engine or a diesel), hydrogen peroxide (as in the German catapult), and explosives. BuAer was already familiar with explosively driven catapults, because they had been used in battleships and cruisers since before World War II. Steam from a ship's boiler, which is what the British used, seems not to have been on the bureau's list. (In view of later developments, it was ironic that while a power source was being developed, one of the small slotted cylinders was tested using steam from a small boiler.) BuAer catapult developers would later argue that it was impractical to take steam from a ship's boiler. The ship would be slowed unacceptably, presumably because so much steam would be lost through the slot. Later, BuAer catapult developers also argued that the interval between launches would be excessive. Both of these problems also concerned British engineers at RAE.[19]

In 1947 BuAer chose explosives, with liquid fuel as a backup. It characterized both as "pressure generators," so presumably their gas products would be vented into the catapult cylinder. For initial tests compressed air was used, but it could not provide sufficient power to launch aircraft. BuAer's focus on explosive catapults was stimulated by the need for a device to launch light loads (five hundred pounds) at unusually high acceleration (170g—that is, exerting 170 times the force of gravity), with an end speed of 1,200 ft./sec. (about seven hundred knots). Such a catapult, the XM1, was built for use at the naval testing ground at Point Mugu, California. It had an expendable piston and launch car, which meant that its designers did not have to brake the piston in a reasonable distance after the end of its stroke.[20]

Between 1945 and 1948, catapult requirements exploded. In 1944–45 BuAer was contemplating accelerating fifteen-thousand-pound jet fighters to end speeds of 120 mph. In 1946 BuAer became interested in hundred-thousand-pound bombers (the largest it bought weighed about seventy thousand). Thus in January 1947, BuAer changed the requirement to a forty-five-thousand-pound airplane at the same speed, but with twice the launching interval. Its catapult designers estimated that a much more massive hydraulic catapult—weighing 675,000 pounds—would be needed. That was simply too heavy.[21]

In November 1947 the Chief of Naval Operations, Fleet Adm. Chester W. Nimitz, approved the design requirements for a new carrier that would operate fifty-thousand-pound fighters and hundred-thousand-pound bombers. That December BuAer reported to the CNO, now Adm. Louis E. Denfeld, that it had completed a design study of a catapult capable of launching hundred-thousand-pound aircraft at a hundred knots airspeed, including twenty-five knots of wind over deck due to the motion of the ship. This far exceeded the performance of any earlier or developmental catapult. BuAer pointed out that using two fifty-thousand-pound and two hundred-thousand-pound catapults would save about a hundred tons in flight-deck weight in comparison to the likely hydraulic design. Although that might not seem like much for what turned out to be a sixty-five-thousand-ton ship, it was so high in the ship that it could have considerable impact.[22]

In January 1948 the bureau further increased desired performance, to a hundred thousand pounds at ninety knots and a maximum speed of 105 knots with a 73,500-pound airplane. (Note that ninety knots is about 103 mph and that 105 knots is the earlier maximum of 120 mph.)[23] BuAer decided in April 1948 that the limit of hydraulic catapult performance had been reached with the H9 and that all future effort should go into slotted cylinders. The C1 slotted-cylinder catapult now seemed too small for future aircraft but too large for experimental work. It was therefore redefined as a test catapult, suited to but not intended for shipboard installation, with a capacity of eighteen thousand pounds and an end speed of a hundred knots (maximum acceleration 3.5g). For the future, lessons learned in its design would be applied to a catapult capable of launching a two-hundred-thousand-pound airplane at 150 knots. Somewhat later there were references in BuAer correspondence to three-hundred-thousand-pound aircraft.

A revised development schedule produced in January 1948 showed plans to complete the final design of the XC1 prototype on 1 April 1948 and the final design of the shipboard version on 1 April 1949.[24] The Naval Air Material Center on 29 June 1948 submitted its design proposal, which was formally approved for development on 21 July. In its proposal, NAMC noted that the XC1 was to serve as the basis for a larger catapult, and its configuration (the shape and size of the braking pit, for example) was modified so that it could be readily scaled up. There was even the possibility that NAMC could develop a twin-tube catapult, to double power in the simplest way. However, braking such a driven-piston device required absorbing 650,000 foot-pounds of energy in four feet, and so BuOrd suggested firing a second powder charge at the oncoming piston. BuAer rejected the idea because a misfire would badly damage the catapult.[25]

In September 1948 BuAer placed an order for the XC1 powder chamber with the Naval Gun Factory at the Washington Navy Yard.[26] Powder tests, presumably using only part of the catapult, began in October 1949.[27] As of October 1949 the catapult was scheduled for completion in March 1950. Tests of a version powered by compressed air were reported in January 1950.

Slotted cylinders seemed to free BuAer to pursue designs for long-range supersonic bombers. At this time the required payload was the early ten-thousand-pound atomic bomb. Given the massive power that supersonic flight seemed to require, any airplane delivering such a weapon had to be enormous. BuAer envisaged a one-way mission, the crew escaping in a smaller aircraft that might return to the carrier or else ditch.[28] This concept recalled the German wartime Mistel composite aircraft, used to deliver ultraheavy warheads. The one-way trip made it unnecessary for BuAer to develop equivalent arresting gear. Two hundred thousand pounds was the maximum takeoff weight of the big B-47 medium jet bomber the U.S. Air Force was then beginning to buy. In some documents the limit was set at three hundred thousand pounds; slotted-cylinder performance seemed potentially limitless. Such hopes collapsed with the cancelation of *United States* in April 1949.

Notwithstanding all this activity, unfortunately, catapult development did not keep pace with aircraft development. Despite its importance for the BuAer aircraft program, catapult work seems to have been underfunded, particularly after deep Defense Department budget cuts were mandated in 1949. The decision to limit C1 to a prototype made sense as part of a protracted development plan, but not if slotted tubes of various sizes were to equip the carrier *United States,* scheduled for laying down in 1949. Since sketch designs of the ship showed slotted tubes, it is not clear what would have been done had the project proceeded.

When the ship was canceled, some of the urgency of heavy catapult development was lost. On 31 May 1949, about six weeks later, BuAer sent BuShips, via the Chief of Naval Operations, a proposal to rebuild the *Midway*s, so as to keep the Navy heavy-attack program alive. Thus in June 1949 the chief of BuAer, Rear Admiral Pride, wrote NAMC that in the near future catapults might be needed to accelerate eighty-thousand-pound aircraft to 125 knots. That was roughly the capacity of the H9D catapult then being developed—whose weight, however, Rear Admiral Pride now said, was prohibitive if applied to existing carriers. The H9D could have been accommodated on board the massive *United States,* but now high performance would have to be provided for existing, but rebuilt, ships of the *Essex* class, and they could not possibly accommodate an H9.[29] The only alternative was a slotted-cylinder catapult.[30]

The new catapult was designated C7 (in its developmental phase, XC7). By January 1950 the projected date for completion of the design was 30 June 1951, and the projected date for completion of all XC7 tests (including calibration) was 30 June 1953. In March 1950, the Chief of Naval Operations, Adm. Forrest P. Sherman, wrote BuAer that it should be pursued with the highest possible priority, for use in all new and converted carriers (i.e., including carriers smaller than the *Midway*s), "in order to permit unrestricted operation of certain aircraft currently programmed, and in order to remove limitations which are seriously restricting new developments and advances in aircraft design."[31] It would launch aircraft weighing between 12,500 and 80,000 pounds at a maximum end speed of 125 knots (average acceleration 3.25*g*, maximum 3.5*g*) and a minimum end speed of sixty knots. Specifications included a launching interval not to exceed 30 seconds for aircraft weighing up to forty thousand pounds and not to exceed a minute for those weighing forty to eighty thousand pounds. Apparently the new A3D Skywarrior heavy (twin-jet, swept-wing) attack bomber was the important airplane that could not be launched *without* a C7 catapult. In 1950 the A3D was expected to enter service within a few years; it was given a particularly high priority. The XC7, however, had not been included in the fiscal year 1950 budget (drawn up in 1949), which was already very tight; given the program's high priority, BuAer had to transfer considerable funds from other projects. For example, work on catapults for surface-to-surface missiles was canceled on 3 May 1950.

USS *Forrestal* (CVA 59), the first of the new postwar U.S. Navy carriers, with an angled deck, steam catapults, deck-edge elevators, and a mirror landing aid. Note the large Douglas A3D Skywarriors.

Thomas C. Hone

Even at this stage, BuAer considered an alternative to the slotted cylinder, one that it called the "solid piston." Presumably the rod extending directly from its piston would have driven the catapult shuttle its complete length, so that the catapult as a whole would have been twice as long as the catapult track. That this alternative was seriously considered in 1950 suggests that building a slotted cylinder was anything but a trivial proposition, at least using the explosive power source that BuAer envisaged. As it was, the solid cylinder was soon rejected as impractical.[32]

The Navy was already modernizing the *Essex*-class carriers, under a program begun in 1946 with the incomplete *Oriskany*. The program involved the H8 hydraulic catapult, but it made sense to replace it with slotted cylinders. Thus in August 1950 BuAer called for a second type of slotted-cylinder catapult. It would have half the performance of C7—an end speed of 125 knots for a forty-thousand-pound airplane, with a thirty-second launch cycle. Heavier airplanes could be launched at lower speeds. The *Essex*-class ships could not accommodate as long a catapult as the C7, so greater acceleration was accepted, 5g maximum (4g average).[33]

Yet development of this catapult proved protracted. Initial powder tests were conducted in May 1950, but apparently they applied only to the catapult combustion chamber. The Naval Air Material Center had to inform BuAer that the catapult would probably not be ready before 1 April 1951. The contractor could not provide cylinder liners, cylinder link forgings, or the sealing strip (to keep the propelling gas from leaking through the slot) quickly enough.[34] Plans to use the C7 as the modernized-*Essex* catapult made such delays particularly unfortunate. BuAer's chief called for completion by 1 November 1950. He also commented that XC1 was very close to what was wanted for the *Essex* class, the main deficiencies being its length, its cooling capacity, and the zipper used to seal it against cylinder reaction. He wanted all tests completed by 1 April 1951, and the XC1 used as the prototype for the *Essex* catapult. Design of the new catapult was scheduled for completion by 31 January 1951. To make this possible, the priority of the XC1 project was raised from three to one. According to a handwritten note in the file, by moving up the priority of the XC1 project, "we stand reasonable chances of providing a very adequate catapult to 27A [*Essex*] conversions by June 1952. This action has full endorsement of CNO."[35] The new catapult was designated "C10," perhaps simply to indicate development from C1. Later documents mention C8 and C9 as target catapults.

In August 1950, the chief of BuAer summarized the situation in response to an urgent oral request (presumably by the Deputy Chief of Naval Operations for Air, Vice Adm. John H. Cassady):

> New model aircraft are designed to take advantage of all the capabilities of our carriers (deck strength, elevator dimensions, arresting capacity, launching capacity, etc.). This procedure is used in the expectation that the carrier construction program and the carrier conversion [i.e., modernization] program will keep reasonable pace with the aircraft development program as they have done in the past. Unfortunately, during the last few years the carrier construction program has been nonexistent and the carrier conversion program has only recently been accelerated. This situation has resulted in the Fleet being supplied with aircraft which crowd very seriously the limitations of the operating carriers. Furthermore, the seriousness of these limitations has been aggravated by the urgent necessity of operating

the new type aircraft at gross weights considerably above the gross weights characteristic of the basic missions for which the aircraft were designed.[36]

The H8 catapult, which was considered a bare minimum to handle new jets, had recently been delivered for installation aboard the first modernized *Essex*, USS *Oriskany*, and it seemed to be developing on schedule. Four more sets were being made for the next four carriers in the program *(Kearsarge, Lake Champlain, Essex,* and *Wasp)*. Further jet-operating carrier modernization had been slowed by pre–Korean War budget cuts, now being reversed. The BuAer chief told DCNO (Air) that, given work already done on the XC1 catapult, XC10s could be available for further ships by June 1952 "if the project is prosecuted at maximum priority and emergency procurement methods are used." That would be possible only if the CNO ordered the other bureaus involved—Ordnance (for the powder charges), Ships, and Yards and Docks (for shipyard work)—to give the catapult project "overriding priority over conflicting projects." As an indication of what scaling up from XC1 meant, each of a hundred C1 charges weighed 2.5 pounds, but each C7 charge was expected to weigh five hundred pounds, and each C10 charge 250 pounds.

At this time the most powerful catapult on board unmodernized carriers was the H4-1 aboard the three *Midway*s, weighing 357,000 pounds. It could accelerate a 52,500-pound airplane to sixty-one knots, or a 23,000-pound airplane to eighty-seven knots. The H4B on board an unmodernized *Essex* (weighing three hundred thousand pounds) could accelerate a thirteen-thousand-pound airplane to eighty-seven knots, or a seventeen-thousand-pound airplane to seventy-eight knots. The difference in power could be traced to different track lengths: 239 feet in a *Midway* versus 170 feet in an *Essex*. In the earliest modernized *Essex*-class carriers, the 245-foot-track H8 (weighing 411,500 pounds) could accelerate a fifteen-thousand-pound airplane, such as a jet fighter, to 104 knots, or a 52,500-pound airplane to sixty-six knots, a bit over what the H4-1 on a *Midway* could do. XC1 had the same track length and similar performance (eighteen thousand pounds to a hundred knots), but it was far lighter, at 213,000 pounds. At this stage XC7 was expected to use a 360-foot track to accelerate an eighty-thousand-pound airplane to 125 knots. Its weight would be 550,000 pounds, probably the upper limit for a flight-deck installation.

Enter the British

By this time the British were well along in developing a steam catapult. The unclassified BuAer catapult file for 1950 thus includes a cover letter from the British Joint Services Mission in Washington, dated 8 August 1950, enclosing "Notes on British Steam Catapults" and eight classified Brown Bros. (manufacturing) drawings. In November 1949, Cdr. R. W. Tunnell and Mr. J. C. Perry from BuAer had visited the United Kingdom, and they may have heard of or even seen the British developments, but they did not return with evidence that sparked interest within BuAer.[37]

Meanwhile XC1 progress was delayed, so that in September 1950 the projected completion date was 15 January 1951, two months later than had been hoped—while the carrier modernization program began to accelerate. However, on 18 January the Naval Air Material Center reported additional delays. With one part still not available, it could promise high-capacity air tests or low-capacity powder shots only beginning about 31 January 1951. The progress of the program was considered unacceptable, and in mid-February BuAer ordered it accelerated.

About February 1951 Rear Admiral Pride listed catapult alternatives for DCNO (Air), Vice Admiral Cassady.[38] He went through the existing program of powder or liquid-fuel slotted cylinders, but this time he mentioned the British steam catapult, as "the only other high capacity catapult development," capable of launching a thirty-thousand-pound aircraft at 126 knots, using 340 pounds of low-pressure steam per shot. "From available data" the British direct-drive slotted cylinder was about 25 percent heavier than its higher-pressure U.S. counterpart.

> Due to the low pressures used . . . its size is sufficiently large to impose a difficult installation problem. Latest information indicates that an aircraft will be launched from the catapult during March 1951 and that consideration is being given to equipping a sister ship of HMS ARK ROYAL with catapults of this type. In any event, *the excessive steam consumption, which has been roughly calculated to require a steam rate of forty thousand pounds per hour, deserves special study before this catapult can be seriously considered* [our emphasis]. A previous study of the advisability of using steam for slotted tube catapults made by personnel of the Bureau of Ships and of this Bureau [BuAer] led to the conclusion that the use of powder has many important advantages over the use of steam.

An attached note describes the BuAer letter as "an attempt to inject a note of realism into the program to replace H8s with C10s." BuAer suggested replacing one rather than two H8s in near-term *Essex* conversions. Delivery of the first production C10 was scheduled, at the earliest, for June 1952. This unit could go aboard the eighth converted carrier, but it could not be tested fully before that ship was completed in June 1953. Thus no ship to be completed before that date could have two C10s. Whether such a mixed installation made sense was important enough an issue for the Chief of Naval Operations to decide. The rest of the letter listed factors that might make it impossible to meet the envisaged schedule. As a further complication, BuAer hoped later to shift from powder to liquid propellant. Although the bureau was not sure how to do this, it expected the cost per shot to fall by three-quarters if it could, justifying extensive work. The *Perseus* (i.e., British steam catapult) file in the BuAer Ships Installation Division catapult papers contains an undated (probably early 1952) cost comparison of "C10-C7" and "C10-H81" programs. The former would install one C10 in the port side of six *Essex* (known as 27C) conversions and in the waist positions of the new carriers

Forrestal and *Saratoga*. The latter two would have C7s in their bows. C10s would serve as backups for H81 (presumably meaning H8 Mod. 1) catapults in the 27Cs and as the only catapult in the new carriers. The C7 project would be abandoned. Adopting the C10-H81 plan would have saved about seventy million dollars through fiscal year '57.

Acceleration of the BuAer program proved impossible. On 4 April 1951 the Naval Air Material Center listed a series of necessary changes that would delay the first powder launches to 1 May. Apparently there were much worse delays, because a 4 October BuAer conference on the catapult program heard that XC1 would begin ten firings (over a two-week period) to "prove out mechanical details of [the] catapult" on 15 October, after which it would fire twenty times (over a week beginning 20 October) to check its ballistics, after which it would undergo further tests of water-injection cooling. Firings at maximum rate would begin only on 19 November 1951.[39]

On 17 May 1951, OPNAV approved a BuAer proposal to study a steam catapult, with the caveat that "an extensive detailed investigation of the relative merits of all the various types of slotted cylinder catapults should be made, however, before selecting steam as an alternative propellant." BuAer proposed completing the study during the next fiscal year, but OPNAV wanted it expedited.[40] Presumably in support of this effort, on 22 May 1951 the new chief of BuAer, Rear Adm. Thomas S. Combs, asked OPNAV (Op-32) to have the naval attaché in London "keep in close touch with the progress of development of the steam catapult and keep this bureau informed . . . at frequent intervals."[41] BuAer did not admit that it was stymied. Rather, it claimed, "great effort is being directed toward the development of powder and liquid fuels as propulsion mediums for slotted cylinder catapults. Present progress in these developments shows promise. Early British results with the steam slotted cylinder catapult aboard HMS PERSEUS have also been encouraging." The bureau merely wanted to "keep pace with all slotted cylinder developments [so as to] keep programs properly oriented."

The Steam Catapult

BuAer set up a steam-catapult design program in June 1951, the stated rationale being that the high cost and complex logistics of powder charges made an alternative source of power economically attractive. At this time the bureau estimated that each naval aircraft would be catapulted about ten times per month, which meant thousands of charges.[42] The bureau's catapult-design R&D organization, the Naval Aircraft Factory in NAMC, was to evaluate steam as a catapult propellant to determine the range of pressures and temperatures most suitable for this purpose; compare the use of the ship's boilers to the use of separate flash boilers; and conduct a preliminary design study of a steam equivalent to the C10 catapult, then under development (launching a forty-thousand-pound airplane at 125 knots end speed, maximum acceleration 3.75g).

Nothing in BuAer's letter to NAMC referred to the existing British program. NAMC's response was less than enthusiastic. It assigned the steam catapult priority three, after the powder C10 (priority one) and H8 (priority two).[43]

British development of the steam catapult was initially classified, and the secrecy surrounding the British effort had prevented Royal Navy officers in the British Joint Services Mission in Washington, D.C., from sharing information with their counterparts in the U.S. Navy.[44] However, though the Bureau of Aeronautics became aware of the Royal Navy's steam catapult work in 1948, its engineers chose to focus their work on powder (i.e., explosive-driven) catapults.[45] The BuAer file on the British steam catapult includes an 8 August 1950 letter enclosing plans of the Type C (BS.4) version of the British catapult, to be provided to BuAer "in accordance with verbal instructions.... This procedure will be continued unless instructions to the contrary are received." The prototype steam catapult (BXS.1) was installed in the aircraft repair ship (ex-carrier) HMS *Perseus,* which was reactivated in 1948 specifically for these tests. For simplicity, all catapult machinery was installed on top of (rather than within) its flight deck, part of which was covered by a false deck.

At Admiralty invitation, two U.S. officers, Capt. H. S. Clarke and Capt. F. H. Horn, visited the ship in Belfast Lough to watch catapulting. By the time of their report, another ten steam catapults were on order for specific Royal Navy ships, with another ten for future installation. The prototype had fired 727 times, including thirty-two manned launchings. The report added that on 27 June 1951 the Admiralty offered to send the ship to the United States the following November for two months of demonstrations. The two captains and the naval air attaché in London, Rear Admiral Apollo Soucek, warmly recommended acceptance, as "it is the opinion of this office that the steam catapult has great possibilities."[46] On 14 July CNO extended an invitation. The attaché worked out arrangements, such as payment for fuel (the British supply of dollars was severely limited). NAMC drew up a test program using deadweights of fifteen, twenty-one, and twenty-eight thousand pounds. The *Perseus* trials in the United Kingdom having succeeded, Rear Admiral Soucek in London forwarded Admiralty catapult drawings. That BuAer wanted them suggests that whatever had been forwarded earlier had been lost, since they included a cross section through the catapult cylinder and various basic system diagrams.

In August 1951, before trials had been run, BuAer asked BuShips to provide studies of installation of direct-drive—as opposed to indirect-drive—catapults in existing and planned carriers, the results to be ready by July 1952. No such change could be realized until a direct-drive catapult had been proven. In January 1952 BuShips pointed out that the British catapult met exactly this requirement. Since the British had produced the very first such catapult, BuShips proposed to include it in the study BuAer had requested. This may not have pleased the NAMC catapult developers, who had already complained of the steam catapult's "excessive steam consumption."[47]

In October 1951 the CNO, Adm. William M. Fechteler, circulated an announcement that *Perseus* was coming (it was actually somewhat delayed). The ship arrived at Philadelphia Naval Shipyard in January 1952 and was expected to return to the United Kingdom late in February. However, at the U.S. Navy's request (see below) further trials were added.

During the *Perseus* trials, C. C. Mitchell, who had invented the British catapult, made the startling claim that it could stand up to American steam conditions (550 pounds per square inch, or psi). Moreover, using such higher-pressure steam it could match planned C10 performance.[48] An anonymous BuAer memorandum writer thought it wise to take up Mitchell's offer for tests not contemplated when *Perseus* had been sent to the United States. The high-pressure steam could be provided by a USN destroyer tied up alongside. "If these tests should verify that the British catapult has approximately the capacity predicted, and if BuShips will underwrite putting this catapult in our ships [with the note, crossed out, "something they have not previously done for any direct-drive catapult"], the Ships Characteristics Board might well be requested ["directed" was crossed out] to examine the feasibility of employing British catapults in our carriers." Clearly this was a sensitive proposition, because the writer added that "in making this recommendation, I do not wish to imply that our own catapult development program will not yield thoroughly reliable catapults. In fact, if allowed to continue our own program aggressively, we will produce catapults by about 1956 which are greatly superior to any possible extrapolation of the present British low pressure catapult." But the writer had to admit that the British had been actually firing their catapult two months before development of the C10 even began. C10 development now was moving rapidly; after only sixteen months the experimental model was ready, and delivery of the production version was expected in December 1952. Even so, the British catapult already existed and worked. The ship's visit was extended specifically so that it could run the high-pressure trials.

In January 1952 BuAer circulated a "brief comparison" of the British and U.S. catapults by Capt. Sheldon W. Brown, head of the Ships Installation Division, the BuAer catapult branch. "The British may make a determined effort to sell their steam catapult to us for use in our carriers. [This] effort could conceivably be motivated by a desire either to be helpful or to acquire dollars or to do both. The following . . . information . . . may be useful in the event the British take this anticipated course of action." The attached

A U.S. Navy AD Skyraider attack plane on HMS *Perseus*.
Naval Aviation History Unit, Navy History and Heritage Command

tabulation showed that the British catapults did not match the desired capacity. The experimental BXS.1 aboard HMS *Perseus* had a 203-foot power stroke, launching a thirty-thousand-pound aircraft at 123 knots (not taking into account Mitchell's proposal to use higher American steam pressures). By way of comparison, the C10 could launch forty thousand pounds at 125 knots, and C7 could launch eighty thousand pounds at that speed. Both had 184-foot power strokes. The projected production version of the British catapult, BS.1, was rated at only thirty thousand pounds at 105 knots using a 144-foot stroke. The British stored boiler steam in an accumulator before firing. It took the accumulator time to build up sufficient steam pressure, and that limited the firing rate. BuAer planned to replace powder with hydrogen peroxide (as then also planned for U.S. submarine propulsion, but later abandoned) or some other gas generator. In contrast to the British, BuAer preferred indirect to direct drive.

The chief advantages of the British catapult were the low cost of its propellant and the fact that it already existed. However, it drained steam from a ship's power plant. BuAer estimated that firing every thirty seconds (to provide C10 capability) it would need about an eighth of the full steam capacity of an *Essex*-class carrier. Firing 150 times a day, it would need 10 percent of the ship's water capacity. BuAer conceded that steam offered the British catapult a considerable logistical advantage but held that it would disappear when the bureau replaced powder with internal combustion or even with steam from a flash boiler. The direct drive used by the British placed much heavier weights at flight-deck level and seemed to require a large cut in the flight deck. That might not matter much in an *Essex*, but in the new carriers the flight deck was the strength deck, and its structural integrity needed to be preserved. BuShips was being asked to look into whether such cuts could be accepted. For Captain Brown, the British catapult had flaws, and he apparently did not see it, before it was tested in Philadelphia, as other than a backup for NAMC's product.

The higher-steam-pressure trials were carried out, up to fifty-five thousand pounds deadweight, but no aircraft were launched at higher pressure (acceleration curves were circulated under an 8 April 1952 cover sheet). Because *Perseus* was tested at Philadelphia and at Norfolk, senior U.S. operational officers watched—and were impressed. The BuAer *Perseus* file includes pointed questions from Commander in Chief, Atlantic Fleet, and from Commander, Naval Air Forces, Atlantic: When will this catapult be tested with U.S. aircraft, and when will it go aboard our carriers? The trials were conducted on the highest-priority basis.

The BuAer memo suggests that the problem of flight-deck structure was in its view the clinching argument against the British catapult. In February 1952 BuShips quashed this objection. The BuAer catapults needed much heavier support to handle lateral loads due to the firing of powder.[49] For example, a C7 or C10 powder catapult had to withstand a chamber pressure of 4,000 psi, compared to 600 psi for a steam catapult. The lateral load on a C7 using indirect drive was 19,500 psi; it was fourteen thousand for an indirect-drive C10. Direct-drive catapults, whether powder or steam, carried no lateral loads. A British-type steam catapult with C10 performance (forty thousand pounds at 125 knots) would weigh about 160 tons, about the same as a direct-drive version of C10 but far less than the 227 tons of the indirect-drive version. Comparable figures for C7 performance (seventy thousand pounds at 125 knots) were 239 tons for the British catapult, 243 for a direct-drive C7, and 300 for an indirect-drive C7. Moreover, BuShips pointed out that the flight decks of the U.S. carriers then planned could be reinforced around the catapult slot to maintain structural strength. Finally, BuShips argued that using hydrogen peroxide or liquid oxygen would take "considerably more weight and space below decks." BuShips also considered boiler capacity in the new carriers quite sufficient.[50] In short, the steam catapult was quite suitable for all the carrier classes envisaged.

With the *Perseus* trials complete, the Naval Aircraft Factory reported details and performance of the BXS.1 catapult. It suggested that considerable weight could be saved by redesign. However, it seems clear that it much preferred its own solutions, drawing up a sketch design of a steam indirect-drive catapult (like the C7 and C10) that, like the C10, could launch a forty-thousand-pound airplane at 125 knots. At this point it still expected the C10 to enter service as a powder catapult. Work was under way to design an air plant to replace the current powder propulsion. The main advantages of the British catapult were its compact brake (at the end of the catapult stroke), its unique sealing strip (possible because it operated at low pressure), and the fact that it needed no cooling water. The C10 was lighter. Its forty-nine-foot (rather than five-foot) brake stroke made it possible to recover the tow bridle after launching (U.S. steam catapults were later fitted with simple "bridle catchers"). To the U.S. catapult developers, deficiencies such as the massive brake could be blamed on an urgent development schedule, and they would be easy to remedy. Once that was done, the U.S. catapult would clearly be superior to the British.

Contrary to the expressed hopes of officers like Captain Brown, the U.S. Navy adopted the British steam catapult, testing it successfully in 1952–54 aboard *Essex*-class carriers. The "C7" and "C10" designations were taken over for British-style direct-drive steam turbines. The record of just how these decisions were taken is not clear, not least because BuAer correspondence files for the period after 1951 have not been declassified as of this writing. Until now, all U.S. carriers have had steam catapults descended from Mitchell's BXS.1 prototype rather than from the intense BuAer effort of the late 1940s and early 1950s.

After World War II, BuAer funded several different catapult technologies through NAMC. Initially, NAMC engineers believed that incremental improvements in existing hydraulic catapult technology would meet BuAer's requirements for power and acceleration. Even before it became clear that those improvements would not be adequate for a loaded A3D Skywarrior, NAMC engineers considered alternative catapult concepts—though the engineers' preference appears to have been to stay with what was known versus what was new (and therefore more of a risk). The British engineers at Farnborough also improved existing hydraulic catapult technology, but they eventually ran up against the same physical limits that the Americans had encountered: "The greatest single shortcoming of the hydro-pneumatic under-deck gear was that of increasing weight and inertia of its moving parts, with the unavoidable increase in demands for power."[51] The catapult engineers at Farnborough, however, had an ally that their counterparts at NAMC did not—Colin C. Mitchell, the steam catapult pioneer.

What "saved" the catapult engineers working for both navies was their willingness and ability to move from the theoretical analysis of the physics of catapult design to actual tests of prototypes. In addition, the engineers were supported by senior officers who were willing to spend scarce funds on actual experiments, especially those carried out on board HMS *Perseus* in the United Kingdom and later in the United States. Both navies relied on parallel development efforts, though the range of parallel efforts was greater for the USN than for the RN, and, as it happened, the most successful parallel effort in the United Kingdom was that conducted by Colin Mitchell, who was something of an "outsider."

At the same time, the surviving documents in the National Archives suggest that there was an element of "not invented here" in the minds of BuAer's catapult experts. One suspects that they did not believe that their British counterparts could develop an effective and efficient steam catapult, especially one that would work at the higher steam pressures generated in the boilers of U.S. carriers. It was fortunate that Rear Admiral Soucek was the USN's air attaché in London in 1951. He grasped what the engineers back in the United States did not—that the USN had to gamble on Mitchell's steam catapult, because the risk of not doing so outweighed the risk of spending funds to support *Perseus* on its journey to the United States and its tests in Philadelphia and Norfolk.

By the late 1940s the U.S. Navy was not inclined to buy foreign innovations, the main exception being the radical aircraft and missile technology the Germans had introduced during World War II. Thus, after a very successful demonstration of the new British Limbo antisubmarine weapon in 1949, the Americans apologized: they knew that the Bureau of Ordnance would prefer its inferior Weapon Alfa. The British understood. The last foreign innovations that BuOrd had willingly adopted had been Swedish and Swiss antiaircraft guns immediately before the United States entered World War II, and the German electric torpedo—all answers to very urgent operational problems. In effect, the steam catapult was the beginning of a short era of adoption of British-invented innovations by a grateful U.S. Navy. Besides carrier improvements, these innovations included the far less well known method of "rafting" to silence a nuclear submarine—a technique adopted in the face of Adm. Hyman Rickover's considerable preference for turboelectric drive, a technology with which he was personally involved.

Finally, catapults were not BuAer's only way of launching the new heavy aircraft. Solid-fuel rockets for jet-assisted takeoff, developed during World War II, represented another alternative. For missiles, they in effect superseded catapults, to become the boosters that are now so familiar. Apparently JATO was considerably less acceptable for carrier aircraft, although it had been used in wartime. In 1949, when it wanted to demonstrate the potential of heavy carrier bombers but had no suitable catapults, the Navy used JATO to launch three Neptune bombers from *Midway*-class carriers. These aircraft became the core of an interim Navy nuclear-attack capability. As such they would have been launched from the same type of carrier in wartime, in the same way. BuAer interest in solid propellants for catapults could be seen as a way of domesticating JATO, to suit it to regular carrier use.

Notes

1. Geoffrey Cooper, *Farnborough and the Fleet Air Arm* (Hersham, Surrey, U.K.: Midland, 2008), p. 219.
2. William F. Trimble, *Wings for the Navy: A History of the Naval Aircraft Factory, 1917–1956* (Annapolis, Md.: Naval Institute Press, 1990), pp. 294–318.
3. The Naval Aircraft Factory submitted a proposal for a high-capacity hydraulic-ram catapult on 2 February 1945; letter, BuAer

Confidential Correspondence file S83-2(C), vol. 5, 1945. NAMC engineers had already distinguished between lower-speed catapults for aircraft and much higher-speed catapults for missiles. A 26 February 1945 letter in this file notes that the factory was also working on a slotted-cylinder catapult, which the head of BuAer's Ships Installation Division considered worth patenting.

4. Copies of the letter sent to potential manufacturers are in BuAer Confidential Correspondence file S83-2(C), vol. 4, 1945 (new series; this is not the vol. 4 in the 1922–44 correspondence series). Written on 30 November 1944, they were sent early in December. The requirement was for a catapult that could accelerate a five-thousand-pound dead load to 250 mph (not knots, as later specified) in 175 feet, with a maximum acceleration of 14g, or a twenty-thousand-pound dead load to 125 mph with a maximum acceleration of 3.5g. Launch interval was twenty seconds.

5. The BuAer *Ten-Year History and Program of Future Research and Development*, completed late in 1945, asserted that slotted tubes had the greatest potential for high power. The BuAer 1949 Confidential Correspondence file (S83-2[C]) includes a note indicating that BuAer had a copy of the Royal Aircraft Establishment report (Technical Note NA 182) of the German catapults. The BuAer S83-2(C) Confidential Correspondence file for 1945, vol. 5, contains a 17 January 1945 Army Air Corps description of the launching procedure for the German catapult, using either flash steam or a chemical propellant, presumably hydrogen peroxide.

6. Letter, BuAer Confidential Correspondence file S83-2(C), vol. 8, 1946. This is the first letter in the file, reading from the back.

7. BuAer Confidential Correspondence file S83-2(C), vol. 8, 1946.

8. A BuAer confidential letter noted that the standard H4-1 on an *Essex* carrier weighed 357,000 pounds, while the H8, then under development, was expected to weigh 400,000 pounds. By way of contrast, the XM1 missile-launching slotted-tube catapult weighed only thirty-two thousand pounds and cost far less to manufacture. The drawback to the slotted-tube design, however, was *cost per launch*. Whereas it cost thirty-five cents each time the H4-1 was used, it cost $1,200 each time the XM1 was used, because in the latter case both the piston and the launch car were lost. See 31 March 1948, ser. 3136587, BuAer Confidential Correspondence file S83-2(C), 1948–1949, to the BuAer representative at the USAF test center at Wright Patterson Air Force Base, Dayton, Ohio.

9. Trimble, *Wings for the Navy*, p. 290.

10. Ibid., p. 318.

11. Letter, April 1948, BuAer Confidential Correspondence file S83-2(C), 1948–1949.

12. See the Confidential Correspondence file S83-2(C), vol. 1, 1949. The letter from the chief of BuAer to NAMC is 14 January 1949.

13. Chief, BuAer, letter to Op-05, date not visible but probably February 1951, ser. 3145432, BuAer Confidential Correspondence file S83-2(C), vol. 1 (box 155).

14. A 25 February 1947 letter from BuShips described the setup at Patuxent River; see BuAer Confidential Correspondence file S83-2(C), 1947.

15. Letter, 20 November 1951, ser. 3138314, BuAer Confidential Correspondence file S83-2(C), vol. 3, 1951.

16. BuAer, letter to Commander, NAMC, 22 December 1948, BuAer Confidential Correspondence file S83-2(C), 1948–1949.

17. NAMC, letter to BuAer, 17 October 1951, BuAer Confidential Correspondence file S83-2(C), vol. 3, 1951.

18. Naval Aircraft Factory (in NAMC), letter to BuAer, 8 October 1951, ser. 0482, BuAer Confidential Correspondence file S83-2(C), vol. 3, 1951. The steam-catapult work was assigned to a private contractor, Steam Generators, Ltd., of Trenton, New Jersey. In 1985, Rear Adm. D. K. Weitzenfeld noted that the NAMC engineers were concentrating on powder catapults, because they knew that the British were working on steam catapults and "we decided not to duplicate their work." See Weitzenfeld's "Colin Mitchell's Steam Catapult: The Heart of Modern Aircraft Carriers," *Wings of Gold* 10 (Summer 1985), p. 42.

19. Cooper, *Farnborough and the Fleet Air Arm*, pp. 278–82.

20. A 28 April 1948 letter from BuAer to the Bureau of Ordnance in the BuAer 1948–1949 S83-2(C) Confidential Correspondence file, ser. 3138868, refers to an earlier BuAer confidential letter (ser. 07497) of 21 October

1947 that described the entire catapult program to BuOrd (which provided the explosives).

21. Naval Aircraft Factory, letter to BuAer, 19 September 1946, BuAer Confidential Correspondence file S83-2(C), vol. 9, 1945–47. This was apparently in response to a 9 August letter from BuAer authorizing the design of the ill-fated H9.

22. Letter, BuAer Confidential Correspondence file S83-2(C), vol. 9, 1947 (photographic copy).

23. BuAer, letter to NAMC, 23 April 1948, ser. 3138638, BuAer Confidential Correspondence file S83-2(C), vol. 1.

24. 29 January 1948, ser. 3134387, BuAer Confidential Correspondence file S83-2(C). This revised a 21 October 1947 schedule sent to BuOrd. Preliminary design of the XC5 was to be completed by 1 January 1950, and of the XC6 by 1 June 1949. In neither case did BuAer estimate a date for completion of the final designs.

25. Letter, ser. 3146104, BuAer Confidential Correspondence file S83-2(C), vol. 1, 1949.

26. BuOrd, letter to BuAer, 7 September 1948, BuAer Confidential Correspondence file S83-2(C), vol. 1. (BuOrd was responsible for the Naval Gun Factory.) However, a 10 February 1948 BuAer letter to BuOrd mentions ongoing construction of an XC1 prototype, as proposed in October 1947. Presumably it was a pre-prototype, since the February letter mentions adaptation to powder (i.e., explosive) operation and asks BuOrd to develop the necessary powder charge. The contemporary XC2 used liquid oxygen and gasoline to generate its propelling gas; ser. 313244, BuAer Confidential Correspondence file S83-2(C), vol. 1, 1949.

27. Letter, 25 November 1949, ser. 91128435, BuAer Confidential Correspondence file S83-2(C), vol. 2, 1949.

28. See examples in Jared A. Zichek, *Secret Aerospace Projects of the U.S. Navy: The Incredible Attack Aircraft of the USS* United States, *1948–1949* (Atglen, Pa.: Schiffer, 2009).

29. Letter, 15 June 1949, ser. 3125989, BuAer Confidential Correspondence file S83-2(C), vol. 2.

30. Letter, 9 June 1949, ser. 3125853, BuAer Confidential Correspondence file S83-2(C), vol. 2. This letter describes the 31 May 1949 proposal, which is not enclosed.

31. Letter, 13 March 1950, ser. 3232992, BuAer Confidential Correspondence file S83-2(C), vol. 1, 1950.

32. Chief, BuAer, letter to Commander, NAMC, 4 May 1950, BuAer Confidential Correspondence file S83-2(C), vol. 2.

33. BuAer, letter to NAMC, 8 August 1950, ser. 3147484, BuAer Confidential Correspondence file S83-2(C), vol. 1, 1950. This letter refers to C7 as an indirect-drive catapult, requiring considerable hangar-deck space, whereas the unit proposed for the *Essex* conversions was a direct-drive type. BuShips had proposed indirect drive because that would have less impact on the ship.

34. NAMC, letter to BuAer, 3 August 1950, BuAer Confidential Correspondence file S83-2(C), vol. 1, 1950.

35. Chief, BuAer, letter to Commander, NAMC, 5 August 1950, BuAer Confidential Correspondence file S83-2(C), vol. 1, 1950.

36. Chief, BuAer, letter to the DCNO(Air), 18 August 1950, ser. 0805, BuAer Confidential Correspondence file S83-2(C).

37. Cover sheet for a report of a 10 November 1949 visit, BuAer Confidential Correspondence file S83-2(C), 1948–1949, record group [hereafter RG] 72, box 146, National Archives. Only the cover sheet was found.

38. Chief, BuAer, letter to Op-05, date not visible but probably February 1951, ser. 3145432, BuAer Confidential Correspondence file S83-2(C), vol. 1 (box 155).

39. BuOrd, letter to BuAer, 31 October 1951, ser. 27784, BuAer Confidential Correspondence file S83-2(C), vol. 3, 1951, enclosure.

40. CNO, letter to BuAer, 17 May 1951, ser. 1051851, BuAer Confidential Correspondence file S83-2(C), vol. 2, 1951.

41. Chief, BuAer, letter to Op-32, ser. 3132831, BuAer Correspondence file S83-2, 1951. (Op-32 was part of OPNAV, the Office of the Chief of Naval Operations.)

42. BuAer, letter to NAMC, 12 June 1951, ser. 3141490, BuAer Confidential Correspondence file S83-2(C), vol. 2, 1951.

43. Naval Aircraft Factory (in NAMC), letter to BuAer, 8 October 1951, ser. 0482, BuAer Confidential Correspondence file S83-2(C), vol. 3, 1951.

44. Rear Adm. John P. Stevens, RN, British Joint Services Mission, letter to Rear Adm. Felix Johnson, USN, Director of Naval Intelligence, subject "HMS *Perseus,* visit to the United States," 28 August 1951, RG 72, box 3, entry 133, Perseus folder, National Archives.

45. D. K. Weitzenfeld, "Colin Mitchell's Steam Catapult: The Heart of Modern Aircraft Carriers," *Wings of Gold* 10 (Summer 1985), p. 42.

46. Undated attaché report in BuAer Ships Installation Division file on *Perseus* trials. Records of the Bureau of Aeronautics, Project Records Relating to Catapults, Launchers, Missiles, 1941–1953, RG 72, box 3, entry 133, National Archives.

47. BuShips memo in BuAer Ships Installation Division file on *Perseus* trials, RG 72, box 3, entry 133.

48. BuAer Ships Installation Division file on *Perseus* trials.

49. Memorandum, 14 February 1952, Ships Installation Division file on *Perseus* trials.

50. Ibid.

51. Cooper, *Farnborough and the Fleet Air Arm,* p. 214.

CHAPTER NINE

Analysis

> *Our method . . . can be compared with that used by people assembling a complicated jigsaw puzzle. We will first put together the pieces of one corner, then pieces of another corner. Gradually, we will link our assembled sections.*
>
> HONE, FRIEDMAN, AND MANDELES,
> *AMERICAN & BRITISH AIRCRAFT CARRIER DEVELOPMENT, 1919–1941*

In one corner of our complicated jigsaw puzzle are engineer Lewis Boddington and his colleagues in the Naval Aircraft Department at the Royal Aircraft Establishment.[1] As we pointed out in chapter 4, they had accepted as early as February 1945 the concept that future naval fighters would have to be "pure" jets and that therefore launching and recovering them from carriers would demand significant changes in equipment and procedures. In June 1945, Boddington and his colleagues had decided to embark on a program to experiment with jets without undercarriages in order to increase the very limited range of the early jet aircraft. By mid-July Boddington had noted that future carrier aircraft would need assisted takeoff and that they would land at higher speeds than propeller-driven planes. By mid-September, he was certain that it would be best if jet aircraft landed with their engines running at 90 percent of full power, and he knew that having them do so would require somehow separating the landing and take-off decks.

The Individuals: Royal Navy

But there were more people involved in this string of developments than engineer Lewis Boddington. Test pilot Eric Brown noted in his memoir, *Wings on My Sleeve*, that in January 1945 Maj. F. M. Green, whom Brown identified as "the veteran aero-engine inventor," described in detail to an audience of engineers and test pilots a "carpet deck" that would accept jets without undercarriages. The idea clearly caught (or had already captured) the attention of Boddington, because he ran with it during the summer and fall of 1945. What matters to us is that Boddington, his colleagues, and his superiors had identified the military requirement (jets on carriers as *routine*) and had also recognized that some dramatic changes would have to be made to carriers if they were to operate jets safely while generating enough sorties to fulfill the required mission.

Boddington continued to be influential in the effort to adapt carriers to jet aircraft. On 7 August 1951, a meeting was held in the Ministry of Aviation to discuss ways of handling aircraft on carriers with "flexible" decks. Capt. Dennis R. F. Cambell of the RN, a naval aviator and assistant chief naval representative to the ministry, was chair, and Boddington and others attended. Just before the meeting, eating his lunchtime sandwich, Captain Cambell had been staring at a large model of the carrier *Illustrious* on his desk. As he recalled, "I kept trying to picture how this crazy deck [i.e., the flexdeck] could be installed to allow a reasonable speed of successive landings. I sketched a few ideas[,] . . . none of which looked really practicable."

But then, "right out of the blue it came to me—why not angle the deck about 10 degrees to port?" Later, in the meeting, Captain Cambell waited until "it had become clear to all that the paramount need in accepting the rubber mat idea was to retain the deck park. When it was coming to be seen that no simple solution was in the offing, I presented a large sketch . . . showing the mat and the four arresting wires offset 10 degrees to port. I admit I did this with something of a flourish, and was accordingly somewhat miffed at not getting the expected gasps of gratifying amazement." But Boddington was taken with the idea, and he stayed after the meeting to look carefully at Cambell's sketch.

On 28 August 1951, Lewis Boddington sent detailed drawings of an angled deck applied to the planned carrier *Ark Royal* to the Deputy Director of Naval Construction and to Captain Cambell.[2] The drawings were sent on to the Board of Admiralty. In September, during the semiannual air show at Farnborough, Cambell mentioned his angled-deck concept to visitors from the U.S. Navy. He remembered "that they exchanged significant looks."[3] What Cambell apparently didn't know at the time was that Brown had taken the idea of the angled deck with him when he was sent to the Naval Air Test Center at Patuxent River.[4] As Brown later recalled, the idea of the angled deck "was seized on eagerly by the Americans." They were ready for it. In his *Nuclear Weapons and Aircraft Carriers,* retired vice admiral Jerry Miller noted that Capt. James D. Small, who in 1951 was a young engineering officer in the Navy's Bureau of Ships, admitted years later that "it is too bad that our naval architects, naval aviators, or bystanders didn't see [the angled-deck concept first]—but they didn't."[5] Yet they quickly took advantage of it, converting the *Essex*-class carrier *Antietam* to the angled-deck configuration by mid-December 1952.[6]

An unmodified carrier, USS *Leyte* (CV 32), on the left and a carrier given an angled deck, USS *Antietam* (CV 36), on the right, October 1954. As Vice Adm. Robert Dunn noted to the authors, the angled deck eliminated the demand from pilots for a flush-deck carrier.

Navy Department, National Archives

Boddington and Cambell first tested the angled-deck concept by directing the painting of a ten-degree-offset landing path on the deck of the carrier *Triumph*. Royal Navy pilots then made touch-and-go landings along the path. As Cambell would recall, "These trials were completely successful, and the pilots concerned were most enthusiastic." Yet it took a visit of and demonstrations by USS *Antietam* in May 1953 to convince "the Admiralty that retrofit action [on existing RN carriers] should be started forthwith."[7]

Cambell and his assistant, Cdr. Nicholas Goodhart, polished a scheme of Goodhart's to replace a carrier's landing signal officer with "visual indication of the optimum approach and landing path . . . [using] a steady light source." According to an article in *Naval Aviation News* in 1955, Goodhart had served as an exchange pilot at the Patuxent Naval Air Test Center in 1948–49, and he had witnessed U.S. Navy efforts to find a way to improve the coordination between landing signal officers (LSOs) and pilots of jet aircraft.[8] Engineers at Farnborough had already been working on a mechanical replacement for LSOs, and Goodhart took his idea to them.[9] The first component of his system was a large light placed at the after end of the flight deck. About 150 feet from the stern, Goodhart and the Farnborough engineers set up the second component—a large concave mirror, eventually gyrostabilized, that would reflect the light at an angle suited to the type of aircraft coming in to land. On each side of the mirror would be a row of three green lights. The pilot's task would be to keep the reflection of the light level with the green lights.

Cambell's account of how they tested the idea in the office he shared with Goodhart is classic: "We borrowed a small vanity mirror from Miss Montgomery, our secretary, and propped it up at a simulated 3 degrees approach angle. . . . [W]e then borrowed Monty's lipstick and stood it on end a few feet away. Looking at the lipstick in the mirror, we found it easy to keep it in view while we moved forwards and downwards."[10]

The mirror landing aid on USS *Bennington* (CV 20) in August 1955. It is stabilized to remain steady while the ship rolled and pitched.

Navy Department, National Archives

Cambell and Goodhart realized that it was "blindingly obvious that the two revolutionary inventions [angled deck and landing mirror] would be complementary."[11] When this "visual glide slope system" was tested first at Farnborough and then at sea on HMS *Illustrious* in November 1953, two U.S. Navy pilots were part of the test team, and one, Lt. Cdr. Donald D. Engen, wrote a report to the Chief of Naval Operations recommending "that the Navy procure the mirror immediately."[12] Engen was at that time one of two U.S. Navy exchange pilots at the Royal Air Force's Empire Test Pilots School at Farnborough.

Eric Brown was involved in more than the development of the angled deck and the mirror landing aid. He also had a hand in the U.S. Navy's adoption of the steam catapult. When HMS *Perseus,* modified but not used for regular fleet operations, arrived at the Philadelphia Navy Yard in February 1952, Brown was at Patuxent River as an exchange pilot. He was ordered north to Philadelphia to fly an F9F Panther jet from *Perseus,* moored to a dock at the Navy Yard. Brown was probably selected for this task because, as he noted, he had worked closely with C. C. Mitchell "many times on catapult trials in Britain."[13]

On the day of the test, there was no headwind blowing over the flight deck; instead, there was a five-knot tailwind. As Brown later wrote, "A huddle of frustration gathered. The Americans shook their heads firmly at the idea that a jet could be shot off with the ship tied up and a tail wind blowing over the catapult." Developer Mitchell, however, insisted that the trial launches take place as scheduled. As Brown stood by, the senior engineer officer on *Perseus* said, "We'll risk the British pilot if you'll risk the aircraft." That was it. There was no backing down. Brown, "the innocent in this drama," climbed into his cockpit and "was flung off . . . through a maze of dockyard cranes and workshop chimneys." But he and the other pilots made it, and they repeated their performances the next day—when the tailwind was even worse.[14] His success garnered Brown an interview with the Chief of Naval Operations, Adm. William M. Fechteler. As Brown remembered, the admiral "expressed his gratitude for the way in which the British had co-operated in handing over the steam-catapult, the angled-deck and the flexible-deck ideas."[15]

The individuals in the Royal Navy who were prominent in the development of the steam catapult, angled deck, and mirror landing system and in the sharing of these innovations with individuals in the U.S. Navy left a trail of papers, memorandums, drawings, and recollections. In reviewing this material, we infer that one reason the British naval officers and civilians were able to come up with their innovative concepts was that at least some of them—in particular, Eric Brown, Lewis Boddington, Dennis R. F. Cambell, and Nicholas Goodhart—had worked together effectively over an extended period of time. They weren't strangers to one another, and they were also not strangers to the problems. They appear to have realized in 1945 or soon thereafter that jet aircraft were both the future of naval aviation and also a challenge to launch and recover safely and quickly from aircraft carriers. They then built on their shared knowledge of the problem—mating the new jet aircraft to a carrier's flight deck—to find ways to recover and launch jet aircraft rapidly.

The Individuals: U.S. Navy

In the U.S. Navy, individuals also mattered, but they worked within a setting that was very different from that of their counterparts in the RN. In early 1945, while senior officers in the Royal Navy had already accepted the idea that British carriers would have to operate jet aircraft, U.S. Navy officers at sea and ashore were thinking about current operational problems in their fight against Japan. Could the carrier force fight off the kamikazes? Could its strike aircraft actually succeed in attacking the Japanese mainland? Could the carriers be constantly supplied with new aircraft, fuel for those planes, and enough ordnance?

It wasn't clear in January or February 1945 that the war against Japan would end that August, and U.S. Army and Navy ordnance specialists had begun developing new weapons to attack targets in Japan, including missiles with conventional warheads. The Navy was also concerned that the Japanese might develop missiles that their manned aircraft could launch against any U.S. invasion force, much as Germany had used radio-guided bombs and missiles against Allied forces in the Mediterranean in 1943. In July 1944, for example, the Navy's Bureau of Ordnance had asked the scientists who had developed the antiaircraft proximity fuse to evaluate the possibility of using ship-launched missiles for fleet air defense. In early December 1944, the Commander in Chief, U.S. Fleet, Adm. Ernest J. King, had directed BuOrd to push ahead "on an urgent basis" with work to develop and field antiaircraft missiles, and he simultaneously created a committee to study the postwar implications of wartime missile developments in the Allied and Axis nations.[16]

More importantly, the Manhattan Project had developed nuclear weapons. The need to have a carrier-based bomber that could carry nuclear weapons drove both aircraft and carrier development after World War II. In January 1946, the Navy's Bureau of Aeronautics issued a request for proposals to major aircraft manufacturers that specified a carrier-based bomber able to carry an eight-thousand-pound weapon. In the interim, while the new aircraft was being designed and built, the Navy reconfigured P2V Neptune patrol bombers so that these large machines (wingspan one hundred feet, loaded weight over sixty-one thousand pounds) could actually take off from the large *Midway*-class carriers.[17]

A modified Lockheed P2V Neptune patrol bomber takes off from the USS *Midway* (CV 41) in April 1949, accelerated to launch speed by JATO units.

Thomas C. Hone

The story of the development of the AJ carrier-based attack plane has been told in some detail by various authors, especially Vice Adm. Jerry Miller, USN (Ret.), in his *Nuclear Weapons and Aircraft Carriers*, published in 2001.[18] From our perspective, what matters is how the development of an airplane capable of carrying an early-design (and therefore bulky and heavy) nuclear weapon consumed the attention of some of the finest minds in the U.S. Navy. After the end of World War II, the Chief of Naval Operations, then Admiral King, and the Secretary of the Navy, James Forrestal, had to decide just where in the Navy's organizational hierarchy to put an office for nuclear weapons and their delivery systems. Rear Adm. William R. Purnell, who had served during the war on the Military Policy Committee, which had advised President Franklin D. Roosevelt on nuclear weapons issues, apparently favored creating a special office within OPNAV to be headed by Capt. William S. Parsons, an ordnance expert who had armed the bomb dropped on Hiroshima and had worked closely with the atomic scientists at Los Alamos. Captain Parsons had already recruited Cdrs. Frederick L. Ashworth and Horacio Rivero to assist him in fashioning a postwar Navy policy covering nuclear weapons. Parsons was apparently able to persuade Purnell to convince Admiral King in November 1945 to establish a Deputy Chief of Naval Operations/Special Weapons, appoint Vice Adm. William H. P. Blandy to the post, and ensure that Captain Parsons and his assistants served under Blandy.[19]

With Blandy's support, Parsons prepared a memorandum in March 1946 for the Deputy Chief of Naval Operations for Plans and Policy in which he predicted that reductions in the size and weight of the "fission bomb," coupled with advances in the range and accuracy of long-range surface-to-surface guided missiles, would allow the Navy to launch nuclear attacks from submarines and surface ships.[20] Vice Admiral Miller, in *Nuclear Weapons and Aircraft Carriers,* notes that Commander Ashworth had "started thinking about mixing carrier aircraft and the atomic bomb not long after he concluded his duties with the wartime operations of the atomic weapon program."[21] Parsons and Ashworth were supported by Vice Adm. Arthur W. Radford, who was then (1946) the Deputy Chief of Naval Operations (Air) and later (1947–48) the Vice Chief of Naval Operations.

The focus on the nuclear mission for aircraft carriers and the resulting conflict between the Navy and the newly created U.S. Air Force over which service should have control of nuclear bombardment took the time, energy, and talent of a number of Navy aviators, especially those with scientific or technical backgrounds. In addition to the officers mentioned thus far, there were others, including the war hero Rear Adm. Daniel V. Gallery. Gallery's antisubmarine group, built around the escort carrier *Guadalcanal,* had captured the German submarine *U-505* in June 1944, garnering for the Navy its first war prize since the war against Great Britain in 1812. Gallery was a colorful character, articulate and outspoken, but he was also a good writer and a specialist in aviation ordnance, and he waded energetically into the debate over how nuclear weapons should be delivered. His advocacy almost cost him his commission. It apparently did cost him his third star.[22]

Navy aviation in World War II had developed a powerful land-attack capability, and, as we have shown in an earlier chapter, the Navy had already experimented with the launching and recovery of large, twin-engine carrier aircraft. After the war, both aviators and nonaviators (such as Captain Parsons) argued that carriers could serve as nuclear-strike platforms. In the summer of 1946, President Harry Truman granted the Navy permission to begin "planning to equip its ships and aircraft for atomic operations."[23] This meant that much of the Navy's aviation community would focus on developing planes for carrying nuclear weapons and on modifying carriers so that they could store nuclear weapons and launch the large aircraft that carried those weapons.

An illustration of this focus on nuclear capability is the composition of the Navy's team that reviewed North American Aviation's mock-up of the XAJ (Savage) in October 1946.[24] The leader of the BuAer team was Cdr. Roger B. Woodhull, the project officer for the XAJ. Woodhull had served as a combat aviator during the war and was Design Branch head for torpedo planes in BuAer's Engineering Division at war's end. Also on the team was Capt. Joseph N. Murphy, who headed the Armament Branch of BuAer's Engineering Division. As a young lieutenant before World War II, Murphy had both studied and taught at the California Institute of Technology. During the war, as a lieutenant commander, he headed the scout bomber branch in BuAer. By 1947, he was head of BuAer's Piloted Aircraft Division. Working with Woodhull and Murphy were civilians William Z. Frisbie and George A. Spangenberg. Frisbie led BuAer's Design Coordination Branch and Contract Airplane Design Branch in 1942. Spangenberg became his deputy during the war. Both were talented engineers.

Acting as an observer was Cdr. John T. Hayward, then, like William Parsons, one of the more technically astute officers in the Navy.[25] Before World War II, Hayward had worked as a lieutenant at the Naval Aircraft Factory on aircraft navigation instruments and flight controls. He taught at the Royal Air Force's navigation school in Canada in 1940 and in 1942 organized the Navy's first long-range, land-based bomber squadron. In 1944, he was selected to be the Navy officer in charge of experiments at the new Naval Ordnance Test Station at Inyokern, California, including work on the trigger mechanism for a nuclear weapon. Before taking his position there, he developed contacts with the science faculty at the California Institute of Technology and began working on a graduate degree in physics. He studied the effects of the nuclear explosions at Hiroshima and Nagasaki in Japan right after the war, and then he managed high-speed photography of the nuclear weapons tests at Bikini in the summer of 1946. By the time he examined the XAJ mock-up in October 1946, he had a reputation as one of the best heavy-attack aircraft evaluators in the U.S. Navy. He also knew enough about the early nuclear weapons to evaluate the XAJ's capability to carry them.

Not surprisingly, given the haste in developing the XAJ, the airplane turned out to be less than satisfactory. In 1949, retired Navy test pilot James Pearce, just hired by North American Aviation, flew the XAJ and wrote this evaluation of the aircraft: "When everything was working properly—it handled like a fighter. The problem was that everything was working properly only about five percent of the time; the rest of the time the pilot was coping with some sort of problem ranging from some minor annoyance to struggling to stay alive. . . . Amongst those of us who tested the AJ, none were left without vivid memories of some moment of terror."[26] In his memoir, Vice Admiral Hayward notes that he had recommended that the XAJ be rebuilt with jet engines but that Rear Adm. Theodore Lonnquest, assistant chief of BuAer for research and development, rejected Hayward's recommendation.[27] Given the troubles with turbojet engine development described in chapter 5 of this study, Lonnquest—under pressure to help get the XAJ into the air—was understandably unenthusiastic about reworking the XAJ around jet propulsion.

Individual officers such as Parsons, Hayward, Rivero, and Ashworth knew each other by war's end and were familiar with one another's abilities. During World War II, Hayward had worked for Rear Adm. Mitscher when Mitscher commanded Fleet Air Wing 2 in Hawaii. In fact, Hayward, by his own account, had first met Mitscher in 1934 and had worked with him again in 1940, when Mitscher was assistant chief of BuAer. At that time, the Naval Aircraft Factory was manufacturing models of the Curtiss SO3C (Seamew) two-seat amphibian. "Chick" Hayward flew one out of the Navy's air station at Anacostia, Maryland, and dumped it into the Potomac. In his memoir Hayward says that he promptly went to BuAer headquarters on Constitution Avenue in Washington, "wet flight suit and all," to tell Mitscher that the SO3C was "a lousy airplane." Mitscher had then christened the SO3C "Chick's airplane."[28] That was Mitscher. Hayward was a character, but he was also very bright and a good pilot. Mitscher liked him, and Admiral King, whose airplane Hayward had flown, evidently listened to him.

Under the leadership of Admirals Blandy and Radford, officers such as Parsons, Ashworth, Rivero, and Hayward developed Navy policy regarding nuclear weapons and managed the aircraft and ordnance projects that gave the Navy its nuclear striking arm. They were aided by aircraft designers like Douglas Aircraft's Edward H. Heinemann. Heinemann began designing bombing aircraft for the Navy in the 1930s, including the very versatile and reliable SBD-1 Dauntless dive-bomber. George A. Spangenberg, one of BuAer's best aircraft design evaluators and eventually something of a legend in his own right, noted years later that "Heinemann's real strength was a good understanding of the entire airplane. He did a superb job of trying to find out what the Navy needed and trying to give them what they needed and he also had a superb engineering organization."[29]

Heinemann also knew the officers and civilian engineers in BuAer. His memoir, *Ed Heinemann, Combat Aircraft Designer*, is peppered with the names of BuAer personnel. Heinemann also spent several weeks in the fall of 1944 on carriers in the Pacific, where he met and talked at length with then–rear admiral Arthur Radford and Capt. Frederick M. Trapnell, who was the first Navy pilot to test the Bell Aircraft XP-59A jet prototype (in April 1943). In addition, Heinemann was a member of a delegation of Douglas engineers who headed for Germany in 1945 to examine the results of wartime German aeronautical research.[30] In short, he was an "insider" when it came to the development of Navy aircraft, especially attack aircraft.

As a consequence, he was one of the first to consider what it would take to create a nuclear-armed jet bomber that could be flown off a carrier and then recovered after its mission.[31] After watching Navy tests of the Douglas AD-1 attack plane on board the light carrier *Saipan* in 1948, Heinemann "went to Washington to visit BuAer." As he recalled, "I had seen the CNO's memorandum regarding weight parameters for the [successor to the AJ Savage] and was aware that other company representatives had been in and out of Navy offices getting a feel for what the final requirement figures would be." Heinemann learned that BuAer would accept design proposals from the aircraft manufacturers using one of three turbojets—the Westinghouse J40, Pratt & Whitney's J57, and Curtiss-Wright's J65.[32] He returned to Douglas determined to design a jet bomber weighing the existing upper limit on loads for the *Midway*-class carriers—sixty-eight thousand pounds.

With a concept in hand, Heinemann returned to Washington and showed—unofficially—drawings of the proposed Douglas aircraft to Captain Murphy, who had been one of the BuAer officers involved in developing the AJ Savage. Heinemann's account has Murphy reacting with disgust: "You know good and well that you can't produce an airplane of that capability for that weight!" Heinemann was furious, but he persuaded Murphy to keep the drawings and weight estimates. The next day, Heinemann was in BuAer's spaces and was accosted by Ivan H. Driggs, the director of BuAer's Design Research Division. Driggs was quick to apologize, telling Heinemann that "we have checked your figures [and] your concept looks valid."[33] According to George Spangenberg, Driggs and his colleagues had assumed that the successor to the AJ Savage would have to rely on *turboprop* engines to carry the heavy nuclear weapon (at least eight thousand pounds) the necessary range and would therefore weigh in at takeoff at about a hundred thousand pounds.[34]

Heinemann had gambled that both the size and weight of nuclear bombs would come down, and his gamble paid off.[35] Douglas got the contract for the follow-on to the AJ and produced a mock-up in 1949. The airplane was huge—seventy-six feet long, with a wingspan of over seventy-two feet and a loaded weight of about seventy thousand pounds. By comparison, the Navy version of the B-25 that had flown off the carrier *Shangri-La* in November 1944 had been about fifty-three feet long, with a wingspan of just over sixty-seven feet and a loaded weight of thirty-five thousand pounds. Heinemann was not surprised to find Capt. John Hayward on the team inspecting the mock-up.[36] It was the same cast of Navy characters who had been trying to make real the visions of 1946–47. As Vice Admiral Miller puts it, the nuclear bombing mission was the "only game in town," and it attracted the best Navy and industry designers and engineers.[37]

Note the difference with the Royal Navy, which did not have the nuclear bombing mission. We believe that this is important. In effect, the "best and brightest" within the U.S. Navy's aviation community were focused postwar on using carriers as mobile nuclear-strike platforms. For that to happen, BuAer and industry technical and technically sophisticated personnel had to come up with aircraft that could fly from carriers *and* carry the early, very heavy and bulky nuclear weapons. In 1946, it was not clear that this effort could succeed. To reduce the chance that it would not, senior Navy leaders such as Rear Admiral (and then Vice Admiral) Radford supported a cluster of intelligent, accomplished subordinate officers and civilians as they labored to do what often seemed the impossible.

The Organizations: U.S. Navy

We begin an assessment of organizational factors with those of the U.S. Navy, because we are more familiar with them. There were two key events for the USN. First, the General Board, which had been a key integrator of technology and operational concepts in the 1920s and 1930s, lost during the war much of its influence and therefore also its ability to compel developers and fleet operators to review the evidence generated by their own actions. Second, the Secretary of the Navy created the post of Deputy Chief of Naval Operations (Air) in August 1943. Rear Adm. Julius A. Furer, who wrote *Administration of the Navy Department in World War II*, summarizes the change as follows: "Broadly speaking, naval aviation planning, training of flying personnel, logistics, planning and aviation operations were now responsibilities of DCNO (Air); BuAer was responsible for all that related to aviation materiel of the Navy, including 'designing, building, fitting out, and repairing Naval and Marine Corps aircraft, accessories, equipment, and devices, connected with aircraft.'"[38]

The first DCNO (Air) was Vice Adm. John S. McCain. His counterpart at BuAer was Rear Adm. DeWitt C. Ramsey. In effect, the Office of the Chief of Naval Operations would set Navy aviation policy, while BuAer and its subordinate organizations would provide aircraft, aircraft engines and controls, aircraft maintenance manuals and training, and the equipment needed by aircraft carriers to launch and recover their air wings.

In the office of the DCNO (Air), officers such as Arthur Radford, assistant to DCNO (Air) in early 1944, worked to tie together all the elements of Navy aviation. This was no small feat. Before the war, BuAer had begun a program of expanding aircraft production, pilot training, and the training of all the skilled technicians who supported air operations ashore and afloat.[39] This planning, though successful, had not been adequate for the huge surge in the size and missions of the Navy's air forces during the war.[40] There was a perceived need for reorganization, and the first step was the consolidation of the Naval Aircraft Factory, the Naval Aircraft Modification Unit, the Naval Air Experimental Station, and the Naval Auxiliary Air Station into the Naval Air Material Center, in July 1943. Before the war, BuAer and its subordinate organizations had focused on solving problems ranging from how to design an effective tailhook for carrier aircraft to how to maneuver carriers as a group in wartime. Once war began, however, the practice of identifying and solving problems had to compete with the obvious need to expand naval aviation dramatically. Getting the resources for such an expansion required senior Navy aviators to win the battles of resource allocation that took place in the offices of the CNO and the Secretary of the Navy. To do that, the aviators needed direct access to these individuals—hence the August 1943 reorganization.

But the aviators, along with the rest of the Navy, also needed a substitute for the General Board. In late 1944, for example, Vice Admiral Mitscher argued that the new DCNO (Air) needed an informal advisory board to capture both the lessons of wartime experience and the future potential of wartime research and development. In May 1945, the type commander for Navy air forces in the Pacific, Vice Adm. George D. Murray, suggested that the *Essex*-class carriers still under construction be modified to carry and launch large bombers. That same month, BuAer began studying the feasibility of large carrier bombers. There was a need to bring the thinking behind these initiatives together, and, as we have shown, Capt. W. T. Raisseur, working in the new office of the DCNO (Air), did just that with a paper he wrote at the end of June 1945. That paper emphasized the heavy-attack mission and noted that a carrier could generate more sorties if its aircraft elevators were located at the edges of the flight deck, thereby leaving room for longer, more powerful catapults.

In early July 1945, the informal board that Vice Admiral Mitscher had proposed approved the concept of carrier operations presented by Raisseur. In October, BuAer engineers at the newly created NAMC suggested to BuAer headquarters that turboprop engines might give carrier-launched bombers both increased range and heavier bomb loads. After reviewing the available evidence, BuAer chief Rear Adm. Harold B. Sallada endorsed in December the idea that carriers be modified to accept very large and very-long-range aircraft. That led the Chief of Naval Operations to authorize the requirement for what became the XAJ Savage on 28 December. In January 1946, the informal board advising DCNO (Air) suggested that the Navy develop a new carrier for the much larger aircraft, and the DCNO (Air), Vice Admiral Mitscher (who had suggested that the informal board be created in the first place), supported Rear

Admiral Sallada's recommendation. The Bureau of Ships began working on new carrier designs in February 1946.[41]

In short, the new organization seemed to work well when it had the functional equivalent of the General Board. The aviators had a new concept of operations (large aircraft, escorted by long-range fighters, conducting strike operations against land targets), based on an assessment of wartime experience, and that concept had triggered new designs of both aircraft and aircraft carriers. But somehow the insights that had emerged from the Royal Navy's analyses had not come out of the analogous process in the U.S. Navy. It was obvious that the new, heavier, and larger aircraft would need to be catapulted off any new carrier's deck, but that conclusion ran into the fact that the hydraulic catapults then in use had nearly reached the limit of their effectiveness.

This collision of an operational imperative with a technological limit was apparently not appreciated in the office of the DCNO (Air), despite the work of Mitscher's committee. Evidence for this inference is the fact that the new concept of carrier operations first developed by DCNO (Air)'s Captain Raisseur in June 1945 required a clear flight deck. The aircraft elevators would have to move to the edge of the flight deck so that two catapults could work sequentially and rapidly. But which catapults? What catapult technology would work best? Answering those questions was left to BuAer, but the documentary evidence suggests that the effort to develop effective jet aircraft for carriers focused BuAer on improving the reliability of jet engines.

In April 1947, for example, Rear Admiral Pride later recalled of the period just before taking charge of BuAer, "It then dawned on me that I would be up to my neck in jet procurement and that I had better find out a little about them at first hand. Furthermore, since no flag officer seemed to have soloed the things, it seemed appropriate that the Chief of the Bureau set the pace." So Pride drove to the Naval Air Test Center at Patuxent River and asked to fly one of the new McDonnell XFD-1 Phantom prototypes, but "the Patuxent boys were not taking any chances with their new pet." Pride ended up flying an Army P-59, which got into the air but had an engine failure, forcing him to return to the runways at Patuxent.[42]

As a younger naval aviator in the 1920s and 1930s, Pride had been an innovator. In August 1921, as a lieutenant, he had developed the first arresting gear system for the experimental aircraft carrier *Langley*. As BuAer chief, however, he "had to defend the naval aviation budget. That took most of [my] time."[43] But the bureaucratic infighting that characterized budget negotiations was not new to Pride. In World War II, for example, he had strongly and successfully opposed drone attack aircraft as neither particularly "valuable, nor reliable."[44] Once he took over BuAer, Pride tried to acquire the rights to the Rolls-Royce Nene jet engine and ended up purchasing a number of the engines for Navy use. He also pressured the Marine Corps to adopt jet aircraft, and he rejected the concerns of officers in BuAer that jets would not work on carriers. As he put it in his oral history interview, "There were a lot of people out in the fleet that were very dubious about getting [jets] back up to revs again after you came in for a landing and you had to take a waveoff. They were quite convinced that the jet would never be able to take a waveoff [i.e., to resume normal flight after being ordered to abort a landing attempt just before touching down]. Well, I said, 'By God, they'll have to or be made to, or we might as well go out of business now.'"[45]

In his championing of jet aircraft Pride did not consider himself a visionary or a radical, but he "liked new ideas."[46] At the same time, he stayed with BuAer's traditional practice of having the government provide engines that the aircraft designers could build their airplanes around. He also ended the Navy's lighter-than-air program, and he admitted that the angled flight deck was an ingenious British innovation—and one that the U.S. Navy had not foreseen.[47] He acknowledged that the steam catapult was a significant innovation, but he did not approve of the British "flexdeck" or "mat deck."

What is easily forgotten when considering the activities of BuAer under Rear Admiral Pride's leadership is the menu of possibilities that wartime expenditures had produced. There were the obvious ones: jet propulsion, rockets, radar for night fighters, air-breathing missiles, and new supersonic-aircraft designs, such as the delta wing. But there was much more. The BuAer "Research and Development Master Program" for fiscal year 1947—a document put together early in 1946—contained some breathtaking proposals. Perhaps the most audacious was Project JUPITER, an "airborne aircraft carrier" that would carry both "parasite" manned fighters and pilotless aircraft. This flying carrier was to have been "an airplane in the 4–600,000 lb. class, powered by gas turbines, cruising at 35 to 40,000 feet at 400 to 475 MPH, with a radius of action of 2500–3500 miles."[48] The Army Air Forces analog to this behemoth was the November 1945 general operational requirement for the next generation of heavy bombers. Meeting this requirement led U.S. Air Force officers to develop a 1948 design of a swept-wing jet aircraft weighing over three hundred thousand pounds, carrying a ten-thousand-pound payload to forty-five thousand feet, and flying almost seven thousand miles at a speed of approximately 450 knots.[49]

The "Research and Development Master Program" also contained proposals for refining the liquid-fuel and solid-fuel rocket engines for the Gorgon, Super Gorgon, and Lark missiles, plus money proposed for work on pulse-jet engines for missiles and target drones. What drove BuAer's investment in both Project JUPITER and missiles was the need to extend the range of a carrier's striking power against land targets. A 1947 BuAer memorandum argued that "carrier striking power cannot be limited to a range of six to seven hundred miles, otherwise the carrier program would stand in a precarious situation when compared to the long range bombardment plans of the Army Air Forces."[50] As Malcolm Muir notes in his history of Navy surface warfare after World War II, the Bureaus of Aeronautics and Ordnance "advanced a bewildering variety of missile projects during the immediate postwar period."[51] One of Rear Admiral Pride's more difficult tasks, therefore, was to wade through all the proposals and research-and-development efforts and decide which ones really mattered.

But the "Research and Development Master Program" did identify a key short-term problem: "continuous development of installations aboard ship which will permit the safe arrestation [sic] of any future type of carrier airplanes making normal or approximately normal landings." In the words of the master program, "the shipboard arresting gear programs should be kept ahead of the development of the carrier airplane itself."[52] The program also singled out the need to develop a crash barrier that would work with twin-engine planes with tricycle landing gear (like the F7F). As it observed, "The magnitude of the problem of arresting heavy twin-engine airplanes, or jet-propelled airplanes, with high stalling speeds, and tricycle landing gear is very great."[53]

The master program also proposed "utilizing the slotted cylinder principle" for carrier catapults, but admitted that the slotted-cylinder concept was "a considerable departure from the conventional catapult" and needed careful investigation.[54] At the same time, the section of the R&D master program devoted to improving launching techniques on carriers noted that "as the operating speeds of aircraft continue to increase, a decreased launching interval is required to maintain the operating efficiency of the carrier."[55] Here were the same hints that had provoked British engineer Lewis Boddington in the summer and fall of 1945 to move away from the axial (straight) carrier deck and toward an angled deck with a rubber mat. At the same time, these hints were accompanied—and perhaps overshadowed—by more dramatic concerns, especially the need to strike land targets from great distances at sea by the use of missiles or pilotless aircraft launched by a flying aircraft carrier. In effect, what came to be called the "heavy attack" mission had become institutionalized—embedded in the planning and thinking of officers in both OPNAV and BuAer. Moreover, as the 1947 master program pointed out, the need for increasingly powerful catapults appeared to be met by incremental improvement to existing hydraulic systems—just as in the case of arresting gear, where older equipment had been superseded by incrementally improved designs.[56]

One of the most important tasks that leaders of an organization like BuAer have to undertake is determining the priority of the problems that the organization is supposed to deal with. To do this effectively, senior personnel must be able to evaluate reliable evidence about the performance of existing and planned systems in a realistic operational setting. In the case of the Royal Navy, the basic problem was how to adapt carriers to the new jet *fighter* aircraft, because the postwar mission of the Royal Navy's carriers was the protection of seaborne trade from air attack. In the case of the U.S. Navy, the mission was long-range strike, especially nuclear attack, and that forced the U.S. Navy to focus on near-term, high-risk programs like the XAJ Savage, long-term missile programs, *and* high-performance jet fighters with the range to accompany carrier-launched bombers. In his oral history, Vice Adm. Robert B. Pirie, who was DCNO (Air) from May 1958 until November 1962, praises four postwar BuAer chiefs: Rear Adms. Alfred M. Pride, Thomas S. Combs, Apollo Soucek, and James S. Russell.[57] We think Pirie admired these officers because they set and then imposed sensible priorities on BuAer.

We ask readers to place themselves in Rear Admiral Pride's shoes in June 1947. On the one hand, demobilization was still taking its toll on Navy aviation. For example, the number of combat aircraft was dropping—from a high of 29,125 in 1945 to 9,889 in 1948—and the number of Navy pilots was being reduced from a wartime high of 49,819 to 10,861 in 1948.[58] At the same time, the advent of jet aircraft and missiles had made, or would soon make, many Navy aircraft obsolete. The future sketched out in the 1947 "Research and Development Master Program" was both dramatic and expensive. Moreover, the development of nuclear bombs threatened to make the concept of a concentrated task force or fleet obsolete. Finally, the bureaucratic and political conflicts over military service unification and service roles and missions ate up the time and talent of a number of the Navy's most experienced and capable officers. Vice Admiral Miller may have been correct to say that the nuclear mission was the "only game in town," but it was a risky game. The potential for error was high, as was the cost to the Navy if errors were made. Moreover, as Admiral Pride said years later, some of the more stubborn opponents of change were actually younger officers in BuAer: "I got more opposition from juniors than I ever did from seniors in trying to get new programs in."[59]

Pride may have been exaggerating. There were reasons why some BuAer personnel thought that jet aircraft—especially jet heavy attack aircraft—might not be suitable for carriers. As civilian engineer George A. Spangenberg recalled, "The Navy had a very real problem in attempting to get into the jet age" and therefore, "most of us were kind of in the middle. The pure jets at the time [1947] couldn't quite do the job and everybody recognized a composite way to go was [a] poor choice. All of us recognized I think that you couldn't get there from here with a turbo prop if the other guy without carrier constraints was going to be using jets. We would be in trouble."[60] Two things saved jet aircraft on carriers. The first was the persistence of Cdr. (later rear admiral) Alfred B. Metsger, a torpedo-plane pilot who became head of the Fighter Design

Branch in BuAer in the fall of 1945.[61] The second was a simulated-combat test at Patuxent River in the spring of 1946 that pitted an F8F-1 Bearcat against a Navy P-80 Shooting Star. The highly maneuverable F8F-1 could turn inside the P-80, but the report by the F8F-1's pilot made clear the P-80's advantage: "The F8F-1 is without doubt one of the most outstanding performers in the conventional field. Yet I felt ... helpless.... I was completely on the defensive with no option but to counter the P-80's approaches."[62] As George Spangenberg recalled, "The F8F was solely at the mercy of the P-80. You couldn't get away from it. It should have taught a lot of people a lot of lessons.... [I]t educated a lot of the people."[63]

The emphasis on testing, along with the funds to conduct tests at fields such as Patuxent River, is apparent in photographs from the early postwar years, especially in such books as Thomason's *U.S. Naval Air Superiority* (2007) and *Strike from the Sea* (2009), and in the many articles published in *The Hook* over the last generation or so.[64] Experimentation is a valuable tool for deciding among alternatives and in testing assumptions, and BuAer had been committed to rigorous testing ever since its creation in 1921.

The inferences drawn from many such tests conducted when Rear Admiral Pride was bureau chief were summed up in a memorandum he wrote to the Chief of Naval Operations, Adm. Forrest P. Sherman, in December 1949. Pride noted that piston-engine fighters could not "successfully engage jet fighters, either offensively or defensively." He also listed other weaknesses of the piston-engine aircraft: they could not attack jet bombers or "escort attack aircraft of any type in the face of jet fighter opposition." If the skies were free of enemy jet fighters, piston-engine attack aircraft, such as the AD-1 Skyraider, could be very effective. Based on exercises, Pride recommended against building any turboprop fighters, and he informed Admiral Sherman that "jet aircraft should be procured in the necessary numbers for all fighter tasks ... so as to modernize our fleet air forces as rapidly as possible."[65]

Pride was clearly trying to head off criticism that jet fighters were not suitable for use on carriers. He knew that the U.S. Air Force, the Soviet air arm, and the British had already flown swept-wing jet fighters, and he knew that the Navy needed equivalent aircraft if its carriers were to continue to be effective strike platforms. He also knew that Douglas Aircraft was developing the A3D Skywarrior to take the place of the problem-plagued AJ Savage for the nuclear mission; BuAer had awarded Douglas a contract for two prototypes of the new jet bomber at the end of March 1949.

The Organizations: The Royal Navy

We have already mentioned the close contact between the Fleet Air Arm and the U.S. Navy's Bureau of Aeronautics before World War II, when then–rear admiral John Towers was BuAer's chief, culminating in the housing of the naval aircraft portion of the British Aircraft Commission in the spaces of the USN's Bureau of Aeronautics. At the same time, Royal Navy aviators were apparently concerned that the formation of the Ministry of Aircraft Production in their own government would keep them from obtaining high-performance aircraft suited for use at sea by emphasizing the need for numbers of good land-based bombers and fighters.[66] What met the Royal Navy's needs was the quality and quantity of fighters and attack aircraft available from U.S. manufacturers.

What is most interesting, however, is the decision in the summer of 1942 by the RN's First Sea Lord, Adm. Dudley Pound, to create a Future Building Committee within the Admiralty. At the same time, Pound appointed retired admiral Sir Frederic Dreyer to the post of "Chief of the Naval Air Services."[67] Dreyer, as assistant chief of the Naval Staff from 1924 to 1927, had opposed the takeover of the RN's aviation by the Royal Air Force, and Pound may have felt the need for an older air advocate in the Admiralty's wartime aviation staff. But what matters to us is that the FBC was charged to look ahead and create a plan for the development of British *fleet* aviation during and after the war.

The FBC was chaired by the Deputy First Sea Lord. The deputy chairman was the Assistant Chief of the Naval Staff (Weapons). The other permanent members were the Controller (Third Sea Lord); the Director of Plans; the Director, Tactical and Staff Duties Division (responsible for organizing Admiralty staff requirements); the director of the Gunnery Division; the Director of Naval Construction; and the Director, Naval Air Division.[68] As Norman Friedman has pointed out, the FBC "tried . . . to re-think the fleet's air needs as a coherent whole," a remarkable task for some of the most senior officers on the Admiralty staff while war was raging.[69]

There was no organization like it in the U.S. Navy at the time. The USN's General Board had performed a similar function at intervals in the years between World War I and World War II, but once Congress had approved and funded the "two-ocean Navy," the main focus of the Office of the Chief of Naval Operations had been on fulfilling a plan for naval aviation, not on developing a new one.

The leaders of the Royal Navy, however, did not have to produce all new aircraft once its carrier commanders and pilots realized that existing British-made aircraft were inadequate. The RN's leaders could devote their attention to assessing war experience and looking ahead to the implications of new technology. The FBC was an "early proponent of the catapult as the primary means of launching aircraft."[70] It also pressed for the RN to have the most modern fighter aircraft on its carriers. In February 1943, an "interim report" insisting that the carrier was the core of the fleet "shaped British naval aircraft policy for the remainder of the war."[71] In 1943 and 1944, the FBC compared

U.S. Navy and Royal Navy carrier operations, and the Fifth Sea Lord (with responsibility for naval air), Adm. Denis W. Boyd, became convinced by those studies "that a carrier had to be able to fly off her entire air complement in one continuous operation."[72] This meant that the Royal Navy would have to adopt the "open hangar" common to U.S. carriers, so that aircraft could be warmed up while still in the hangar, and also the deck-edge elevator, to move aircraft from the hangar to the flight deck.

In 1943, the position of "Director of Airfield and Carrier Requirements" was created under the Fifth Sea Lord, and the head of that organization joined the new Naval Aircraft Design Committee, which had been a subcommittee of the Future Building Committee.[73] But this change, and other administrative changes, did not disrupt the work of the FBC. The FBC, along with its aircraft design subcommittee—later a separate but still allied organization—assumed that jet aircraft represented the future of military aviation and that carriers would have to launch and recover them.

In effect, the Royal Navy had had to build a new aviation organization once the Fleet Air Arm had moved back into the RN from the RAF in 1938. There were many details that had then to be worked out—matters of training, promotion, personnel, bases, and the like. This took a great deal of time and energy, as Stephen Roskill notes in his second volume of *Naval Policy between the Wars*. Moreover, the aviation doctrine that the RN had developed before the war, wherein carriers complemented battleships, had turned out to be inadequate, and so the aviation officers in the RN had in some sense to start all over again in 1942–43.

That they could do so was the result of the existence of an effective ally, the USN, and effective organization—at the flag-level Future Building Committee inside the Admiralty, and at the Principal Supply Officers Committee, which supported the Committee of Imperial Defence. As G. A. H. Gordon shows in his *British Seapower and Procurement between the Wars*, the RAF and RN fostered an aviation industry in the 1930s that was both innovative and capable of the sustained serial production of aircraft.[74] Like the U.S. Navy, the Royal Navy relied on domestic aircraft manufacturers to build naval aircraft. Unlike the U.S. Navy, however, the RN had not been able to foster a British naval aviation industrial base separately from the other military services. Yet the RN had the necessary technical expertise when it needed it—when the Future Building Committee was casting its plans, especially in 1943 and 1944.[75]

The differences in the approaches to jet aircraft in the USN and RN seem to have been due to the ways in which the two navies defined the problems they faced. A consensus was reached within the Royal Navy by 1945 that jet aircraft—especially fighters—would have to operate from British carriers. Once that decision was made, the focus of attention turned toward finding ways to fit RN carriers to jet aircraft. In the U.S. Navy, by contrast, the argument about whether to equip carriers with high-performance jet fighters continued into Rear Admiral Pride's term as the head of BuAer.

By contrast, the U.S. Navy officers who wanted the Navy to embrace the nuclear-attack mission reached an early consensus on the need to develop aircraft—first a mixed-engine design and then an all-jet design—that could carry large nuclear bombs, but their focus was on showing that a carrier could serve as an adequate launching platform for nuclear-armed bombers. The first aircraft selected by this group to fly off a carrier with a dummy nuclear bomb was a modified version of the Lockheed P2V Neptune. The bombers were not meant to land back aboard the carriers that had launched them; in case of war, they were to hit their targets and then ditch in the water when they got back to their carriers. The experiments with the modified P2Vs were very visible, because the USN wanted to play a role in nuclear deterrence, but the consensus about that policy choice took time, energy, and resources away from investigations of catapults, the angled deck, and visual landing aids.

What we see in comparing the two navies is a successful committee system in the RN and the absence of one in the USN. That does not mean that the RN's process for dealing with an uncertain future always worked, while the USN's did not. As we've seen, the engineers at Farnborough, who were responsible for turning the policy of arming carriers with high-performance jet fighters into a working system, went down what later was recognized as a dead end—flying aircraft without undercarriages into rubber decks. Remember too that the lack of consensus, *even within BuAer,* about the need to fly high-performance jets from carriers did not mean that the U.S. Navy lacked a sensible process for making decisions.

An example of effective decision making was the sequence of steps that led up to the adoption of the steam catapult. The 1947 BuAer R&D master program had provided for work on improving existing catapult technology and on building and testing slotted-tube catapults.[76] The *Naval Aviation Confidential Bulletin* for April 1947 confidently predicted that improved hydraulic catapults would handle jet aircraft, though the short article admitted that the increased weight of the prototype XH8 was a problem for the Naval Air Material Center engineers.[77] The 1949 BuAer research and development plan contained funds for new barriers for aircraft that failed to catch an arresting wire; a system for recovering "wheelless" aircraft, "instrumented tests of full scale dummy models and aircraft to determine arresting and catapulting characteristics"; development of both hydraulic and slotted-cylinder catapults; development of a "smokeless, high specific impulse, solid propellant"; and improvement of jet-assisted takeoff units.[78] As we have pointed out in an earlier chapter, catapult development was not, as had been anticipated in 1947, keeping up with the increasing size and performance of jet aircraft, despite the work of engineers at BuAer's Naval Aircraft Factory (part of the Naval Air Material Center).

In 1948, the Royal Navy brought the light carrier HMS *Perseus* out of mothballs and built an experimental steam catapult on a platform on the ship's flight deck. The Admiralty offered to send *Perseus* to the United States in June 1951. In response, Rear Adm. Apollo Soucek, the U.S. naval air attaché, sent Capts. Ralph S. Clarke and Peter H. Horn to observe catapult launches on the ship. They reported positively on what they witnessed. Rear Admiral Soucek then advised the new Chief of Naval Operations, Admiral Fechteler, to accept the Admiralty's offer, which Fechteler did at the end of August.[79] On 28 August 1951, Royal Navy rear admiral John Stevens, in the British Joint Services Mission in Washington, wrote to Rear Admiral Felix Johnson, the Director of Naval Intelligence, saying that the Royal Navy would reduce the security classification of the documentation on the RN's steam catapult so that the diagrams and performance data could be examined by civilian engineers at NAMC.[80]

On 27 September 1951, Rear Adm. Thomas S. Combs, the head of BuAer, notified the commander of the NAMC that the tests on *Perseus* were "Priority 1."[81] Preparations for the trials on *Perseus* included arranging berths for the British ship, preparing NAMC personnel for their participation in the tests, finding funds to cover the costs of the tests, planning the delivery of fuel for the test aircraft, and drafting a program of test launches. The Royal Navy officers on the staff of the British Joint Services Mission arranged to have information provided to the U.S. Navy regarding the steam catapult but also cautioned BuAer that it would take a relatively long time (five minutes) to charge up the experimental catapult on *Perseus* between launchings.[82] That is, the experimental steam catapult was not up to sustaining the usual operating tempo on USN carriers.

On 8 January 1952, with the expected arrival of *Perseus* less than a week away, Capt. Sheldon W. Brown, director of the Ships Installation Division in BuAer, sent a memorandum to Rear Adm. Lucien M. Grant comparing "British and American Slotted Cylinder Catapults." Brown's concern was that "the British may make a determined effort to sell their steam catapult to us for use in our carriers." Captain Brown noted that the Navy's own C10 powder-driven catapult "has been built and will be installed in a facility at the Naval Air Material Center . . . in March 1952" and that "the C10 for the USS HANCOCK is under contract with a delivery schedule to the Puget Sound Naval Shipyard of January 1953." The catch was that the C10 was a powder-driven (not hydraulic) catapult, and it had not yet been tested with the gas generator that it was supposed to have. Put another way, significant improvements to the hydraulic catapult were becoming harder and harder to achieve, and now the Navy's catapult developers had placed their hopes in a catapult powered by hydrogen peroxide "or other gas generating devices under investigation." Captain Brown's assessment of the British steam catapult was that "the proper attitude to take toward the British catapult is to regard it as a back-up equipment which can be purchased in case of need."[83]

Brown's cautionary memorandum was not "out of bounds" as the process of bringing *Perseus* to the United States moved along. A primary purpose of a staff process is to reveal and consider options. Brown's point was that the Royal Navy's steam catapult was just one option, and not necessarily the best. However, an undated and unsigned "Progress Report on the Perseus Program" prepared—perhaps by Brown—at the conclusion of the initial tests on *Perseus* at the Philadelphia Navy Yard was much more positive. It said that "at capacities even approximating that expected of the C10, the British catapult becomes an object of very definite interest, one which we can not afford to regard any longer as merely a back-up to our own programs." Moreover, "the British catapult is a bird in the hand which our own instrumentation tells us really works, whereas the C10 is a bird in the bush which we have been unable to shoot to date for lack of a facility."[84] The Naval Aircraft Factory responded on 12 February 1952 by doing its own comparison of the BXS British steam catapult and the C10. Its memorandum argued that, with improvements, "the C-10 catapult will be, in the opinion of the Chief Engineer, far superior and more suitable for use in the U.S. Fleet than the British BS type catapult."[85]

But the pressure to adopt the British steam catapult offset the desire on the part of Naval Aircraft Factory personnel to pursue their own program. One of the witnesses of the tests conducted on *Perseus* was a young Navy engineering officer named Daniel K. Weitzenfeld. Weitzenfeld was working on developing the C10 at the Naval Aircraft Factory. As he would recall years later, Vice Adm. John J. Ballentine, then commander of Navy air forces in the Atlantic, watched the demonstrations of Colin Mitchell's steam catapult and insisted that the Navy acquire it.[86] Ballentine had had a very impressive career: first commanding officer of the *Essex*-class carrier *Bunker Hill* during World War II, two years (1947–49) as a carrier-division commander in the Mediterranean after the war, and then two years (1949–51) as the commander of the Sixth Fleet before taking his post as the type commander for aviation in the Atlantic. He was a friend of Rear Admiral Pride, who had been BuAer's chief from May 1947 to May 1951, and Ballentine had made it a point to visit Philadelphia to monitor the tests on *Perseus*.[87] Weitzenfeld, who eventually became the vice commander of the Naval Air Systems Command (a successor organization to BuAer), believed that the pressure from officers like Ballentine overcame the commitment of Naval Aircraft Factory engineers to their own catapult development program.

The engineers in the USN's Bureau of Ships too were impressed with the tests of the British steam catapult. On 14 February 1952, the assistant chief of BuShips informed the chief of BuAer and the staff of the Chief of Naval Operations that an analysis by BuShips engineers "has determined that a steam catapult installation of the [British] type . . . is technically feasible in the CV 9 Class [*Essex*] conversions, the CVB 41 [*Midway*] Class conversions, and the CVB 59 [*Forrestal*] Class new construction."[88] The staff of BuShips at once began planning a series of conferences on how best to procure and then install the British steam catapult. On 21 February, the Chief of Naval Operations approved a further series of tests of the British catapult at Philadelphia. The goal of these additional tests was to find out whether the BXS.1's performance could be improved by simply increasing the steam pressure used.[89] It was so improved, and the U.S. Navy decided in April 1952 to purchase the manufacturing rights for the RN's steam catapult. An American contractor was hard at work developing pilot models for the USN by March 1953.[90] In December 1953, Captain Brown was awarded the Navy League Award of Merit for his work as Director, Ships Installation Division, in BuAer.[91] Work with the new steam catapults at sea began in the late spring of 1954 and continued through the rest of that year on the *Essex*-class carriers *Hancock* and *Intrepid*.[92]

We have worked through the story of HMS *Perseus* and the steam catapult in detail in order to highlight how organizational factors—particularly organizational structure and process—influence innovation and the diffusion of innovation. Organizations are effective to the degree that their standard operating procedures allow the personnel governed by those procedures to

- Formulate programs of action
- Identify discrepancies between what they anticipate and what they see when they take action
- Adapt, if necessary, future action to reach the organization's goals.

When we began our study, we wondered whether the creation of the office of the Deputy Chief of Naval Operations for Aviation in 1943 might have inhibited innovation in U.S. naval aviation after World War II by separating the makers of aviation policy from the officers charged with aviation procurement and with the fitting on carriers of equipment that would allow carriers to operate modern jet aircraft effectively. It is clear to us that the leaders of BuAer aggressively pursued high-performance aircraft.[93] But did this pursuit—this focus on aircraft power plants and supersonic flight—keep BuAer from paying enough attention to shipboard catapults, arresting gear, and flight deck barriers? The answer seems to be no.

Engineers in the organizations that made up the Naval Air Material Center tried very hard to fit arresting gear, barricades and barriers, and carrier catapults to the new aircraft. Plans to modify the *Essex*-class carriers for heavier aircraft with higher landing speeds were made toward the end of World War II;[94] BuShips and BuAer continued that planning after the war ended. So why did the USN have to borrow the steam catapult, the angled flight deck, and the mirror landing aid from the Royal Navy? Was it because NAMC's engineers didn't see the problems associated with mating high-performance jet aircraft with carriers? It would be tempting to say that the Naval Aircraft Factory (even NAMC generally) failed as an organization. But a review of the evidence by Prof. William F. Trimble of Auburn University suggests otherwise.[95] Was it because the USN lacked effective professional contacts with the RN? No. There was often a very intensive back-and-forth between the two navies.

In 1948, for example, there were several senior Royal Navy staff officers serving as liaison officers in support of Rear Admiral Combs, then the deputy chief of BuAer.[96] They were joined in November of that year by two senior RN civilian engineers. As the engineers later noted in their report of their trip, "We obtained a mass of information, drawings and pamphlets, including the only set of plans of C.V.A. 58 [the carrier *United States*] outside America."[97] BuShips also provided the visitors with the plans for modernizing the *Essex*-class carrier *Oriskany,* which was incomplete at the end of World War II and was finally completed at the end of 1950 to a postwar standard, with a strengthened flight deck, stronger catapults, and new antiaircraft guns.[98] In their turn, the RN engineers gave the USN information and drawings of the control valve of the carrier *Ark Royal*'s arresting gear.[99] There were also useful exchanges regarding what were known as "safety barriers" to the RN engineers, who were surprised, for example, that the idea for a water brake for steam catapults was "quite new to the Americans."[100] But they were pleased with what their USN counterparts had learned about strengthening aircraft arresting-gear hooks to bear the loads imposed by increasingly heavy aircraft, and they were impressed with the relatively low landing speeds of the McDonnell F2H Banshee and the North American FJ-1 Fury. As they asserted, "there is no doubt that the Americans have a much more effective control of the landing speeds of their Naval aircraft than we have for our own."[101]

Exchanges were not always so productive. The quality of the exchange depended a great deal on the personalities on both sides, but the cooperation was extensive. In late June and early July 1953, for example, the "Officer-in-Charge of the [RN's] School of Aircraft Handling, the Senior Instructor, and a party of twenty senior ratings of the School of Aircraft Handling" went aboard carrier *Antietam* to observe operations with the ship's new angled deck.[102] This delegation was impressed with a number of the aircraft handling procedures used on *Antietam* and made a number of recommendations.[103] The RN also had a copy of the 5 February 1953 report from *Antietam*'s commanding officer to the type commander for aircraft, U.S. Atlantic Fleet.[104] The report was sent to London by the RN staff serving on the British Joint Services Mission in Washington.

If there was extensive sharing of information between the RN and the USN, and if the creation of the DCNO (Air) position within the Office of the Chief of Naval Operations did not isolate BuAer from OPNAV, then what was it, if anything, at the organizational level that kept the U.S. Navy from developing in parallel with the Royal Navy the innovations that made it possible for the USN to adapt carriers to modern jet aircraft? The two navies exchanged pilots and technical and operational information. But was there something about the RN's organization that gave it an edge in developing these innovations? We don't know. We do know that USN officers almost immediately grasped the potential of the angled flight deck once they saw drawings of it, being already aware of the challenges of operating jet aircraft from an axial deck. They were ready for a solution to the many problems it created, and the angled-deck innovation caught hold quickly within the USN. As Norman Friedman points out, the contract for the carrier design that became *Forrestal* (CVA 59) was signed on 12 July 1951, over a year before *Antietam* was modified for tests of the angled-deck concept. *Forrestal*'s design was altered while it was being built, in 1953, as soon as OPNAV realized that the experiments with *Antietam* were a success; the new carrier received both an angled deck and steam catapults.[105]

One organizational factor that worked to the RN's advantage was the creation of a special committee by then–rear admiral Abel Smith, Chief of Naval Air Equipment, to consider the problems of using jets on carriers. The committee sought out and evaluated empirical evidence from tests and experiments. The members of this committee included three RN captains (one was Dennis Cambell) who later attained flag rank and Mr. Lewis Boddington, whose papers in the summer and early fall of 1945 so eloquently laid out the problems of operating jets from carriers.[106] In effect, Rear (later Vice) Admiral Smith put together a "winning team," and that team more or less stayed together—the sort of advantage that a smaller navy can have over a larger one. Moreover, because both Cambell and Boddington "were also ex-officio responsible for the occasional carrier trial in *Triumph*," it was possible to move quickly from the formation of a concept to a test of that concept.[107]

The Institutional Level of Analysis

The individuals and organizations examined in our study worked within a framework of rules and expectations set by institutions, the most important of which were the RN and the USN. We have noted the very different expectations that applied to the RN and the USN after World War II. Specifically, the RN did not have the mission of nuclear strike, or even what the U.S. Navy aviators referred to as "heavy attack." In a memorandum written in November 1952, Rear Adm. Arleigh Burke (later admiral and Chief of Naval Operations), the head of OPNAV's strategic plans division, argued to the Vice Chief of Naval Operations that "the British do not believe in, nor do they know how to conduct, fast carrier task force operations."[108] In some sense, this was true, and it is a sign of the different expectations that the U.S. Navy had of its aviation arm.

But because of this, the RN may have found it easier to think about jets on carriers. Eric Brown, the RN's deservedly famous test pilot, recalled years later that he first flew a jet airplane in May 1944, at the Royal Aircraft Establishment at Farnborough. After gaining experience with the early jets, he made suggestions that were acted on in modifying a de Havilland DH-100 Vampire, chosen to be the first jet flown on and off a Royal Navy carrier. In an article he wrote for *Air International* many years later, he commented that there was an air of competition with the U.S. Navy as both services worked to modify jet aircraft for carrier operations.[109] The RN had been very much in second place behind the USN in terms of carrier operations during World War II, but the advent of jets meant that both navies were in some sense starting from scratch in the race to fly a jet from a carrier. As Brown recalled, the RN "won the race to be first to operate a pure jet aircraft from a carrier, a feat that was not to be emulated by the US Navy until seven-and-a-half months later."[110]

There is a note in his remarks of the poorer but still very professional navy showing off its talent to its richer and larger ally. But competition will lead nowhere unless there is talent to sustain a race and rules to decide who has won, and what was common to both navies was the emphasis on professionalism and on listening to the "real" professionals, who knew what they were doing. In our earlier book, *American & British Aircraft Carrier Development,* we described just such a sense of competition tempered by professionalism in the late 1920s, when the U.S. Navy was trying to come from second place and overtake the Royal Navy's lead in carrier aviation.[111] We see the same evidence of friendly competition in this case, though it was the RN that was pushing the competition in the '20s.

The RN may actually have found the competition easier to engage in because of the smaller size of its air arm. Proximity can facilitate serendipitous creativity. For example, RAE put engineers, pilots, and new jet aircraft side by side. They were all together—for thinking, debating, working, flying, and testing. In the USN, the testing was done in one place (Patuxent River), while the thinking tended to be done in Washington (at BuAer and within OPNAV), and the catapult and barrier development was carried on in Philadelphia. Just how important geography (defined as physical separation or the lack of it) was we cannot determine, but the productive interaction among a relatively small group of pilots and engineers at RAE is striking. What really matters, though, is that the interaction was governed by certain rules, especially informal ones that did not discourage frank discussions among individuals like Boddington, Cambell, and Brown.

What is impressive on the U.S. side is the rapidity with which both the angled deck and the mirror landing aid were adopted by the USN. Part of this was due, we are sure, to a growth of knowledge regarding the problems involved. American naval aviators were well aware of the hazards of using jets on an axial carrier deck, and they were also well aware of the problems of communication between pilots and LSOs posed by the higher landing speeds of jets. Having the angled deck and the mirror landing aid—which actually aided LSOs—were obvious improvements. That did not mean both could be incorporated into carrier operations quickly and effortlessly, but a preexisting consensus that there is a problem can often speed resolution by focusing attention and spurring remedial action. The availability of resources is also a major facilitating factor, and the U.S. Navy, though demobilized, was not as desperately short of funds after World War II as the RN.

We have commented already on the way in which the issues of nuclear war, military service unification, and service roles and missions dominated the agenda of the postwar U.S. Navy. In effect, higher-level issues created what might be thought of as a "noisy" or "cluttered," even "distracting," background to discussions about adapting jets to carriers. In our study of RN and USN carrier developments between World Wars I and II we noted a similar problem affecting the RN before World War II. What was the real danger facing Great Britain then? An attack from a rearmed and hostile Germany? A confrontation with Italy over Italian military operations in Ethiopia? An attack by Japan in the Far East? The "worst case" for the British then was a war on three fronts, and that is exactly what they got, but the British economy could not sustain, *in peacetime*, forces adequate to deter all three dangers simultaneously, and so it was difficult for the officers leading the RN to plan effectively for future operations.

Something like that affected the USN after World War II. Senior officers had to struggle simultaneously with a number of thorny issues. We have mentioned demobilization, service unification, and the responsibility for nuclear operations, but there was also what came to be called the Cold War, the creation of the Defense Department, the hot war in Korea, the creation of the North Atlantic Treaty Organization (NATO), and the deployment of the fighting power of the U.S. fleet to the western Pacific and the Mediterranean. One crisis or dramatic change followed another.[112] As retired Navy captain Peter Swartz noted some years ago, "the pace in the U.S. Navy in the first postwar decade was hectic—even frenetic—operationally, organizationally, and technically."[113]

What sustained the U.S. Navy during this time was its commitment to professionalism, which meant a commitment to fairly and reasonably evaluating the evidence of tests and experiments. Professionalism also implied a willingness to adopt proven innovations, even if they were developed—as indeed they were in this case—by another navy. Stephen Roskill put it very well in his discussion of the disagreements within the British government over the issue of transferring naval aviation personnel from the RAF and to the RN in 1936 and 1937: "How extraordinarily difficult it was to frame sound policy as long as experience was confined to theoretical argument backed only by the sometimes dubiously valid experience of peacetime exercises."[114] Both navies in our story had officers who well understood this. War experience had demonstrated a lot, yet both navies had to look beyond that immediate experience and make some hard choices for the futures of their respective air arms. Both could do this difficult task, because both possessed officers who were seasoned professionals—who had the ability to evaluate evidence because they could generate evidence through analysis, demonstrations, experiments, and exercises.

Moreover, the links between the two navies were strong. The end of World War II, and especially the end of Lend-Lease, did not shut down the many organizational and personal contacts that had grown up during the war. People and ideas went back and forth. We have mentioned aviation exchanges, but information regarding steam boilers, steam turbines, fuel filters, electrical systems, submarine propulsion, sonobuoys, and even midget submarines was routinely exchanged and shared.[115]

There were definitely *policy* differences between the two governments that affected their respective navies, especially when it came to the U.S. government's efforts to encourage postwar European rearmament. In 1952, for example, the British service chiefs agreed that the United Kingdom could not "afford the American technique of building up large naval forces to support continental land battles," and that the role of the Royal Navy was to "keep open communications."[116] But two governments can have policy differences while their respective navies can continue cooperating. Away from the attention of the media, communication and exchanges can and do continue unabated. As Captain Swartz puts it, after World War II "U.S. Navy leaders appreciated British technological prowess and exploited that strength, even when budget problems prevented the Royal Navy from doing so."[117]

Notes

1. In Geoffrey Cooper, *Farnborough and the Fleet Air Arm* (Hersham, Surrey, U.K.: Midland, 2008), p. 232, there is a photograph of the whole Naval Aircraft Department (NAD) in November 1951. There were about fifty people in the NAD. On p. 201, there is a photograph of those involved in the first successful test of the flexdeck at Farnborough. There were thirteen individuals.

2. Boddington's plan view of an angled deck is illustrated in Paul Beaver, *The British Aircraft Carrier* (Cambridge, U.K.: Patrick Stephens, 1983), pp. 132–33.

3. See Rear Adm. Dennis R. F. Cambell, "The Angled Deck Story (DRFC's Own Account)," *Rear Admiral Dennis Royle Farquharson Cambell, C.B., D.S.C.*, March 2008, pp. 3, 4, www.denniscambell.org.uk.

4. Eric Brown, *Wings on My Sleeve* (London: Orion Books–Phoenix, 2007), p. 220.

5. Jerry Miller, *Nuclear Weapons and Aircraft Carriers: How the Bomb Saved Naval Aviation* (Washington, D.C.: Smithsonian Institution Press, 2001), p. 185.

6. Norman Friedman, *U.S. Aircraft Carriers: An Illustrated Design History* (Annapolis, Md.: Naval Institute Press, 1983), p. 264. See also Scott MacDonald, "Summing Up: The Turbulent Postwar Years," in *Aircraft Carriers in Peace and War*, ed. Joseph A. Skiera (New York: Franklin Watts, 1965), pp. 201–204.

7. Cambell, "Angled Deck Story," p. 4.

8. "It's Done with Mirrors," *Naval Aviation News* (November 1955), pp. 20–22.

9. Cooper, *Farnborough and the Fleet Air Arm*, pp. 207–12.

10. Cambell, "Angled Deck Story," p. 6.

11. Ibid.

12. Donald D. Engen, *Wings and Warriors: My Life as a Naval Aviator* (Washington, D.C.: Smithsonian Institution Press, 1997), p. 150.

13. Brown, *Wings on My Sleeve*, p. 219.

14. Ibid.

15. Ibid., p. 224.

16. See "Annotated Bumblebee Initial Report," February 1945, repr. *Johns Hopkins APL Technical Digest* 3, no. 2 (1982), pp. 171–79.

17. William E. Scarborough, "The North American AJ Savage, Part One: Establishing the Heavy Attack Mission," *Hook* (Fall 1989), p. 31.

18. Miller, *Nuclear Weapons and Aircraft Carriers*, 2001.

19. Albert B. Christman, *Target Hiroshima: Deak Parsons and the Creation of the Atomic Bomb* (Annapolis, Md.: Naval Institute Press, 1998), pp. 209–11.

20. Miller, *Nuclear Weapons and Aircraft Carriers*, p. 31.

21. Ibid., p. 33. Admiral Miller based his remarks on Ashworth's oral history.

22. For more on the controversy over which service should control nuclear weapons, see Jeffrey G. Barlow, *Revolt of the Admirals: The Fight for Naval Aviation, 1945–1950* (Washington, D.C.: Naval Historical Center, 1994).

23. Ibid., p. 107.

24. Scarborough, "North American AJ Savage," pp. 28–43. The mock-up review is described on p. 33.

25. John T. Hayward and C. W. Borklund, *Bluejacket Admiral: The Navy Career of Chick Hayward* (Annapolis, Md., and Newport, R.I.: Naval Institute Press and Naval War College Foundation, 2000). Oddly enough for an officer with as distinguished a career as Hayward's, some of the details of his career (especially dates of promotion) are difficult to establish. His oral history in the Naval War College archives does not help confirm such dates.

26. Scarborough, "North American AJ Savage," pp. 34–35.

27. Hayward and Borklund, *Bluejacket Admiral*, p. 168. Hayward and Borklund list Rear Admiral Lonnquest as the chief of BuAer, but he was not. This and other small errors detract from the value of Hayward's memoir.

28. Ibid., p. 88.

29. George A. Spangenberg, "Oral History," 31 August 1997, *George Spangenberg Oral History*, 2010, p. 61, www.georgespangenberg.com.

30. Edward H. Heinemann and Rosario Rausa, *Ed Heinemann, Combat Aircraft Designer* (Annapolis, Md.: Naval Institute Press, 1980), chap. 10 for his trip to the Pacific Fleet, pp. 186–87 for his investigation of German military aircraft designs.

31. Ibid., pp. 199–200.

32. Ibid., p. 201.

33. Ibid., pp. 202–203.

34. Spangenberg, "Oral History," p. 105. In December 1948, Lt. Gen. Howard A. Craig, the senior USAF officer in charge of R&D, thought that reliable turboprop engines would be developed earlier than turbojets. As he noted, "The XB-52 is designed to supersede the B-36 as a long range strategic bomber. Its combination of aerodynamic refinement and turbo-propeller engines are

[sic] the only presently known means of achieving characteristics of both long range and high speed—large improvements in this class of aircraft will come with radical developments which will require completely new airframe developments—[u]nless supersonic propellers become a reality, future [large bombers] will be powered by turbo-jet engines. However, neither of these developments are sufficiently near at hand that the turboprop step can be eliminated." Less than two weeks after Craig wrote the memorandum, the XB-47 turbojet bomber, powered by six J35 turbojet engines, made its first flight. Lt. Gen. H[oward] A[rnold] Craig, DCS/M, memorandum to Gen. [Lauris] Norsted, DCS/O, 16 October 1948, subject "XB-52 Long Range Bombardment Airplane." See also Mark D. Mandeles, *The Development of the B-52 and Jet Propulsion: A Case Study in Organizational Innovation* (Maxwell Air Force Base, Ala.: Air Univ. Press, 1998).

35. Vice Admiral Miller says that there was a security scare when Heinemann estimated that the newer nuclear weapons would have a diameter of just thirty-two inches and a much lower weight than the weapon that the AJ had been built to carry. See Miller, *Nuclear Weapons and Aircraft Carriers*, p. 100.

36. But according to Heinemann, Hayward was not happy with the mock-up's cockpit layout. Heinemann and Rausa, *Ed Heinemann, Combat Aircraft Designer*, p. 205.

37. Miller, *Nuclear Weapons and Aircraft Carriers*, p. 94.

38. Secretary of the Navy, Op-01-MD, ser. 71802, 18 August 1943, created DCNO (Air), and Secretary of the Navy, Op-01-MD, ser. 71902, 18 August 1943, transferred the planning, personnel, training, and flight divisions from BuAer to OPNAV. The quote from Julius A. Furer, *Administration of the Navy Department in World War II* (Washington, D.C.: U.S. Government Printing Office, 1959), is on p. 393.

39. See Clark G. Reynolds, *Admiral John H. Towers: The Struggle for Naval Air Supremacy* (Annapolis, Md.: Naval Institute Press, 1991), esp. chaps. 11, 12. During the war, the Naval Air Technical Training Command produced an illustrated review of its activities entitled *Technicians' War* (Atlanta, Ga.: Albert Love, n.d. but probably late 1945). This magazine-style book is an excellent survey of the expansion of the Navy's aviation ratings during World War II.

40. See Thomas Hone, "Naval Reconstitution, Surge, and Mobilization," *Naval War College Review* 47, no. 3 (Summer 1994), pp. 67–85.

41. See Friedman, *U.S. Aircraft Carriers*, pp. 204–33.

42. Roy A. Grossnick, *United States Naval Aviation, 1910–1995*, 4th ed. (Washington, D.C.: Naval Historical Center, 1997), p. 745.

43. Adm. Alfred M. Pride, "Oral History" no. 84, Naval Historical Collection, Naval War College, Newport, R.I., pp. 171–72.

44. Ibid., p. 175.

45. Ibid., p. 183.

46. Ibid.

47. Ibid., p. 197.

48. "Research and Development Master Program," Fiscal Year 1947, Bureau of Aeronautics, "Parasite Fighter Study" section (no page number). This document was in "Navy Department, Bureau of Aeronautics," subhead 4, "Appropria. Aviation, Navy 1947, 1771502.004, Experimental."

49. See Mandeles, *Development of the B-52 and Jet Propulsion*.

50. See Norman Friedman, *U.S. Naval Weapons* (Annapolis, Md.: Naval Institute Press, 1982), p. 217.

51. Malcolm Muir, Jr., *Black Shoes and Blue Water: Surface Warfare in the United States Navy, 1945–1975* (Washington, D.C.: Naval Historical Center, 1996), p. 29. For wartime developments, see Buford Rowland and William Boyd, *U.S. Navy Bureau of Ordnance in World War II* (Washington, D.C.: U.S. Navy Dept., Bureau of Ordnance, 1953).

52. "Research and Development Master Program," Fiscal Year 1947, the section entitled "Shipboard Arresting Gear."

53. Ibid.

54. Ibid., sections on "Catapults for Shipborne Aircraft" and "Catapults for Pilotless Aircraft."

55. Ibid., section on "Development of Improved Launching Technique."

56. Ibid., section on "Shipboard Arresting Gear."

57. Robert B. Pirie, "1958: The Transition Year," in *Into the Jet Age: Conflict and Change in Naval Aviation, 1945–1975*,

ed. E. T. Wooldridge (Annapolis, Md.: Naval Institute Press, 1995), p. 68.

58. Grossnick, *United States Naval Aviation, 1910–1995*, app. 4 (p. 448), app. 10 (p. 593).

59. Pride, "Oral History," p. 182.

60. Spangenberg, "Oral History," pp. 102–103.

61. Tommy H. Thomason, *U.S. Naval Air Superiority: Development of Shipborne Jet Fighters, 1943–1962* (North Branch, Minn.: Specialty, 2007), p. 30. Rear Admiral Metsger wrote an unpublished autobiography upon which Thomason drew.

62. Ibid., p. 31.

63. Spangenberg "Oral History," p. 103.

64. Tommy H. Thomason, *Strike from the Sea: U.S. Navy Attack Aircraft from Skyraider to Super Hornet, 1948–Present* (North Branch, Minn.: Specialty, 2009).

65. Thomason, *U.S. Naval Air Superiority*, p. 125.

66. Geoffrey Till, *Air Power and the Royal Navy, 1914–1945* (London: Jane's, 1979), p. 135.

67. Stephen Roskill, *Naval Policy between the Wars* (New York: Walker, 1968), vol. 1, p. 391, for Admiral Dreyer's actions as assistant chief of the Naval Staff. In his *Churchill and the Admirals* (London: William Collins, 1977), Captain Roskill notes that Admiral Pound had made Dreyer "Chief of the Naval Air Services" without also making him Fifth Sea Lord and therefore a member of the Board of Admiralty (p. 231).

68. Norman Friedman, *British Carrier Aviation: The Evolution of the Ships and Their Aircraft* (London: Conway Maritime, 1988), p. 20.

69. Ibid.

70. Ibid., p. 272.

71. Ibid., p. 275. Roskill, in his *Churchill and the Admirals* (South Yorkshire, U.K.: Pen and Sword Military Classics, 2004, a reprint of the 1977 volume published by William Collins, London, cited above), makes the same point on p. 233.

72. See Friedman, *British Carrier Aviation*, p. 272.

73. See ibid., p. 268.

74. G. A. H. Gordon, *British Seapower and Procurement between the Wars* (Annapolis, Md.: Naval Institute Press, 1988).

75. Till, *Air Power and the Royal Navy, 1914–1945*, p. 136.

76. Indeed, that work was done. See Upshur Joyner and Walter Horne, "Considerations on a Large Hydraulic Jet Catapult," National Advisory Committee for Aeronautics (NACA), 12 April 1951. This research memorandum, prepared for BuAer's Ships Installation Division, reviewed a catapult system that would have the required capacity, a low procurement cost, and a relatively low operating cost. Project Records Relating to Catapults, Launchers, Missiles, 1941–1953, record group [hereafter RG] 72, box 3, entry 133, National Archives.

77. "Naval Aviation Confidential Bulletin" (April 1947), pp. 46–47.

78. "Research & Development Plan for 1949" (Approved Projects), Bureau of Aeronautics, 1 February 1948, National Archives.

79. U.S. Naval Attaché, London, Information Report, Office of Naval Intelligence, 134-C-51, 27 July 1951, to CNO, subject "Trials of prototype steam catapult in HMS Perseus," RG 72, box 1, entry "Catapults, Launchers & Missiles," Perseus folder, National Archives. The response to Rear Admiral Soucek is discussed in BuAer Confidential memorandum Aer-SI-11, 24 August 1951, to Head, Catapult Branch and Head, SACO Branch, subject "Visit of HMS PERSEUS to the United States," RG 72, box 1, entry "Catapults, Launchers & Missiles," Perseus folder, National Archives. Adm. Forrest P. Sherman, Fechteler's predecessor as CNO, had accepted the Admiralty's offer to send *Perseus* on 14 July, but Admiral Sherman died a week later, and the offer was renewed for Admiral Fechteler.

80. Rear Adm. John Stevens, RN, letter to Rear Adm. Felix Johnson, USN, 28 August 1951, B.N.S. 923/51-1, in RG 72, box 1, entry "Catapults, Launchers & Missiles," Perseus folder, National Archives.

81. Chief, BuAer, letter to Commander, NAMC, subject "TED NAM SI 330.0—Visit of HMS PERSEUS to the United States; test program, authorization of," Aer-SI-34, S83/2, 013567, 27 September 1951, RG 72, box 1, entry "Catapults, Launchers & Missiles," Perseus folder, National Archives.

82. Staff Engineer Officer (Air), letter to Chief of the Bureau of Aeronautics, subject "Visit of HMS PERSEUS," 3 December 1951 (RNAS-2/8709), RG 72, box 1, entry

"Catapults, Launchers & Missiles," Perseus folder, National Archives.

83. Capt. Sheldon W. Brown, memorandum to Rear Adm. L. M. Grant, subject "Brief Comparison of British and American Slotted Cylinder Catapults," 8 January 1952 (Aer-SI), RG 72, box 1, entry "Catapults, Launchers & Missiles," Perseus folder, National Archives.

84. "Progress Report on the Perseus Program," no signature, n.d., RG 72, box 1, entry "Catapults, Launchers & Missiles," Perseus folder, National Archives.

85. Warren W. Ford, Naval Aircraft Factory, letter and memorandum to Capt. Sheldon W. Brown, BuAer, 12 February 1952, PE-WWF:dc, RG 72, box 1, entry "Catapults, Launchers & Missiles," Perseus folder, National Archives. The quotation is from p. 5 of the attached memorandum.

86. D. K. Weitzenfeld, "Colin Mitchell's Steam Catapult: The Heart of Modern Aircraft Carriers," *Wings of Gold* 10 (Summer 1985), p. 43.

87. Admiral Ballentine's papers are in the Naval Historical Foundation Collection in the Library of Congress. Entries in his personal diary in box 3 for January and February 1952 indicate his interest in the tests on *Perseus*.

88. Chief, Bureau of Ships, memorandum to Chief, Bureau of Aeronautics, subject "Slotted cylinder catapults, shipboard installation of," 14 February 1952 (C-CV/S83 [440]), RG 72, box 1, entry "Catapults, Launchers & Missiles," Perseus folder, National Archives.

89. Chief of Naval Operations, letter to Commander in Chief, U.S. Atlantic Fleet, Chief, Bureau of Aeronautics, and Chief, Bureau of Ships, subject "Extension of visit of H.M.S. PERSEUS to the USA to permit additional catapult tests," 21 February 1952 (Op-551F/mgt, ser. 055P551), RG 72, box 1, entry "Catapults, Launchers & Missiles," Perseus folder, National Archives.

90. Chief, Bureau of Aeronautics, letter to Commander, Naval Air Material Center, subject "Steam Catapult Operational Films showing launching aboard HMS PERSEUS (BXS-1); request for furnish of," Aer-41-31 (27 March 1953), Catapult Branch, item no. 6, 1952, RG 72, box 1, entry "Catapults, Launchers & Missiles," Perseus folder, National Archives.

91. "From David to Brown," *Naval Aviation News* (February 1954), p. 5.

92. Test Project Coordinator Project Steam II, report to Commander Air Force Atlantic Fleet, subject "Project Steam II Summary Report," SI-2 (20 November 1954), RG 69, box 1, entry A960, National Archives.

93. BuAer did not constrain the imaginations of aircraft designers, as a recent book (Jared A. Zichek, *Secret Aerospace Projects of the U.S. Navy: The Incredible Attack Aircraft of the USS* United States, *1948–1949* [Atglen, Pa.: Schiffer, 2009]) makes clear—quite the reverse.

94. Friedman, *U.S. Aircraft Carriers,* p. 231.

95. William F. Trimble, *Wings for the Navy: A History of the Naval Aircraft Factory, 1917–1956* (Annapolis, Md.: Naval Institute Press, 1990). Trimble documents a number of technical achievements at the Naval Aircraft Factory and at the other organizations within NAMC, including the Aeronautical Instruments Laboratory's development of an autopilot for helicopters and the Naval Aircraft Factory's design and development of the famous "Davis Barrier" to capture jet aircraft that failed to catch a wire when landing on a carrier.

96. The RN liaison officers are listed in the BuAer telephone book. The phone books for BuAer are in the Naval Aviation History archives, box 88, "BuAer, Directories & Correspondence Designations, 1 February 1946, 1 July 1946, 15 January 1947, 15 April 1947, 10 November 1947," Washington Navy Yard, Washington, D.C.

97. "Report of the visit of Mr. J. L. Bartlett & Mr. D. W. Smithers to the U.S.A., November 1948," Naval Construction Department, (Admiralty, Bath), folder ADM 281/109, Public Records Office [hereafter PRO], p. 4.

98. Friedman, *U.S. Aircraft Carriers,* pp. 288–91.

99. "Report of the visit of Mr. J. L. Bartlett & Mr. D. W. Smithers to the U.S.A., November 1948," p. 34.

100. Ibid., p. 39; for the reference to catapult technology, p. 41.

101. Ibid., p. 43 for arresting-gear hook; p. 50 for comparative landing speeds.

102. "Report by School of Aircraft Handling on Period Spent on Board of U.S.S. Antietam," 27 July 1953, attached to Flag Officer, Ground Training, memorandum to Flag Office Air (Home), folder ADM 1/24536, PRO, p. 1.

103. Ibid., p. 7.

104. Commanding Officer, USS *Antietam* (CVA 36), report to Commander Air Force, U.S. Atlantic Fleet, subject "Monthly Report of Canted Deck Evaluation Number 1, period 12 January 1953 through 31 January 1953," CVA-36/15, S1-4, ser. 181, folder ADM 1/24536, PRO.

105. Friedman, *U.S. Aircraft Carriers*, pp. 257–65.

106. Beaver, *British Aircraft Carrier*, p. 131.

107. Ibid., p. 133.

108. Op-30, memorandum to Op-09, subject "Comments on SGM 2538-52," 15 November 1952 (Op-30/nm), Burke Papers, Personal File no. 46, Naval Historical Center.

109. Eric Brown, "Dawn of the Carrier Jet," *Air International* 28, no. 1 (January 1985), pp. 31–37.

110. Ibid., p. 34.

111. See Thomas C. Hone, Norman Friedman, and Mark D. Mandeles, *American & British Aircraft Carrier Development, 1919–1941* (Annapolis, Md.: Naval Institute Press, 1999), p. 47.

112. Jeffrey G. Barlow, *From Hot War to Cold: The U.S. Navy and National Security Affairs, 1945–1955* (Stanford, Calif.: Stanford Univ. Press, 2009).

113. Peter M. Swartz, "The U.S. Navy and Europe in the First Postwar Decade" (Naval Historical Center Colloquium on Contemporary History, Seminar 8, 22 September 2003), p. 2.

114. Roskill, *Naval Policy between the Wars*, vol. 1, p. 398.

115. See, for example, Engineer-in-Chief's Department, "Report on Mission to United States of America, April–May 1951," folder ADM 265/18, 3 W 382, PRO. See also file ADM 1/20176, "Review of state of collaboration between staff officers and their corresponding divisions in the U.S. Navy Dept.," 1946, also PRO.

116. Cited in Andrea Ellner, "Carrier Airpower in the Royal Navy during the Cold War: The International Strategic Context," *Defense & Security Analysis* 22, no. 1 (March 2006), p. 27.

117. Swartz, "U.S. Navy and Europe in the First Postwar Decade," p. 8.

Conclusion

The story of the development of the steam catapult, the angled flight deck, and the mirror landing aid—the innovations that made the modern aircraft carrier possible after World War II—is usually given little attention in general histories of the U.S. Navy.[1] We believe that this relative lack of attention is in fact a sign that senior U.S. Navy officers were confronted by so many new developments—in technology, strategy, and operations—after World War II that the Navy as an institution had difficulty finding time to deal adequately with them all. The stories behind the three innovations that we have studied look insignificant when compared to the debates over service responsibilities and unification or the arguments within the U.S. government regarding what became known as the Cold War. Nobel laureate Herbert Simon argued almost forty years ago that attention, not information, is the really scarce resource in complex organizations. As historians of the U.S. Navy's actions and policies after World War II have found, Navy leaders were constantly time pressured.[2]

Looking at the Evidence

Moreover, the way the Navy was managed changed during World War II. In our earlier comparative study of British and American carrier aviation, we identified three organizations that played the key roles in the development of the U.S. Navy's carrier arm: the Bureau of Aeronautics, the General Board of the Navy, and the Naval War College.[3] Of the three, only one—BuAer—retained a central role in the development of postwar carrier aviation, and its influence in the process of developing naval aviation policy was much diminished. The primary organizational actor after World War II was the Office of the Chief of Naval Operations. But officers in OPNAV had to develop Navy policy in a number of other significant areas as well, including nuclear war and deterrence, service unification, and when and how Navy task forces would be deployed on a regular and recurring basis to the western Pacific and the Mediterranean.

The quality of officers assigned to OPNAV somewhat made up for the lack of multiple organizational "actors," but the Navy nonetheless lacked in 1946 what an earlier generation of Navy leaders had possessed in 1926, which was a systematic means of identifying conceptual errors and possibilities. In the 1920s, Navy doctrinal development began at the Naval War College, where existing and possible doctrines for fleet deployment were tested in rigorous war games. Inferences drawn from the war games were then tested in the annual "fleet problems," where the U.S. fleet was divided into two "teams" and the "teams" engaged in operational maneuvers and mock battles.[4] The results of the fleet problems were funneled back to both the Naval War College and the Navy's technical bureaus, such as BuAer. Thus the Navy had a rolling cycle of concept development, war gaming, tests of concepts at sea in major maneuvers, and post–fleet problem assessment. Then there were more war games, fleet problems, and postexercise assessment.[5]

This rolling cycle was complemented by the way the General Board conducted secret hearings on ship design and other issues of interest to the senior civilian and military leaders of the Navy. In the hearings, those called to testify were asked to present evidence to support their claims, and the members of the General Board encouraged those present to voice their views and to disagree when they felt the evidence could be interpreted in a different way. In effect, the board's rules of procedure for its very confidential hearings promoted and sanctioned a give-and-take regarding problems of strategy, technology, and doctrine. The board kept a stenographic record of its hearings, and that record was made available to both the Secretary of the Navy and the Chief of Naval Operations. The combination of the give-and-take at the hearings and the ability of the CNO and the secretary to monitor that debate gave the Navy an effective organizational tool in Washington to identify problems and then weigh the value of potential solutions. That organizational tool complemented the institutional tool of the cycle of war game/fleet problem/maneuver assessment used in the 1920s and 1930s.[6]

These tools were not available after World War II. Major policy and doctrinal issues had to be dealt with by officers assigned to OPNAV. Though the quality of these officers was high, the organizational distance between them and the engineering specialists charged with, for example, adapting aircraft carriers to jets was great.[7] *If a particular issue mattered enough, that distance could be closed.* That was clearly the case with the development of the AJ Savage nuclear-capable bomber, first ordered in June 1946 and first flown just over two years later. But officers in OPNAV could not deal effectively with every problem facing the Navy after the war. For example, Captain George B. Chafee, the director of BuAer's Ships Installation Division, gave a speech in 1947 in which he acknowledged that the effort to develop new barriers on existing axial-deck carriers that would safely handle jet aircraft "has been the No. 1 priority project at the Naval Air Material Center for nearly 2 years."[8] Chafee also admitted that "designs of future aircraft are being hampered to a degree by catapult capacity," though he also noted that the Naval Air Material Center was working on a slotted-tube device.[9] Chafee informed his listeners that the aircraft elevators of future carriers would need to be "of the deck-edge type," and that they would need to be able to lift a 60,000-pound aircraft. Aircraft hangars on carriers would have to be larger to accommodate the bigger planes, and large jet bombers would "require so much fuel that it will be necessary to double the stowage capacity of carriers."[10]

Chafee's list of new requirements for future carriers suggests the need to design the carrier to the aircraft, yet he also told his audience that the AJ Savage "was designed around the *Midway* class characteristics." The design of this aircraft did not provoke a reassessment of the way in which carriers were designed because the Savage "was conceived as a plane for a special operation with no requirement for entry into the hangar."[11] Reading this speech in hindsight, we wanted to shout, "You need to redesign the whole flight deck! Stop adapting and start innovating!" The signs of a major problem are there, from the inability to develop a satisfactory barrier to the limits of hydraulic catapults, and from the need for dramatically more fuel to the need to find ways to load new and larger (10,000 and 12,000 lb.) bombs. But Captain Chafee made it clear that BuAer was constrained both by a lack of funds and by the need to examine wholly new concepts, including "the submarine aircraft carrier and the airplane aircraft carrier," pilotless aircraft, and guided missiles.[12] Put another way, there was almost too much on the Naval Air Material Center's plate.

The engineers and other specialists responsible for the new carriers and for the aircraft-related equipment on the new ships believed that incremental improvements to existing technologies would work satisfactorily with the new aircraft being developed. It took OPNAV intervention—when Rear Admiral Soucek dealt with CNOs Sherman and Fechteler—to shove the engineers in a new direction.

As we have shown, matters were different in the Royal Navy. Senior RN officers recognized the deficiencies in their aircraft carrier forces during World War II and then set aside the past and grasped the nature of the future, seeing the necessity for jet aircraft in their postwar carrier force. As they did this, the engineers in the United Kingdom charged with developing catapults and arresting gear realized that operating jet aircraft from a carrier meant changing the carrier. The engineers were able to show a logical progression from "Jets are the future" to "The carrier must be suited to jets." That logical progression led to a set of interrelated problems, including efforts safely to recover the jets, which landed at higher speeds than propeller planes, and the adoption of the steam catapult, which was needed by the jets because they accelerated more slowly than propeller-driven aircraft. Because the first jets consumed so much fuel compared with their propeller-driven predecessors, engineer Lewis Boddington and his colleagues at Farnborough worked to adapt the carrier to jets that lacked landing gear, hoping that the weight saved by eliminating the landing gear could be devoted to fuel. The imperative to conserve fuel led to the undercarriage-less airplane, which led to the flexible deck, which led to the angled deck.

When we first looked at the evidence, it appeared that the Royal Navy's invention of the angled deck was the result of an accident. In some sense, that was a consequence of the way that Rear Adm. Dennis R. F. Cambell, RN (Ret.), told the story of its adoption.[13] However, as Geoffrey Cooper's detailed *Farnborough and the Fleet Air Arm* shows, Boddington and his colleagues had laid the groundwork for the angled-deck idea through their careful work on the "flexdeck" concept and prototype.[14] For that reason, we choose to consider the angled deck less an accidental *discovery* than a serendipitous *development*. The terms "accidental," "serendipitous," and "fortuitous" are near synonyms, but "accidental" suggests finding something by chance, whereas we believe that "serendipitous" implies the ability to recognize something as new or innovative while trying to solve a problem. Our point is that Boddington was prepared to perceive the implications of Cambell's sketch design because of his earlier extensive work on the flexdeck.

The notion of serendipity also accounts for the speed with which the U.S. Navy's aviators adopted the angled-deck idea from the British. Its aviators were prepared for the idea by their experiences landing jets on the existing axial flight decks of the *Essex*- and *Midway*-class carriers. The USN's carrier aviators in OPNAV were already committed to modifying a number of *Essex*-class carriers for jet aircraft operations, and so they were open to, and even eager for, ideas that they could "borrow."

Contrast that situation to the initial resistance of BuAer's catapult engineers to the British steam catapult. The Americans were strongly committed to an explosive or gas-driven catapult design, because they could not see a workable solution to the seepage of steam from a slotted-tube catapult. Indeed, when the Navy tested steam catapults on the *Essex*-class carrier *Hancock* (CVA 19) under operational conditions off San Diego, California, in July 1954, the jet aircraft being launched were usually enveloped by clouds of steam from the catapults. It took time for an effective seal to be developed that would work with the higher-pressure steam generated by the U.S. carriers' propulsion plants. As we have pointed out, BuAer catapult

The first test of a U.S. Navy steam catapult at sea, July 1954. USS *Hancock* (CVA 19) is launching . . . what? The plane is completely obscured by steam leaking from the catapult.

Navy Department, National Archives

engineers continued to consider the British steam catapults only an interim solution to the problem of launching very heavy bombers from carriers.

But the BuAer engineers were not in charge of USN aviation policy. It was aviators like Rear Adm. Apollo Soucek who identified the steam catapult as a viable alternative to the hydraulic systems used in U.S. carriers, and it was apparently a senior aviator—Vice Adm. John J. Ballentine, the type commander for aviation in the Atlantic—who insisted that the steam catapult be adopted. In the case of the mirror landing aid, we find a similar pattern. Both navies had been experimenting with new ways of guiding the faster jets safely to carrier flight decks, and hence the U.S. Navy was "ready" to consider a system that complemented or replaced the landing signal officers then employed on carriers. When Lt. Cdr. Donald Engen tested the British "optical landing system" on HMS *Illustrious* in November 1953, his recommendation was enough to convince senior officers to procure it for use on U.S. carriers. Engen was then one of two U.S. Navy pilots assigned to the famous Empire Test Pilot school at Farnborough, and both were directed to test British innovations.[15]

Our study has examined both innovations and adaptations. At the end of World War II, the Royal Navy's engineers at Farnborough decided that the introduction of jet aircraft would require an innovation in carrier design—a different kind of carrier suited to the characteristics (landing speed, takeoff speed, fuel consumption rate, etc.) of the new jet aircraft. The U.S. Navy's counterparts to the engineers at Farnborough decided that their task was to adapt existing carriers and aircraft-handling equipment to the new jet aircraft. But the senior aviators in OPNAV were innovators; they wanted to create "heavy attack" jet bombers that could carry the large and heavy nuclear weapons that had been used in World War II. Launching and recovering those bombers required a very different approach to a carrier's flight deck and its equipment.

The Royal Navy's aviators and its engineers shared a common vision and also shared an understanding of the obstacles that would have to be overcome to turn that vision into reality. We do not see that same level of shared vision on the U.S. side, except between the Navy's aviators and the aircraft designers in industry. Perhaps one reason for the apparent gap between aviators in OPNAV and the catapult engineers in BuAer was that the two groups were not in constant contact, as the BuAer aviators were with industry aircraft designers and engineers. The human, or personal, link between aviator officers in OPNAV and BuAer, on the one side, and BuAer catapult engineers, on the other, was weak—probably too weak for the innovators to challenge and stimulate the engineers who thought their task was to *adapt*.

In World War II, Adm. Ernest J. King shunted aside the Naval War College and the General Board. Major decisions about acquisition and the future of the Navy were to be made within OPNAV, which meant that innovative proposals from the fleet or from BuAer had to catch the attention of the senior admirals there in order to be evaluated. As Friedman has shown, the origins of the Navy's heavy and large carrier-aircraft attack program stemmed from a detailed memorandum sent by the BuAer chief, Rear Adm. Harold B. Sallada, to the CNO in December 1945.[16] Adm. Marc Mitscher, then the Deputy Chief of Naval Operations for Air, was a strong supporter of Rear Admiral Sallada's recommendation and also of a flush-deck carrier concept suited to the new and as yet undeveloped large carrier bombers.[17] The General Board still operated in late 1945, but it did not play the same analytic role that it had before the war, and therefore Mitscher's support was essential if the Navy's leaders were to endorse the heavy-attack concept for carrier aircraft.

With the end of the prewar war-game/fleet-problem/problem-assessment cycle, the process of carrier-concept development was open to influence from officers in OPNAV, BuAer, and the fleet. Disciplining this process was left in the hands of a new organization of bureau representatives called the Ship Characteristics Board (SCB), and major decisions taken by this board were decided by voting—one vote for each bureau, including the Bureau of Medicine and Surgery.[18] In the immediate postwar years, the members of the SCB, as well as the OPNAV staff, were officers with wartime operational experience. The same went for the chiefs of BuAer. That shared experience gave the members of the SCB and the staff of OPNAV a shared set of reference points—a common grounding. But that common grounding did not lead to a carrier design built around heavy-attack aircraft until serious planning for the "supercarrier" *United States* began in June 1946.[19] Put another way, the postwar carrier program was more a product of the views of senior officers than it was the result of back-and-forth before the General Board based on consideration of systematically gathered evidence. And those senior officers in OPNAV decided after World War II that they would not concede the nuclear strike mission to the Army (later Air Force) land-based bomber commanders.

It is ironic that BuAer, which had lost its policy-making responsibilities to OPNAV during the war, nonetheless continued after the war as an organization with major influence within the Navy, because Navy aviation leaders like Admiral Mitscher came out of the war convinced of the importance of the heavy-attack mission. In effect, the requirement for a carrier aircraft that could carry large (ten-thousand-pound and more) bombs merged with the desire of Navy aviators for a carrier-based nuclear bomber. As Lewis Boddington had decided in the summer of 1945, it was time that the characteristics of the carrier's aircraft determined the design of the carrier. The result in the U.S. Navy was the large but canceled *United States* and the later somewhat smaller but still very large *Forrestal* (CVA 59).

In 1944–45, the Royal Navy considered the U.S. Navy the world leader in aircraft carrier technology and operations, and thus the last wartime British carrier design, for the never-built *Malta* class, was inspired by U.S. Navy carrier characteristics, which facilitated the rapid launching and recovery of multiple strike missions. When the RN was forced by financial limitations to rebuild its existing carriers instead of constructing new ones, it made efforts to incorporate such U.S. Navy features as the deck-edge elevator, which greatly simplified the flow of aircraft between the hangar and flight decks.[20] The two navies diverged, however, when in 1949 the British chiefs of staff rejected an RN proposal that its carriers be given the nuclear-strike mission.

By that time, the mission of RN carriers was well understood. They would shield shipping en route from the United States and Canada from attack by Soviet surface warships and land-based attack aircraft. RN carrier aircraft could also intercept Soviet minelaying aircraft trying to close European and British ports. To perform these missions RN carrier aircraft had to have the necessary range, hence the strong interest by Lewis Boddington in carrier fighters without landing gear.

The strategic context in which engineers such as Boddington and officers like Dennis Cambell worked was a classified planning assumption that the Soviet Union would not be capable of attacking Western Europe until 1957. In British parlance, 1957 became the "year of maximum danger." This assumption mattered, because it allowed time for the British economy—as well as the Soviet economy—to recover from World War II. Once the economy was back on its feet, the British assumed, their military services would have the funds to purchase quantities of advanced weapons. Until then the British would invest in research and development and, they hoped, stay in roughly the same technological league as the comparatively wealthy Americans. When the Soviet Union tested its first nuclear weapon in 1949, however, the "year of maximum danger" seemed much closer. When North Korea invaded South Korea in June 1950, military leaders on both sides of the Atlantic feared that the Korean conflict might be the first round of World War III. The United States was already rearming and quickly increasing its spending on research, development, and acquisition. The British government could not do the same.

The steam catapult, angled flight deck, and optical landing aid made *Forrestal* an effective carrier and a strategic weapon. However, by the mid-1950s (the end point for our research), the size and weight of nuclear bombs had been dramatically reduced; it no longer took a massive (eighty-two-thousand-pound loaded weight) aircraft like the Douglas A3D Skywarrior to deliver nuclear weapons. New "tactical" nuclear weapons could be carried by such fighters as the North American FJ-4B Fury, and a lightweight attack plane—the Douglas A4D Skyhawk—was designed specifically for nuclear attack.[21] Deep attack, however, did still require a large, supersonic airplane, and for that purpose the North American A3J Vigilante was supposed to serve as the successor to the A3D. However, by the mid-1950s the Navy had another way to deliver strategic nuclear weapons—the Regulus cruise missile. As Naval Warfare Publication 10, *Naval Warfare,* noted in 1954, "Newer submarines have been equipped with missiles and will provide a tremendous strategic deterrent capability to our Navy."[22]

The first Navy Long-Range Objectives Group (Op-96) study, completed in 1955, envisaged a fleet using such missiles for long-range attack, hence no longer requiring heavy bombers—or heavy carriers.[23] In effect, just as the new carriers were entering service, it seemed, they and their heavy-attack aircraft would soon be unnecessary. But as it happened, the combination of the large carrier and the heavy-attack bomber had kept alive the heavy-attack mission itself long enough for the Navy to demonstrate the strategic value of its dispersed nuclear striking force. Within five years, the Navy shifted from reliance upon heavy-attack aircraft for the nuclear-strike mission to air-breathing cruise missiles and then to ballistic missile–launching submarines.

But the large carriers survived, because fleet air defense required carriers to operate large, high-performance fighters, and the newer, heavier fighters were every bit as demanding of flight-deck equipment as the heavy-attack aircraft. They were probably even more demanding in terms of landing requirements. The F-14, at a loaded weight of fifty-five to sixty thousand pounds, was three times as heavy as a loaded Douglas AD-2 Skyraider and about 70 percent as heavy as a loaded North American RA-5C Vigilante. The routine of bringing it back aboard a carrier would not have been possible without the angled flight deck and the optical landing aid. These innovations, along with the steam catapult, made it possible for the large carrier to continue to field modern, high-performance aircraft.

A Regulus-1 air-breathing, long-range missile catapulted from *Hancock* in 1957. The trolley holding the missile and pulled by the steam catapult is lost when the missile is launched.

Navy Department, National Archives

Lessons

In his *Military Transformation Past and Present,* Mark D. Mandeles observes that "in the real-life world of people in organizations considering military problems, nothing is simple." Moreover, "risk, uncertainty, and ambiguity are constant companions," and therefore the "key to unlocking the process of innovation is attention to multiple sets of relationships among individuals, organizations, and multiorganizational systems."[24] Our study has followed this plan; we have examined the actions of individuals, how individuals have influenced the organizations in which they have worked, and the interactions of different organizations.

One obvious "lesson learned" from this study is that it is difficult for people working in a complex organization like the Navy to identify correctly a technical or tactical problem unless they have procedures and organizations that facilitate their doing so. This is particularly important when—as was the case for the USN after World War II—an organization is confronted almost simultaneously with multiple challenges. So we find that BuAer approached the problem of developing effective and efficient jet engines the way it had approached the problem of developing powerful and reliable piston engines in the 1920s and 1930s—by financing engine development. The new jet engines were provided to the airframe manufacturers as "government furnished equipment." OPNAV, which after the war was the center of aviation policy making, did not object to BuAer's relying on an established method of engine procurement. OPNAV officers also did not object when BuAer proposed testing the RN's flexdeck. There were established, reliable procedures for testing new equipment.

On its part, the RN had a system of committees to review wartime experience and anticipate postwar requirements. Norman Friedman has discovered that the Aircraft Design Subcommittee of the RN's Future Building Committee initiated the study of aircraft without landing gear and the use of flexible carrier-landing decks.[25] Once the subcommittee had identified that possibility as legitimate, Lewis Boddington could begin the studies that led to his papers in the summer of 1945 on what modifications to carriers would be necessary in order to operate jets from them successfully. Boddington's papers did not result from a flash of individual insight. They were based on a good deal of quantitative analysis conducted over a period of several months in pursuit of a possibility approved by a standing committee of experienced officers. But what guided that analysis was a consensus among the relevant military and civilian personnel that jets were the future and that bringing them on board aircraft carriers would be difficult and quite dangerous unless a different approach to landing was developed. The subcommittee's deliberations were essential to developing that consensus.

In the U.S. Navy, by contrast, it took longer for a similar consensus to emerge. One reason was that there were significant "distractors," including competing problems that ate up the time and energy of the people charged with making the transition from piston-engine aircraft to jets. Perhaps the most important of these was the desire to turn carriers into nuclear-strike platforms. Related to this distractor was another—the larger debate about the proper organization of national defense in the United States after World War II. There were still others, including the USN's role in what became NATO, whether the Navy would have what are now called "forward-deployed forces," and, of course, the war in Korea.[26]

For example, why wasn't Rear Adm. Alfred Pride, BuAer chief (May 1947–May 1951) in the critical years after World War II, more concerned about the bureau's catapult program? When the first jets came in, he went down to the Naval Air Test Center to fly one, and he stayed actively involved in BuAer's engine and supersonic-aircraft development efforts. It was under his leadership that BuAer spent scarce funds on some very innovative and secret carrier-launched nuclear bomber designs.[27] Though Rear Admiral Pride had made his mark as a young officer by designing catapults, as BuAer chief his concern was more effective aircraft. One reason—perhaps the main reason—for that concern was the need to show that the Navy's new carrier (the ill-fated *United States* program) and even its modified *Essex* carriers could launch nuclear-weapon-armed bombers that could rival or exceed the performance of bombers being fielded and designed by the U.S. Air Force. But another reason for his focus on aircraft was the lack of what might be called an "integrating mechanism," an organization like the General Board that, through its investigations, could look across different areas of technology and operations.

What else have we learned? We have learned something obvious, something so very obvious that people usually don't stop to consider it—the *value of experimentation*. The perception of a need to experiment and an imperative to learn from experimentation are critical to innovation. The classic illustration is the visit of HMS *Perseus* to the United States in 1952. The USN spent funds (by 1952 not so scarce as before the Korean War) to bring the ship to the United States and support it and its crew during critical experiments in Philadelphia and Norfolk, in an episode we have already described. What is so impressive is the willingness of all the professionals involved to accept the results. The USN catapult experts were concerned that the British steam catapult would not work using steam at six-hundred-pound pressure, so the USN supplied steam at that higher pressure, and Colin C. Mitchell's steam catapult was tested once more—again successfully. That was it. The steam catapult became the primary U.S. carrier catapult, from being an alternative to what BuAer's catapult developers had been working on. Experiments cost money. They take time. They must be carefully planned. But they are priceless as tools for learning—and for convincing the stubborn that something they think little of can actually work.

We have also learned that innovations will be communicated faster if there is an existing "track" to take them from one organization or institution to another. In this case, the track was built during World War II, through the close cooperation between BuAer and the British Mission in Washington, through the Joint Aircraft Committee. Much of the credit for this goes, we believe, to then–rear admiral John H. Towers, who was BuAer chief.[28] But the track was maintained by a whole crowd of military and civilian officials engaged in the war effort. Some of them kept up their contacts after the war. For example, Rear Adm. James S. Russell, who was BuAer chief in 1955, was a good friend of Rear Adm. Dennis R. F. Cambell, and Vice Adm. John J. Ballentine, already mentioned as keenly interested in the steam catapult in 1952, made sure that *Antietam* went to the United Kingdom in the summer of 1953 so that Fleet Air Arm pilots could get some exposure to landing and taking off from an angled deck.

Maintaining this track, or path, has become harder as innovation has shifted out of government organizations and into private ones. Recent studies of defense cooperation have focused on the policy-making role of government rather than on its role as an innovator.[29] Or they have emphasized the "global context" within which defense industries must compete and work.[30] Put bluntly, private, even semipublic, manufacturers and research establishments take great risks in communicating innovations with their present or perhaps future business rivals. Recent policies for "outsourcing" in the United States have therefore probably reduced the likelihood that multiple tracks for communicating innovations will exist. After the Cold War, the going assumption in Washington was that much of Europe's defense industry would wither for lack of funding and that therefore there was little need for a clear link with the research and developmental organizations of allies. Put another way, the advocates of outsourcing in the United States have assumed that there is little to be learned from even close allies, such as the United Kingdom—despite the cases we have described (as well as others, including the Martin-Baker ejection seat, midair refueling, and the submarine-launched Harpoon).

In an age when aircraft are flown by software, those who doubt the value of close contacts with allies in the development of high-tech sensors, software, and weapons may be right, though we have our doubts. Software development is still very much a matter of lines of code, and a relatively small number of firms control the production of code relevant to the operation of manned and unmanned aircraft from aircraft carriers. Indeed, the military may today be doing as good a job as private industry in contracting for the production of reliable software for aircraft and carriers. It is very hard to know for sure. We do know that "military professionalism" in modern navies, as understood by the professional officers of those navies, includes an emphasis on experiments, technological education, and open-mindedness. These traits were essential to navies in the years right after World War II. We believe that they still are.

At the end of an earlier book, *American & British Aircraft Carrier Development, 1919–1941,* we noted that the U.S. Navy mastered carrier strike aviation as it went along, using experimentation (including war games at the Naval War College) and fleet exercises to develop, refine, and even sometimes cast off carrier operating concepts. We did not find the same pattern in postwar U.S. Navy aviation. Postwar, the naval forces of the United States continued a practice that had been required by war—forward deployment. The agenda, the mission, of U.S. naval aviation changed dramatically—from taking on an enemy carrier force to launching nuclear strikes against the heart of the Soviet Union. *But the way in which the Navy explored problems changed too.* Postwar, there was no longer a concentrated fleet that could divide itself in half to try out new tactics and operational concepts in exercises that set one half of the fleet against the other. Postwar, the Naval War College did not resume its role as an "idea generator" or "idea filter" through the use of extensive and repeated war games. Instead, ideas came from officers in OPNAV, from the fleet, from test centers (like that at Patuxent, Maryland), and from industry reacting to "seed money" sowed by BuAer. This was a confusing and almost disorganized situation, especially given the high level of secrecy that cloaked information about nuclear weapons. The amazing thing is that this disorganized, ad hoc process led to a carrier force that was effective throughout the Cold War.

Why was that? First, both the RN and the USN had some wonderfully talented professionals, from test pilots like Eric Brown to engineers like Lewis Boddington, to aircraft designers such as Edward Heinemann, and on to naval officers like the relatively junior Donald Engen and the senior Arthur Radford. Second, both navies had the benefit of the talent that aircraft manufacturers and their own organizations (such as BuAer) had trained during the war. Third, both benefited from having test centers, wind tunnels, and other facilities (to say nothing of the carriers themselves) that had been built with wartime funds. This "stuff" is called "infrastructure," and it matters.

Finally, leadership matters, and at multiple levels. It is difficult to follow all the twists and turns involved in the development of the modern carrier in the U.S. Navy. *Forrestal,* the modern carrier prototype, was developed, and it "worked"—but it was not a sure thing. There again were multiple and pressing "distractors." There was even the possibility that key individuals, like Eric Brown, would be killed or seriously injured in flying accidents.[31] It was impossible to say at the end of 1945 just how things would come out ten years later. Very different people pushed things along in ways that could not have been predicted beforehand. The idea that certain technology developments are preordained is mistaken.

Some of the leaders in our story were relatively easy to identify. There was, for example, Rear Admiral Soucek's monitoring of the Royal Navy's experiments with the steam catapult in 1950 and his subsequent recommendation to the Chief of Naval Operations, Adm. Forrest P. Sherman, that the U.S. Navy pay to bring HMS *Perseus* to the United States for tests. There was also the decision by Admiral Sherman's successor, Adm. William M. Fechteler, to take up where Sherman (who perished suddenly from heart failure) left off. These are obvious examples of senior officials willing to take some risk in order to solve clearly identified problems.

But there is a more subtle form of leadership, one found especially *within* an organization, such as BuAer or the Royal Aircraft Establishment at Farnborough, and it involves an honest give-and-take between civilian specialists and their uniformed colleagues. In the papers of engineer Lewis Boddington, for instance, one sees an intelligent mind at work on a problem—working hard because the work *mattered*. Behind his work is the assumption that the inferences he drew from studies, analyses, and trials would be understood and acted on. This assumption is at the heart of a *professional* organization. Because it is so widespread in truly modern navies, it can easily be taken for granted—assumed, as it were, to exist as an essential element of modern life.

But it is not a given. The willingness (and opportunity) to listen to technical specialists must be sustained in organizations through day-to-day leadership within those organizations. We have already argued that the sharing of innovations across organizational and institutional boundaries is not to be assumed, and neither is innovation itself, nor the ability to know which innovations to gamble on and which to ignore. The U.S. Navy invested in a number of innovative aviation concepts after World War II, including the Convair XFY-1 Pogo (a vertical-takeoff-and-landing turboprop fighter intended to be flown from the decks of cargo ships) and the very beautiful Martin P6M SeaMaster, designed to be the world's first supersonic, seaplane, nuclear-capable bomber.[32] In some sense, the 1920s pattern in military aviation was repeated in the late 1940s and early 1950s: airplanes showed up everywhere, as designers, engineers, and Navy officers tried to get the greatest military benefit from the new technologies that wartime research had spawned.

Yet there is always the danger that funds, even lavish funds, will not produce the innovations that the funding sources hope for and need. Choices have to be made. A classic case is the Grumman TB2F concept from 1942, which was abandoned in the spring of 1944 because it no longer could perform the mission for which it was designed. In the late 1940s and early 1950s, many aircraft designs were rejected at some stage of development, and others did not work out well once in service. In our story, the catapult designers and developers responsible to BuAer kept to their own approaches to a catapult for jet aircraft because they thought that just a bit more effort would produce success. National Advisory Committee for Aeronautics researchers were right in that boat with them.[33]

Why? It happened because there was no "test" of the available alternatives—no "forcing function" that could show the BuAer catapult developers that there was another, better alternative available to them. Indeed, the hydraulic catapults were actually dangerous, as serious hydraulic fluid fires on both *Leyte* (CV 32) in late 1953 and *Bennington* (CV 20) in May 1954 showed.[34] Why was that danger not foreseen? We do not know for certain, but we do know from study and experience that it is often not easy for people in an organization to admit that what they have worked on has failed. It takes a special kind of leadership—usually exercised through some mechanism such as the General Board's pre–World War II hearings—to convince them that they have.

Our last comment echoes one we made in *American & British Aircraft Carrier Development, 1919–1941*. Flying is exciting. Pilots wanted to fly jets on and off carriers despite high accident rates in the late 1940s and early 1950s. Eric Brown flew almost everything he could climb into, and his memoir, *Wings on My Sleeve*, is full of accidents, near accidents, and hair-raising aerial adventures. Running through the memoirs and stories from this period in aeronautical history is a strong sense of adventure, coupled with a grim determination to adapt jets to carriers and carriers to jets. It worked. Despite great odds, it worked.

Notes

1. Robert W. Love, Jr., *History of the U.S. Navy, 1942–1991* (Harrisburg, Pa.: Stackpole Books, 1992), pp. 378–79.

2. Jeffrey G. Barlow, *From Hot War to Cold: The U.S. Navy and National Security Affairs, 1945–1955* (Stanford, Calif.: Stanford Univ. Press, 2009).

3. See Thomas C. Hone, Norman Friedman, and Mark D. Mandeles, *American & British Aircraft Carrier Development, 1919–1941* (Annapolis, Md.: Naval Institute Press, 1999).

4. Craig C. Felker, *Testing American Sea Power* (College Station: Texas A&M Univ. Press, 2007).

5. See Thomas C. Hone and Mark Mandeles, "Interwar Innovation in Three Navies: U.S. Navy, Royal Navy, Imperial Japanese Navy," *Naval War College Review* 40, no. 2 (Spring 1987), pp. 63–83.

6. John T. Kuehn, *Agents of Innovation: The General Board and the Design of the Fleet That Defeated the Japanese Navy* (Annapolis, Md.: Naval Institute Press, 2008). See also Albert A. Nofi, *To Train the Fleet for War: The U.S. Navy Fleet Problems, 1923–1940* (Newport, R.I.: Naval War College Press, 2010).

7. See Norman Friedman, *U.S. Destroyers: An Illustrated Design History* (Annapolis, Md.: Naval Institute Press, 1982), p. 3.

8. Capt. George B. Chafee, "Carrier Requirements for Future Aircraft," "Naval Aviation Confidential Bulletin" (July 1947), p. 17, in Aviation History Office, Naval History and Heritage Command, Washington Navy Yard, Washington, D.C.

9. Ibid.

10. Ibid., p. 18.

11. Ibid.

12. Ibid., p. 20.

13. Rear Adm. Dennis R. F. Cambell folder collection, Navy Operational Archives, Navy History and Heritage Command, Washington Navy Yard, Washington, D.C.

14. Geoffrey Cooper, *Farnborough and the Fleet Air Arm* (Hersham, Surrey, U.K.: Midland, 2008).

15. Donald D. Engen, *Wings and Warriors: My Life as a Naval Aviator* (Washington, D.C.: Smithsonian Institution Press, 1997), pp. 138–52.

16. See Norman Friedman, *U.S. Aircraft Carriers: An Illustrated Design History* (Annapolis, Md.: Naval Institute Press, 1983), pp. 231–33.

17. Ibid., pp. 240, 243.

18. See Friedman, *U.S. Destroyers*, p. 3.

19. See Friedman, *U.S. Aircraft Carriers*, p. 244.

20. See Norman Friedman, *British Carrier Aviation: The Evolution of the Ships and Their Aircraft* (London: Conway Maritime, 1988), pp. 272–73.

21. Tommy H. Thomason, *Strike from the Sea: U.S. Navy Attack Aircraft from Skyraider to Super Hornet, 1948–Present* (North Branch, Minn.: Specialty, 2009), chap. 6.

22. U.S. Navy Dept., *Naval Warfare,* Naval Warfare Publication 10, through change 4 (Washington, D.C.: 1954), p. 5-13.

23. See Friedman, *U.S. Aircraft Carriers*, pp. 22–25.

24. See Mark D. Mandeles, *Military Transformation Past and Present: Historical Lessons for the 21st Century* (Westport, Conn.: Praeger Security International, 2007), p. 2.

25. See Friedman, *British Carrier Aviation,* p. 272.

26. See Barlow, *From Hot War to Cold*.

27. Jared A. Zichek, *Secret Aerospace Projects of the U.S. Navy: The Incredible Attack Aircraft of the USS* United States, *1948–1949* (Atglen, Pa.: Schiffer, 2009). At least one of these futuristic designs was supposed to be able to land back aboard an *Essex*-class carrier; see p. 139.

28. See Clark G. Reynolds, *Admiral John H. Towers: The Struggle for Naval Air Supremacy* (Annapolis, Md.: Naval Institute Press, 1991), pp. 339–41.

29. An example is David Gompert, Richard Kugler, and Martin Libicki, *Mind the Gap: Promoting a Transatlantic Revolution in Military Affairs* (Washington, D.C.: National Defense Univ. Press, 1999).

30. Neil Latham, *Defense Industry in a Global Context: Policy Implications for the United Kingdom,* Whitehall Paper 57 (London: RUSI, n.d.).

31. For example, Lt. Cdr. Hugh Wood, the BuAer project officer for the Douglas XA2D turboprop Skyshark, was killed during a test flight in December 1950. Thomason, *Strike from the Sea,* p. 62.

32. See the many beautiful photographs of this large airplane in Stan Piet and Al Raithel, *Martin P6M SeaMaster* (Bel Air, Md.: Martineer, 2001).

33. Upshur T. Joyner and Walter B. Horne, "Considerations on a Large Hydraulic Jet Catapult," NACA Research Memorandum L51B27, 12 April 1951, Langley Aeronautical Laboratory, Langley Field, Va., National Archives.

34. The fires were apparently caused by the overheating of petroleum oils in the hydraulic cylinders. The danger was eliminated by a private manufacturer's development of water-glycol fluid as a substitute. See *Houghton,* www.houghtonintl.com (website of Houghton International Inc.) and "Time Line / Crew Stories," *USS Bennington,* www.uss-bennington.org/.

Appendix A: The Physics of Jet Propulsion

Jets seemed revolutionary because instead of pulling their way through the air like propellers, they relied on the airplane's reaction to a blast of hot gas emitted from their nozzles. In fact the contrast in principle was not so great, because a propeller can be seen as a fan accelerating air back over an airplane, creating a backflow just like that of a jet engine. However, the propeller can also be understood as generating a forward force by the flow of air over its moving blades, which are like wings turned on their sides. This way of generating thrust gets an airplane into the air but ultimately limits the speed of that airplane. This limit was not an issue for designers until military and test aircraft started to reach very high speeds—above 400 mph.

In a propeller-driven plane, the movement of each propeller blade generates lift in a direction that pushes the airplane forward. When the airplane is moving, this wing is moving in a net direction (a combination of the forward motion of the airplane and the rotary motion of the propeller). For a fixed pitch (propeller inclination to the direction of the airplane), the faster the airplane the steeper is, in effect, the angle of the propeller as it is presented to the air. Eventually the propeller, like a wing tilted too steeply, stalls. If it is angled too close to the direction of flight, to avoid stalling, it produces too little lift (force) along the direction the airplane is flying. To make matters worse, if the propeller is lengthened (to absorb more power) it runs the risk that the area near the blade tips will be moving at supersonic speed, with disruptive effects on the airflow over the rest of the blade. The practical limit for propellers appeared to be about 500 mph, although some turboprop fighters flew considerably faster. It may be that the 500 mph figure combined possible power outputs from piston engines with propeller dynamics.

Because the propeller is moving even when the airplane is at rest, the propeller has a considerable effect as soon as the engine is turned on. Even if it is mounted behind an airplane's wing, the propeller creates an airflow over the wing, which generates lift before the airplane begins to move. (Once it is moving, the airflow created by the airplane's forward movement is soon dominant.) A jet engine has less effect when the airplane is at rest, although it maintains its thrust as the engine moves faster and faster. It is fair to say, therefore, that there are two ways of understanding the phenomenon of lift. One way is to think about the low pressure generated on top of a wing because the air flows more quickly there (Bernoulli's principle). But it is also possible to think about the downward thrust created by a wing as it moves through the air (hence the wing-in-ground effect). If you think that an airplane rises because it creates a downward thrust of air, then you are not too far from seeing a propeller as a generator of thrust. If you think that an airplane is, in effect, sucked upward, then you probably view a propeller as a means of carving a screw path through the sky. Hence you might be more open to the suggestion that a jet turbine can do in a different way just what a propeller does. *But not many engineers thought this way before World War II.*

It is also difficult to compare jet and piston engines directly. Power (e.g., horsepower) is force multiplied by speed. For a jet, the conversion factor is that a pound of thrust equals one horsepower at 375 mph. Thus at that speed an airplane with a five-thousand-pound-thrust engine is developing the equivalent of five thousand horsepower, well beyond what any fighter-grade piston engine could do. On the other hand, the same thrust is equivalent to far less power at low speeds, and carrier aircraft needed power at low speeds if they were given "waveoffs" by landing signal officers.

U.S. engine builders, mainly Allison, Pratt & Whitney, and Wright, concentrated on highly successful piston engines. As abroad, there was no service pressure demanding speeds so great that such engines could not provide them. The jet pioneers abroad had to push very hard on closed doors to get official backing, as Britain's Frank Whittle discovered. Moreover, the main new area of aviation engine development in the United States in the late 1930s was the turbo-supercharger, which made it possible for piston engines to function effectively at high altitudes by compressing the "thin" air. The first such devices were tested during World War I, and their descendants made it possible for aircraft such as the B-17 to fly at unprecedented altitudes, which seemed to offer them near immunity to interception by enemy fighters, though during World War II that did not turn out to be altogether true.

Some aircraft researchers certainly were interested in high-speed flight, but their ideas were generally rejected as visionary. Historians of the jet revolution remark that by the 1930s some aircraft engineers were noticing that each jump in engine power seemed to buy a smaller corresponding jump in maximum aircraft speed. Some limit was approaching. By about 1930, seaplane racers with thin wings and propellers set for very fine pitch (for efficiency at high speed) were exceeding 400 mph. The speed records set at the time were not exceeded for at least a decade, suggesting that propeller planes faced a fundamental limitation in speed. The number of engineers who thought that a new kind of power plant would make possible much higher speeds is not clear. What is clear is that they could not find much—if any—financial support for their research.

The push to faster fighters in the 1938 BuAer competition (which produced the powerful piston-engine F4U Corsair) was explained on the basis of higher performance already being demonstrated in Europe rather than on the abstract value of higher speed in U.S. aircraft. That is, U.S. fighters had to outperform those they might meet, especially those flying from land bases, but there was no particular standard of performance they had to meet and hence no pressure to create reliable turbojets.

Appendix B: The Impact of Jet Aircraft on Carriers

The following table lists the carrier aircraft employed as fighter-bombers or as attack aircraft at the close of World War II and at the beginning of the "jet age."

TABLE B-1
Carrier Fighter-Bomber/Attack Aircraft at the End of World War II

AIRCRAFT	YEAR PROTOTYPE ORDERED	STALL SPEED (KNOTS)
F4U-4 Corsair	1938	66.9
TBM-3 Avenger	1940	63.4
SB2C-5 Helldiver	1939	66.2
F7F-3 Tigercat	1941	74.2
AD-1 Skyraider	1944	76.0
AJ-1 Savage	1946	72.4
F9F-5 Panther	1946	94.0
F7U-3 Cutlass	1946	96.0
A-3B Skywarrior	1949	99.0
A-4C Skyhawk	1952	90.4
A-5A Vigilante	1956	106.0

Sources: Norman Friedman, *Carrier Air Power* (New York: Rutledge, 1981), app. 2; Swanborough and Bowers, *United States Navy Aircraft since 1911*.

The stall speed is an indicator of landing speed because carrier aircraft slowed to nearly stall speed as they touched down on their ship's flight deck. Higher stall speed was significant because the energy generated by the plane on landing is the square of the landing speed. It's this energy that the carrier's arresting gear must absorb. Before World War II, engineers at the Navy's Bureau of Aeronautics thought that 60 knots was the maximum safe landing speed for carrier aircraft. Higher landing speeds, however, were the inevitable and unavoidable consequence of adapting jet aircraft to carriers, and Navy officers procuring jet aircraft knew it. The graph of "stall speed vs. prototype year" makes the relationship clear.

FIGURE B-1
Stall Speed vs. Prototype Year

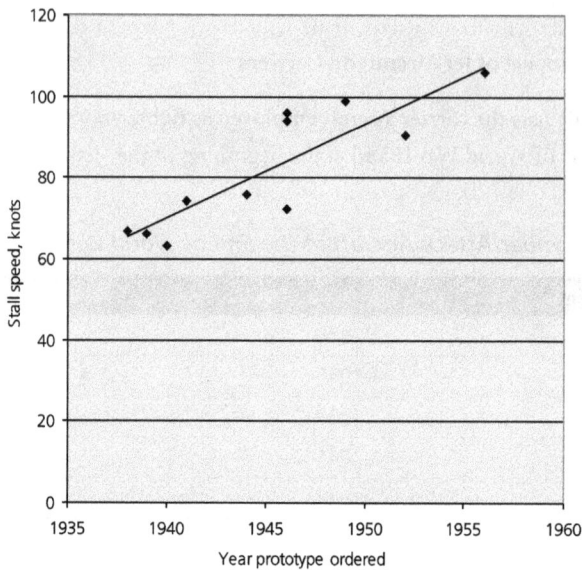

The jets also were heavier than their World War II piston-engine counterparts, as the following table shows.

TABLE B-2
Weight Comparison

AIRCRAFT	YEAR	TAKEOFF WEIGHT (LBS.)	ROLL AT 25 KNOTS WIND OVER DECK	MAXIMUM BOMB LOAD
F4U-4 Corsair	1944	13,597	377 ft.	1,000-lb. bomb
TBM-3 Avenger	1944	16,761	455 ft.	2,000-lb. torpedo
SB2C-5 Helldiver	1945	16,287	584 ft.	2,000-lb. bomb
F7F-3 Tigercat	1945	21,720	495 ft.	2,000-lb. torpedo
AD-1 Skyraider	1945	18,029	455 ft.	Three 2,000-lb. bombs
AJ-1 Savage	1948	49,952	720 ft.	Six 1,600-lb. bombs
F9F-5 Panther	1949	17,766	1,435 ft.	Two 1,000-lb. bombs
F7U-3 Cutlass	1951	28,173	1,650 ft.	Two bombs up to 3,500 lbs. or 32 2.75-inch rockets
A-3B Skywarrior	1955	72,000	1,940 ft.	12,800 lbs.

Source: Friedman, *Carrier Air Power*, app. 2.

The accompanying graphs (of takeoff weight vs. year the aircraft was deployed and then of the roll required at 25 knots "wind over deck" [WOD] vs. the year deployed) are based on the numbers in the preceding chart.

It's true that the first carrier jet fighter—the FH-1 Phantom—was not, at 11,292 lbs., heavier than the World War II F4U Corsair (13,597 lbs.), but the FH-1 did not carry bombs. It was strictly a fighter, and the only advantage it had over the F4U was speed. The next jet fighter, the F2H Banshee, weighed in at 19,602 lbs., and it was heavier than the F4U largely because it had to carry more fuel for its thirstier engines. As in the case of many new types of aircraft of innovative design, the first models often don't outmatch—or outmatch by much—their predecessors. The proper comparison is between the F4U-4 and the F9F-5 Panther. Both were fighter-bombers, but the F9F-5 was both faster than the F4U and able to carry a heavier bomb load.

The table also gives the length of roll required by the aircraft when there was a 25-knot wind blowing over a carrier's deck. As Norman Friedman pointed out in the book from which this information was taken, the long takeoff roll required by the slower-accelerating jets mandated the use of high-capacity catapults. The roll required by the propeller-driven SB2C-5 of 1945 was 584 feet on a carrier deck that did not quite stretch to 900 feet. But the 1,435 feet required by the Panther was simply beyond what wartime or early postwar carrier catapults could provide.

FIGURE B-2
Takeoff Weight vs. Year

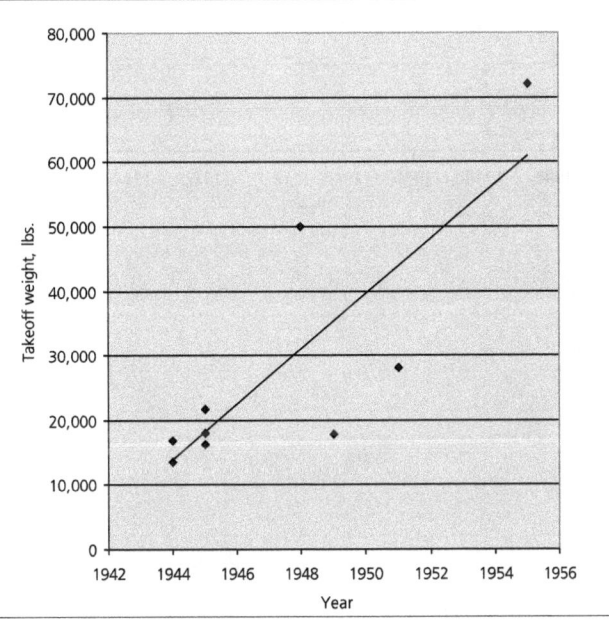

As we've noted, the Navy was aware of the difficulties of operating these heavier jet aircraft. The table that gives the years when BuAer ordered the prototypes shows that the Navy went into the jet age deliberately. Indeed, the Navy had already chosen to adopt larger attack aircraft for its carriers. The F7F Tigercat, powered by twin piston engines and weighing in at over 21,000 lbs., is clear proof of that. The AJ-1, F9F, and F7U were ordered in 1946—before jet engine technology was reliable. All three were analogs to existing fighters and attack aircraft. The F9F was a jet-powered F4U. The F7U was a swept-wing, twin-engine alternative to the F9F. The AJ-1, which was originally designed as a heavy conventional carrier bomber, was modified and rushed into production to prove that the Navy's carriers could conduct nuclear strikes using the heavy and large nuclear implosion weapons.

FIGURE B-3
Roll at 25 Knots WOD vs. Year

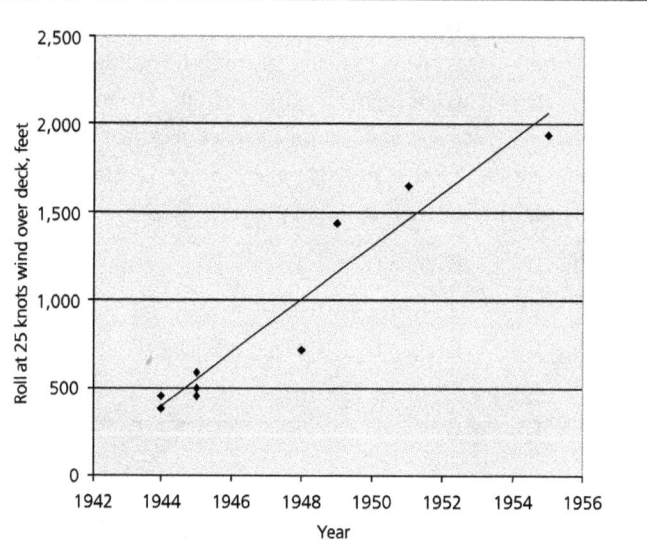

Appendix C: Problem Solving within Bureaucracies

The scholarly literature on organizations assumes that there are certain patterns of behavior common to all complex professional organizations. If so, organizational problems found in one area will probably show up in others. But can the solutions to those problems be the same, or similar? For example, in 1972, in a study done for RAND, counterinsurgency expert Robert W. Komer identified what he called "the inevitable tendency of bureaucracies to keep doing the familiar and to adapt only slowly and incrementally" to changed circumstances.[1] It might seem inappropriate for us to draw on the rich literature on counterinsurgency for insights into our case, but we don't think it is. Komer was an experienced and extraordinary bureaucrat, a perceptive analyst, and a dogged problem solver. As he recognized, "atypical problems demand specially tailored solutions, not just the playing out of existing institutional repertoires."[2]

Did we see that in our study of USN–RN cooperation after World War II? Yes. In effect, the Royal Navy was in the process of reconstructing its air arm even during World War II. Its Fleet Air Arm (FAA) was an institution "under reconstruction" while the Royal Navy was still fighting a war. As a consequence, it was somewhat simpler than it would have been for the Americans—if very demanding in terms of time and energy—for the FAA to start from scratch, so to speak. The RN recognized by 1942 that its prewar carrier aviation program was not meeting wartime challenges. It proceeded from that recognition to positive action with the creation of the Future Building Committee in 1942. As we have pointed out, the way that the FBC proceeded was rather extraordinary. It defined the Fleet Air Arm's future problem, changed Royal Navy fleet doctrine (placing the aircraft carrier at the fleet's center), and set out a "way ahead" that assumed the need for jet aircraft on carriers.

One of Komer's arguments in his 1972 RAND study was that dealing with "atypical" situations requires "setting up autonomous ad hoc organizations to manage specially tailored programs which are not in conventional organizational repertoires."[3] The Future Building Committee was, we think, just such an organization. So was its offspring, the Naval Aircraft Design Committee. Moreover, as Komer well knew, innovative ideas go nowhere if an organization lacks "flexible and imaginative conflict managers at all levels," and this requirement is one that the RN's officers and engineers seemed to meet—from Lewis Boddington and his associates at the Royal Aircraft Establishment to the more senior officers on the Future Building Committee and its postwar successor. This is not to say that the Royal Navy's approach was perfect. It was not, as our case study shows. But it built upon a tradition that Komer said in 1972 was essential if innovation was to take place: "a capability for thorough evaluation and analysis."[4]

That same capability existed in the U.S. Navy. If it had not, U.S. Navy officers would not have embraced the angled flight deck and the mirror landing aid so quickly, and they would have refused to accept HMS *Perseus* as a test bed for the Royal Navy's steam catapult. In the case of the catapult, engineers at the Naval Aircraft Factory thought that they could do what Komer says people working in a bureaucratic setting always do, which is to do more of the same but better. But the resistance to change or to a new idea or piece of equipment can be overcome if competing alternatives can be put to the test. This was done twice in the case of *Perseus*—first at Philadelphia using lower steam pressures and then again, later, at Philadelphia using higher steam pressures.

The tests of the steam catapult on *Perseus* would not have taken place, however, if the U.S. Navy's aviation community had not had a history of rigorously testing aircraft and carrier arresting gear, aircraft crash barriers, and aircraft catapults. We do not think that it was an accident that the U.S. officer in London who promoted the use of *Perseus* as a test platform for the British steam catapult was Rear Adm. Apollo Soucek. Soucek had been a test pilot in the late 1920s and early '30s, and in June 1930 he had established an altitude record for military aircraft of over forty-three thousand feet. He was "air boss" of the carrier *Hornet* in 1942 and served on a special board in the spring of 1943 to revise the cruising instructions of the U.S. Pacific Fleet. The board "exceded [*sic*] its instructions to the extent that all existing Pacific Fleet Tactical Bulletins and numerous Fleet confidential letters in effect, were overhauled and included in the new instructions," giving the Pacific Fleet as a result the new *Tactical Orders and Doctrine* (known as "PAC-10").[5] In short, Soucek was an outstanding officer, and *he understood the need for what Komer called thorough evaluation and analysis*. It is no accident that he did or that he was where he was when a need arose for a new approach to catapulting aircraft from carriers.

At the end of our previous book we cited a 1946 quotation from Adm. Marc A. Mitscher: "Aviation was a relatively new weapon and we learned as we went." After World War II, jet engines made aviation a new weapon yet again, and a lot of learning was required—again. For the U.S. Navy, learning about jets was made all the harder because of the self-imposed requirement to adapt large, nuclear-capable jet bombers to carriers. Meeting this requirement transformed naval aviation. It was an extraordinary achievement—yet one understandable in light of what is known about complex professional organizations.

Notes

1. R. W. Komer, *Bureaucracy Does Its Thing: Institutional Constraints on U.S.-GVN Performance in Vietnam,* RAND Corporation Report R-967-ARPA (Santa Monica, Calif.: RAND, August 1972), p. xii.
2. Ibid.
3. Ibid.
4. Ibid.
5. Pacific Fleet Board to Revise Cruising Instructions, memorandum to Commander in Chief, United States Pacific Fleet, subject "Revision of Pacific Fleet Cruising Instructions," 18 May 1943 (A16-3/P/A17), p. 1, record group 38, "World War Two, Plans, Orders and Related Documents," box 22 (CINCPAC), National Archives.

Appendix D: Chronology

Sources for U.S. Navy dates are U.S. Navy Dept., *United States Naval Aviation, 1910–1980*, NAVAIR 00-80P-1 (Washington, D.C.: Naval Air Systems Command, 1981); Jeffrey G. Barlow, *Revolt of the Admirals: The Fight for Naval Aviation, 1945–1950* (Washington, D.C.: Naval Historical Center, 1994); Norman Friedman, *U.S. Aircraft Carriers: An Illustrated Design History* (Annapolis, Md.: Naval Institute Press, 1983); and Donald D. Engen, *Wings and Warriors: My Life as a Naval Aviator* (Washington, D.C.: Smithsonian Institution Press, 1997).

Sources for Royal Navy dates are Norman Friedman, *British Carrier Aviation* (London: Conway Maritime, 1988); Eric Brown, *Wings on My Sleeve* (London: Orion Books–Phoenix, 2007); and Geoffrey Cooper, *Farnborough and the Fleet Air Arm* (Hersham, Surrey, U.K.: Midland, 2008). RN entries are *italicized*.

1938	*Steam catapult patented in the United Kingdom. In September, the Royal Aircraft Establishment creates a separate Catapult Section, headed by Lewis Boddington.*
Sept. 1940	*Tizard Mission to the United States. The mission brings the cavity magnetron and information on Frank Whittle's jet engine. To further the initial work of the Tizard Mission, the United States and the United Kingdom set up scientific liaison offices in Washington and London.*
Feb. 1942	The chief of the Bureau of Aeronautics approves a decision within BuAer to develop large single-seat attack aircraft.
1942	BuAer contracts with Grumman to build a twin-engine, long-range, large-bomb-load bomber (XTB2F-1) that can operate from *Essex*-class carriers. Its loaded weight is about forty-five thousand pounds.
1942	*The Joint Technical Committee (RN and RAF) draws up new recommendations for naval aircraft. For example, maximum aircraft weight goes from eleven to thirty thousand pounds, and stall speed grows to seventy-five knots.*
Spring 1943	BuAer solicits proposals from industry for large, long-range, single-seat attack aircraft.
Spring 1943	*The RN tests rocket-assisted takeoff gear.*
1943	Navy tests first jet-assisted takeoff units.
1943	*First landing and takeoff of a twin-engine Mosquito on a carrier take place. Approval is given to produce a modified Sea Mosquito.*
Jan. 1944	*Lt. Eric Brown is appointed naval test pilot at Farnborough.*
Sept. 1944	*Admiral Cunningham requests specially modified Mosquitoes from the Chief of the Air Staff (RAF) for use on British aircraft carriers; wants them early in 1945.*
Nov. 1944	PBJ-1H bomber is launched from and recovered back aboard USS *Shangri-La*.

Dec. 1944	The Naval Aircraft Factory develops slotted-cylinder catapult to launch target drones.
Jan. 1945	British test afterburner.
Jan. 11, 1945	Meeting at Farnborough to discuss ways to operate aircraft without undercarriages from carriers. Maj. F. M. Green proposes a "carpet."
Spring 1945	British give an American delegation plans of the M.52 supersonic aircraft. (The British government will cancel the M.52 in February 1946.)
Late spring 1945	BuAer begins studying carrier aircraft capable of carrying eight to twelve thousand pounds of bombs. This is triggered by the results of the U.S. Strategic Bombing Survey, which showed that the twelve-thousand-pound bombs could damage hardened submarine pens.
Summer 1945	Navy's Bureau of Ships begins studying thirty-five-to-fifty-thousand-ton carrier designs. Study completed in April 1946. Recommends 39,600-ton carrier. Ship Characteristics Board created in 1945.
July 1945	SCB recommends a new carrier design with 1945 F7Fs (each weighing twenty-five thousand pounds at takeoff) and thirty-six BT3Ds (each weighing approximately fourteen thousand pounds at takeoff).
July 1945	An informal board reporting to DCNO (Air) endorses report by Capt. W. T. Raisseur that carriers need a radically redesigned flight deck and a new mode of operations.
Aug. 10, 1945	Hornet, a variant of the Mosquito, lands and takes off from HMS Ocean.
Sept. 1945	Engineer Lewis Boddington provides conceptual justification for the angled flight deck.
Oct. 1945	Navy Air Development Research organization proposes to BuAer that BuAer develop turboprop aircraft for bombing from specialized carriers.
Oct. 1945	The Committee to Evaluate the Feasibility of Space Rocketry recommends that the Navy study the possibility of an earth satellite. (BuAer will respond to this recommendation by contracting with three firms and one university for studies of possible launch vehicles and their liquid fuels.)
Dec. 1945	BuAer chief Rear Adm. Harold Sallada tells CNO that carrier aircraft must carry larger bombs and that BuAer had options for new aircraft based on combined propeller and jet-turbine propulsion. Sallada recommends development of a new bomber with a gross weight of forty-one thousand pounds and a landing weight of twenty-eight thousand pounds. (This proposed design will become the AJ-1 Savage.) CNO approves the program.
Dec. 1945	First jet takeoff from and landing on a Royal Navy carrier. This is only a demonstration. There are no operational RN jet carrier squadrons.
Jan. 1946	Vice Adm. Marc Mitscher, DCNO (Air), recommends that CNO approve the development of hundred-thousand-pound bombers.
1946	Admiralty decides to adopt slotted-cylinder catapults. (In 1942, the RN had used catapults that were compatible with USN aircraft being procured through Lend-Lease.)
Feb. 1946	CNO directs DCNO (Air), Vice Adm. Arthur W. Radford, to begin detailed design study of the hundred-thousand-pound bomber. (The weight and size of this aircraft will drive the Navy away from the first postwar carrier design and toward a very large ship—what will become United States.)
Feb. 1946	BuAer technical divisions are aligned into two groups: Research, Development and Engineering; and Material and Services.
March 1946	The Secretary of the Navy approves converting two submarines into air-breathing guided-missile carriers and launchers.

March 1946	The Chief of Naval Operations directs BuAer to adopt ground-controlled approach equipment for landing aircraft in poor visibility.
Spring 1946	BuShips uses BuAer's hundred-thousand-pound (gross weight) design study ADR-42 in working out the characteristics of a new, large carrier. Study completed in May 1946. (Friedman notes that the preliminary characteristics were reviewed by the Ship Characteristics Board in June 1946.)
April 1946	Contract issued to Douglas Aircraft for the design and construction of the night fighter XF3D-1.
June 1946	North American Aviation is given a contract for the design and construction of three XAJ-1 aircraft (a long-range bomber able to carry nuclear weapons).
June 1946	Investigation begins of the suitability of jet aircraft for carrier use at the Naval Air Test Center at Patuxent River, with the Navy pilots using a P-80A.
July 1946	First tests of jets on carriers take place. An FD-1 lands on and takes off from carrier *Franklin D. Roosevelt* on July 21.
July 1946	DCNO (Air) recommends to the Vice Chief of Naval Operations that the new carrier not be included in the 1948 shipbuilding program but be funded as a design study.
Sept. 1946	DCNO (Air) is organized into four groups—Plans, Personnel, Readiness, and Air Logistics. An Air Planning Group is also established. This reorganization reflects the shift of aviation policy to the Office of the Chief of Naval Operations.
Oct. 1946	Naval Air Missile Test Center, Point Mugu, California, is established.
Oct. 1946	First live test of a pilot ejection seat is conducted.
Oct. 1946	Development of XF9F-1 four-engine night fighter is halted. BuAer decides to develop the XF9F-2 instead. (To get this plane, BuAer will substitute the Rolls-Royce Nene engine for Westinghouse 24Cs. Later, U.S. firms will produce the Nene engine.)
Nov. 1946	Responsibility for guided-missile development is assigned to a newly created Office of the Assistant Chief of Naval Operations (Guided Missiles).
Nov. 1946	A P-80A, piloted by a Marine, makes two catapult launches, four free takeoffs, and five arrested landings on carrier *Franklin D. Roosevelt*. This is part of the series of tests run at Patuxent River starting at the end of June 1946.
Feb. 1947	SCB produces first preliminary characteristics for a new carrier.
Feb. 1947	A surfaced submarine fires a Loon guided missile for the first time.
March 1947	*Serious work on the flexible deck begins at RAE, Farnborough.*
June 1947	CNO approves the characteristics for a carrier improvement program called "Project 27A." This is the first modification of the *Essex*-class ships. The modifications are designed to enable the carriers to launch and recover jets, which requires blast deflectors, more fuel, and jet fuel mixers. *Oriskany*, the first ship so modernized, begins conversion in October 1947.
June 1947	BuAer awards contract to Douglas Aircraft for a study of a delta-winged fighter. (This study will lead to the XF4D-1.)
June 1947	BuAer awards contract to Chance Vought for development and construction of three XF7U-1 aircraft. (This plane will later be produced as the Cutlass.)
July 1947	Adm. Robert Carney, senior member of SCB, tells General Board that *Essex*-class carriers must be modernized and that the new carrier (with flush deck) must be in the fiscal year (FY) 1949 Navy program. (It will be.)

Aug. 1947	BuAer establishes an organization to develop guided missiles and aircraft electronics.
Sept. 18, 1947	Executive Order 9877 defines the roles and missions of the newly created U.S. Air Force. The National Security Act of 1947, which created the USAF, had been signed by President Truman on July 26, 1947.
Sept. 1947	CNO approves new carrier characteristics.
Oct. 1947	*Tests of operational Attacker jet fighter on HMS* Illustrious *occur.*
Dec. 1947	The President's Air Policy Commission, headed by Thomas Finletter, submits its report.
Dec. 1947	*First landing of a jet fighter on the flexible deck at Farnborough takes place.*
1948	*British Admiralty adopts a nine-year fleet modernization plan. Plans for a test unit steam catapult are completed.*
March 1948	Test Pilot Training Division is set up at the Naval Air Test Center, Patuxent River.
March 1948	Carrier suitability of the FJ-1 Fury is tested on carrier *Boxer* with landings and takeoffs.
April 1948	Two P2V-2 Neptunes make JATO takeoffs from the carrier *Coral Sea.*
May 1948	The Navy establishes first carrier-qualified jet squadron (using FH-1 Phantoms).
May 1948	DCNO (Air) presents new carrier design to the Joint Chiefs of Staff. The USAF Chief of Staff objects. The Navy defends new ("6A") design as a prototype.
May 1948	The Michelson Laboratory for rocket and guided-missile research at Naval Ordnance Test Station, China Lake, opens.
June 1948	*First landing and takeoff of a twin-jet Meteor on HMS* Implacable *take place.*
June 1948	Meetings of the Quarterly Air Board (DCNO [Air], BuAer, and the Commanders, Air Forces Atlantic and Pacific) begin.
June 1948	Congress authorizes construction of large (6A) carrier in the FY 1949 program.
June 1948	BuShips initiates development of the TACAN (Tactical Air Navigation) system for carriers.
July 1948	The first carrier-based AEW squadrons (VAW-1 and VAW-2) are commissioned. (They will organize and train future AEW squadrons.)
July 1948	Construction of carrier *United States* is approved by President Truman.
Aug. 1948	Aeronautical Board is dissolved.
Sept. 1948	*First "navalized" Sea Hawk jet flies. (Deck trials are in May 1949, but no production aircraft will enter the fleet until the end of 1951.)*
Nov. 1948	The Naval Aircraft Factory begins work on the design of the Mark 7 high-energy-absorbing arresting gear (to capture planes weighing up to fifty thousand pounds and landing at speeds as high as 105 knots).
Nov. 1948	The Office of Naval Intelligence informs General Board that the Royal Navy is "well advanced" in experimenting with a "flexible, rubber and pneumatic" flight deck for carriers.
Nov. 1948	*First sea trials of flexible deck with a prototype Vampire take place.*
Nov. 1948	*Representatives of the RN visit BuShips and BuAer in Washington. They obtain a full set of deck plans for CVA 58* (United States) *and detailed drawings of USS* Midway. *They also get information on the slotted-tube catapult for CVA 58 and detailed information about arresting gear being developed by the USN.*

March 1949	A P2V-3C is launched from carrier *Coral Sea* with a ten-thousand-pound load. It flies across the country, drops its load, and then returns to Patuxent River.
April 1949	Secretary of Defense Louis Johnson cancels the carrier *United States*.
Feb. 1950	A P2V-3C Neptune makes a 5,060-mile flight after being launched from a carrier.
March 1950	The staff of DCNO (Air) informs General Board that the critical factor in the modernization of the *Essex*-class carriers is the catapult.
April 1950	First carrier takeoff of the AJ-1 occurs, made from *Coral Sea* by Capt. J. T. Hayward.
April 1950	A P2V-3C, weighing 74,668 pounds, takes off from *Coral Sea*.
July 1950	Navy pilots fly F9F Panthers from the carrier *Valley Forge* off Korea.
1950	*NATO navies agree on a standard form of jet fuel.*
Aug. 1950	The first squadron of AJ-1 Savage bombers qualifies on *Coral Sea*.
Oct. 1950	DCNO (Air) tells General Board that any new carrier must have a flush deck.
Feb. 1951	The first heavy attack wing is commissioned at Norfolk.
March 1951	First test of ramjet Talos long-range antiaircraft missile is conducted.
March 1951	BuAer contracts with Convair for the propeller-driven vertical takeoff fighter XFY-1. Three weeks later, BuAer orders an alternate design from Lockheed.
April 1951	First Navy use of a jet fighter as a bomber takes place off Korea.
April 12, 1951	Langley Aeronautical Laboratory recommends "hydraulic jet catapult" to BuAer for an aircraft with a gross weight of a hundred thousand pounds.
June 1951	BuAer issues a contract to Convair for development of delta-winged, hydro-ski seaplane fighter.
June 27, 1951	*The Admiralty offers to send HMS* Perseus *to the United States.*
July 1, 1951	The Naval Air Turbine Test Station is established at Trenton, N.J.
July 14, 1951	CNO accepts the Admiralty offer of a visit by HMS *Perseus*.
July 27, 1951	Rear Admiral Soucek, the naval air attaché, sends memorandum from London to CNO via Office of Naval Intelligence detailing results of a visit to *Perseus* by two USN captains.
Aug. 1951	*Angled-deck concept presented at a Ministry of Supply conference by Capt. Dennis Cambell. Lt. Cdr. Nick Goodhart, Cambell's assistant, conceives of a landing-light system.*
Aug. 24, 1951	Preliminary discussions among representatives of BuAer, the Royal Navy, and OPNAV regarding the trip of *Perseus* to the United States.
Aug. 28, 1951	Adm. Sir Cyril Douglas-Pennant, RN, corresponds with CNO regarding the visit of *Perseus*.
Sept. 7, 1951	A Terrier surface-to-air missile (SAM) fired from test ship *Norton Sound* intercepts target drone.
Sept. 27, 1951	Chief, BuAer makes *Perseus* visit a priority one.
Oct. 12, 1951	Work gets under way to accommodate *Perseus* at Philadelphia Naval Shipyard.
Oct. 15, 1951	The shipyard at Philadelphia conducts catapult tests on the World War II escort carrier *Block Island*. Because these could conflict with tests on *Perseus,* the shipyard decides to put the *Perseus* tests ahead of those on *Block Island*. The shipyard promises to have the dead loads ready by November 15, 1951.
Dec. 1951	First test assembly of nuclear warheads on a carrier at sea takes place.

Dec. 3, 1951	British Joint Services Mission–Air establishes an office inside the Main Navy Building on Constitution Avenue. The mission plans tests of *Perseus* at both Philadelphia and Norfolk. (*Perseus* had been launching jets at five-minute intervals, but the target for launches at Philadelphia is thirty seconds.)
Dec. 6, 1951	Schedules place *Perseus* in United States from mid-January to March. *Perseus* will visit Philadelphia first and then Norfolk.
End of 1951– early 1952	*Eric Brown promotes idea of angled deck while serving as an exchange pilot with Flight Test Division at Naval Air Station Patuxent River, Maryland.*
Dec. 13, 1951	A CNO letter establishes responsibilities of "interested commands" for the *Perseus* visit.
Jan.–Mar. 1952	A British-developed steam catapult is tested at the Philadelphia Navy Yard, at Norfolk, and then again (with six-hundred-pound steam) at Philadelphia. A U.S. aircraft is launched from HMS *Perseus*.
Jan. 8, 1952	Capt. Sheldon W. Brown of BuAer compares U.S. and RN catapults for Rear Adm. Lucien M. Grant, USN.
Feb. 1952	CNO approves a modification of the "Project 27A" carrier conversion program to give each ship more powerful arresting gear, better catapults, and a deck-edge elevator in place of its number-three centerline elevator. (Three *Essex*-class conversions will be completed in 1954—Project 27C, axial deck.)
Feb. 12, 1952	W. W. Ford of the Naval Aircraft Factory/NAMC writes to Ships Installation Division of BuAer (headed by Capt. Sheldon Brown), asking whether BuAer wants the British steam catapult for the 27C conversion instead of the U.S.-developed C10 (powered by a powder charge).
Feb. 1952	*Eric Brown flies an F9F Panther from anchored* Perseus *in Philadelphia Navy Yard.*
Feb. 14, 1952	BuShips says steam catapult will work structurally in CV 9 and CVB 41 conversions, and also in CVB 59 (*Forrestal*).
Feb. 15, 1952	First BuShips steam catapult conference is held.
Feb. 20, 1952	Second BuShips steam catapult conference is held.
Feb. 20, 1952	Tests of *Perseus* are made part of a program called TED NAM SI 330.0, established under a BuAer confidential letter of September 27, 1951.
Feb. 21, 1952	DCNO (Air) extends *Perseus*'s visit schedule to permit additional tests.
1952	*HMS Eagle's arresting gear takes a twenty-thousand-pound aircraft landing at ninety-two knots. (Compare this with the standard set by the Joint Technical Committee at the end of 1942.)*
March 19, 1952	Chief, BuShips notes successful conclusion of "an extremely high priority Chief of Naval Operations directed project." This is the test of the steam catapult on *Perseus*.
March 26, 1952	Commander in Chief, U.S. Atlantic Fleet asks in a letter to CNO whether the British steam catapult will be installed in USN carriers.
April 1952	The USN announces that the steam catapult will be adopted, with the first installation on *Hancock*.
May 1952	Tests of a simulated angled deck on carrier *Midway*.
June 25, 1952	Capt. Sheldon Brown arranges a July trip to Brown Bros. in Scotland (the builders of the British steam catapult) and asks for data from the firm.
July 1952	Keel of carrier *Forrestal* is laid.
Aug. 8, 1952	U.S. embassy in London asks Brown Bros. to forward catapult drawings to BuAer directly rather than through NAMC.
Sept. 3, 1952	First test of fully configured Sidewinder air-to-air missile takes place.

Dec. 1952	An air-breathing Regulus missile is launched successfully from a ship at sea and guided to a safe landing ashore.
Jan. 1953	Landing and takeoff tests are conducted on board the first angled-deck carrier, *Antietam*.
Mar. 1953	*Tunny* (SSG 284) is outfitted to launch Regulus surface-to-surface missiles. (The first successful live firing will be held on July 15, 1953.)
April 1953	The first flight of XF2Y-1 experimental jet seaplane fighter occurs.
June 1953	*Antietam*'s pilots demonstrate angled-deck landings to the RN in the English Channel. RN jets also participate. (Engen)
Aug. 1953	The first successful shipboard launching of Terrier SAM against a target drone occurs.
Aug. 1953	The D558-2 Douglas Skyrocket sets a new altitude record.
Sept. 1953	A plan is promulgated officially to covert the *Midways* to an angled-deck configuration. But they will have modified C11 steam catapults in the angled-deck area.
Sept. 1953	The first successful interception of a drone by Sidewinder air-to-air missile takes place.
Nov. 1953	USN pilots land jets on HMS *Illustrious* in the United Kingdom.
Dec. 1953	The Steam Catapult Facility at Philadelphia is commissioned.
May 1954	CNO approves Project 125 to install angled decks and enclosed bows on the carriers that had been modernized under Project 27A.
1954	*The landing light (or mirror) system is tested on HMS* Albion.
June 1954	Initial at-sea tests of C11 steam catapult on carrier *Hancock*.
June 1954	The Naval Air Development and Material Center is established at Johnsville, Pennsylvania.
Aug.–Nov. 1954	Tests of the vertical-takeoff-and-landing XFY-1 delta-wing experimental fighter.
July 1955	The P6M SeaMaster jet seaplane bomber makes its first flight.
Aug. 1955	VX-3 successfully tests the mirror landing system on *Bennington*.
Sept. 1955	Guided Missile groups 1 and 2 are commissioned to train detachments to launch Regulus missiles from aircraft carriers, cruisers, and submarines.
Oct. 1955	USS *Forrestal* (CVA 59) is commissioned.
Nov. 1955	CNO decides to equip each angled-deck carrier with a mirror landing system.

Bibliography

BOOKS

Barlow, Jeffrey G. *From Hot War to Cold: The U.S. Navy and National Security Affairs, 1945–1955*. Stanford, Calif.: Stanford Univ. Press, 2009.

———. *Revolt of the Admirals: The Fight for Naval Aviation, 1945–1950*. Washington, D.C.: Naval Historical Center, 1994.

Beaver, Paul. *The British Aircraft Carrier*. Cambridge, U.K.: Patrick Stephens, 1983.

Borowski, Harry R., ed. *Military Planning in the Twentieth Century*. Washington, D.C.: U.S. Government Printing Office, 1986.

Brown, Eric. *Wings on My Sleeve*. London: Orion Books–Phoenix, 2007.

Christman, Albert B. *Target Hiroshima: Deak Parsons and the Creation of the Atomic Bomb*. Annapolis, Md.: Naval Institute Press, 1998.

Connery, Robert H. *The Navy and Industrial Mobilization in World War II*. Princeton, N.J.: Princeton Univ. Press, 1951.

Constant, Edward W., II. *The Origins of the Turbojet Revolution*. Baltimore: Johns Hopkins Univ. Press, 1980.

Cooper, Geoffrey. *Farnborough and the Fleet Air Arm*. Hersham, Surrey, U.K.: Midland, 2008.

Cressman, Robert J. *USS Ranger: The Navy's First Flattop from Keel to Mast, 1934–1946*. Washington, D.C.: Brassey's, 2003.

Davis, Vincent. *Postwar Defense Policy and the U.S. Navy, 1943–1946*. Chapel Hill: Univ. of North Carolina Press, 1962.

Engen, Donald D. *Wings and Warriors: My Life as a Naval Aviator*. Washington, D.C.: Smithsonian Institution Press, 1997.

Friedman, Norman. *British Carrier Aviation: The Evolution of the Ships and Their Aircraft*. London: Conway Maritime, 1988.

———. *The Fifty-Year War: Conflict and Strategy in the Cold War*. Annapolis, Md.: Naval Institute Press, 2000.

———. *Network-centric Warfare: How Navies Learned to Fight Smarter through Three World Wars*. Annapolis, Md.: Naval Institute Press, 2009.

———. *The Postwar Naval Revolution*. Annapolis, Md.: Naval Institute Press, 1986.

———. *U.S. Aircraft Carriers: An Illustrated Design History*. Annapolis, Md.: Naval Institute Press, 1983.

———. *U.S. Naval Weapons*. Annapolis, Md.: Naval Institute Press, 1982.

Furer, Julius A. *Administration of the Navy Department in World War II*. Washington, D.C.: U.S. Government Printing Office, 1959.

Gillcrist, Paul T. *Feet Wet: Reflections of a Carrier Pilot*. New York: Presidio, 1990.

Gompert, David, Richard Kugler, and Martin Libicki. *Mind the Gap: Promoting a Transatlantic Revolution in Military Affairs*. Washington, D.C.: National Defense Univ. Press, 1999.

Gordon, G. A. H. *British Seapower and Procurement between the Wars*. Annapolis, Md.: Naval Institute Press, 1988.

Green, William, and Roy Cross. *The Jet Aircraft of the World*. New York: Hanover House, 1956.

Grossnick, Roy A. *United States Naval Aviation, 1910–1995*. 4th ed. Washington, D.C.: Naval Historical Center, 1997.

Guinn, Gilbert, and G. H. Bennett. *British Naval Aviation in World War II: The US Navy and Anglo-American Relations*. London: Tauris Academic Studies, 2007.

Hayward, John T., and C. W. Borklund. *Bluejacket Admiral: The Navy Career of Chick Hayward*. Annapolis, Md., and Newport, R.I.: Naval Institute Press and Naval War College Foundation, 2000.

Heinemann, Edward H., and Rosario Rausa. *Ed Heinemann, Combat Aircraft Designer*. Annapolis, Md.: Naval Institute Press, 1980.

Holley, Irving B. *Buying Aircraft: Materiel Procurement for the Army Air Forces*.

Washington, D.C.: Office of the Chief of Military History, U.S. Army, 1964.

Holloway, James L., III. *Aircraft Carriers at War.* Annapolis, Md.: Naval Institute Press, 2007.

Hone, Thomas C., Norman Friedman, and Mark D. Mandeles. *American & British Aircraft Carrier Development, 1919–1941.* Annapolis, Md.: Naval Institute Press, 1999.

Isenberg, Michael T. *Shield of the Republic.* Vol. 1, *1945–1962.* New York: St. Martin's, 1993.

Jones, Glyn. *The Jet Pioneers: The Birth of Jet-Powered Flight.* London: Methuen, 1989.

Jones, Lloyd S. *U.S. Naval Fighters.* Fallbrook, Calif.: Aero, 1977.

Knaack, Marcelle Size. *Encyclopedia of U.S. Air Force Aircraft and Missile Systems.* Vol. 1, *Post–World War II Fighters, 1945–1973.* Washington, D.C.: Office of Air Force History, 1978.

Lamb, J. Parker. *Evolution of the American Diesel Locomotive.* Bloomington: Indiana Univ. Press, 2007.

Latham, Neil. *Defense Industry in a Global Context: Policy Implications for the United Kingdom.* Whitehall Paper 57. London: RUSI, n.d.

Love, Robert W., Jr. *History of the U.S. Navy, 1942–1991.* Harrisburg, Pa.: Stackpole Books, 1992.

Mandeles, Mark D. *The Development of the B-52 and Jet Propulsion: A Case Study in Organizational Innovation.* Maxwell Air Force Base, Ala.: Air Univ. Press, 1998.

Melhorn, Charles M. *Two-Block Fox: The Rise of the Aircraft Carrier, 1911–1929.* Annapolis, Md.: Naval Institute Press, 1974.

Mersky, Peter B., ed. *From the Flight Deck: An Anthology of the Best Writing on Carrier Warfare.* Washington, D.C.: Brassey's, 2003.

Miller, Jerry. *Nuclear Weapons and Aircraft Carriers: How the Bomb Saved Naval Aviation.* Washington, D.C.: Smithsonian Institution Press, 2001.

Miller, John Anderson. *Men and Volts at War: The Story of General Electric in World War II.* New York: McGraw-Hill, 1947.

Milward, Alan. *War, Economy and Society, 1939–1945.* Berkeley: Univ. of California Press, 1977.

Muir, Malcolm, Jr. *Black Shoes and Blue Water: Surface Warfare in the United States Navy, 1945–1975.* Washington, D.C.: Naval Historical Center, 1996.

Piet, Stan, and Al Raithel. *Martin P6M SeaMaster.* Bel Air, Md.: Martineer, 2001.

Reynolds, Clark G. *Admiral John H. Towers: The Struggle for Naval Air Supremacy.* Annapolis, Md.: Naval Institute Press, 1991.

———. *The Fast Carriers.* Annapolis, Md.: Naval Institute Press, 1992.

Roskill, Stephen. *Churchill and the Admirals.* London: William Collins, 1977.

———. *Naval Policy between the Wars.* Vol. 1. New York: Walker, 1968.

Rowland, Buford, and William Boyd. *U.S. Navy Bureau of Ordnance in World War II.* Washington, D.C.: U.S. Navy Dept., Bureau of Ordnance, 1953.

Schlaifer, Robert. *Development of Aircraft Engines.* Boston: Graduate School of Business Administration, Harvard University, 1950.

Simpson, Michael, ed. *The Cunningham Papers.* Vol. 2. London: Ashgate and the Navy Records Society, 2006.

Skiera, Joseph A., ed. *Aircraft Carriers in Peace and War.* New York: Franklin Watts, 1965.

Swanborough, Gordon, and Peter M. Bowers. *United States Navy Aircraft since 1911.* Annapolis, Md.: Naval Institute Press, 1976.

Taylor, H. A. *Fairey Aircraft since 1915.* Annapolis, Md.: Naval Institute Press, 1974.

Taylor, Theodore. *The Magnificent Mitscher.* New York: W. W. Norton, 1954.

Thomason, Tommy H. *Strike from the Sea: U.S. Navy Attack Aircraft from Skyraider to Super Hornet, 1948–Present.* North Branch, Minn.: Specialty, 2009.

———. *U.S. Naval Air Superiority: Development of Shipborne Jet Fighters, 1943–1962.* North Branch, Minn.: Specialty, 2007.

Till, Geoffrey. *Air Power and the Royal Navy, 1914–1945.* London: Jane's, 1979.

Trimble, William F. *Wings for the Navy: A History of the Naval Aircraft Factory, 1917–1956.* Annapolis, Md.: Naval Institute Press, 1990.

von Kármán, Theodore, with Lee Edson. *The Wind and Beyond.* Boston: Little, Brown, 1967.

Wagner, Ray. *American Combat Planes.* 3rd ed. New York: Doubleday, 1982.

Wood, James B. *Japanese Military Strategy in the Pacific War: Was Defeat Inevitable?* New York: Rowman & Littlefield, 2007.

Woodbury, David O. *Battlefronts of Industry: Westinghouse in World War II.* New York: Wiley, 1948.

Wooldridge, E. T., ed. *Into the Jet Age: Conflict and Change in Naval Aviation, 1945–1975.* Annapolis, Md.: Naval Institute Press, 1995.

Zichek, Jared A. *The Boeing XF8B-1 Fighter: Last of the Line.* Atglen, Pa.: Schiffer, 2007.

———. *Secret Aerospace Projects of the U.S. Navy: The Incredible Attack Aircraft of the USS United States, 1948–1949.* Atglen, Pa.: Schiffer, 2009.

Zimmerman, David. *Top Secret Exchange: The Tizard Mission and the Scientific War.* Montreal: McGill–Queen's University Press and Alan Sutton, 1996.

ARTICLES

"Annotated Bumblebee Initial Report." February 1945. Repr. *Johns Hopkins APL Technical Digest* 3, no. 2 (1982).

Brown, Eric. "Dawn of the Carrier Jet." *Air International* 28, no. 1 (January 1985).

Ellner, Andrea. "Carrier Airpower in the Royal Navy during the Cold War: The International Strategic Context." *Defense & Security Analysis* 22, no. 1 (March 2006).

"From David to Brown." *Naval Aviation News* (February 1954).

Hill, Richard. "British Naval Thinking in the Nuclear Age." In *The Development of British Naval Thinking,* edited by Geoffrey Till. London: Routledge, 2006.

Hobbs, David. "Naval Aviation, 1930–2000." In *The Royal Navy, 1930–2000: Innovation and Defence,* edited by Richard Harding. London: Frank Cass, 2005.

Hone, Thomas C., Norman Friedman, and Mark D. Mandeles. "The Development of the Angled-Deck Aircraft Carrier." *Naval War College Review* 64, no. 2 (Spring 2011).

"It's Done with Mirrors." *Naval Aviation News* (November 1955).

Jacobs, Jan. "Follow the Bouncing Cougar: The Flexdeck Program." *Hook* 12, no. 1 (Spring 1984).

Kennedy, Paul. "History from the Middle: The Case of the Second World War." *Journal of Military History* 74, no. 1 (January 2010).

MacDonald, Scott. "Summing Up: The Turbulent Postwar Years." In *Aircraft Carriers in Peace and War,* edited by Joseph A. Skiera. New York: Franklin Watts, 1965.

Moore, John. "The Wrong Stuff: Flying on the Edge of Disaster." In *From the Flight Deck: An Anthology of the Best Writing on Carrier Warfare,* edited by Peter B. Mersky. Washington, D.C.: Brassey's, 2003.

Pirie, Robert B. "1958: The Transition Year." In *Into the Jet Age: Conflict and Change in Naval Aviation, 1945–1975,* edited by E. T. Wooldridge. Annapolis, Md.: Naval Institute Press, 1995.

Ramage, James D. "Taking A-Bombs to Sea." *Naval History* 9, no. 1 (January/February 1995).

Rubel, Robert C. "The U.S. Navy's Transition to Jets." *Naval War College Review* 63, no. 2 (Spring 2010).

Scarborough, William E. "The North American AJ Savage, Part One: Establishing the Heavy Attack Mission." *Hook* (Fall 1989).

Weitzenfeld, D. K. "Colin Mitchell's Steam Catapult: The Heart of Modern Aircraft Carriers." *Wings of Gold* 10 (Summer 1985).

MANUSCRIPTS AND ORAL HISTORIES

Cambell, Rear Adm. Dennis R. F. "The Angled Deck Story (DRFC's Own Account)." *Rear Admiral Dennis Royle Farquharson Cambell, C.B., D.S.C.* March 2008. www.denniscambell.org.uk.

History Unit, DCNO (Air). "Aviation Procurement, 1939–1945, Part II." *Monographs in the History of Naval Aviation* 19 (1946).

Pride, Adm. Alfred M. "Oral History" no. 84. Naval Historical Collection, Naval War College, Newport, R.I.

Ramage, James D. "The Atom Bomb and the Fast Carrier Task Force." Junior thesis, Naval War College, (May 1947). Record group 13. Naval War College Naval Historical Collection.

Spangenberg, George A. "Oral History." 31 August 1997. *George Spangenberg Oral History.* 2010. www.georgespangenberg.com.

Wylie, Joseph C., Jr. "The Reminiscences of Rear Admiral Joseph C. Wylie, Jr." Annapolis, Md.: U.S. Naval Institute Press, 2003.

About the Authors

Dr. Thomas C. Hone is a retired professor at the Center for Naval Warfare Studies in the Naval War College. He is a former senior executive in the Office of the Secretary of Defense and was a special assistant to the Commander, Naval Air Systems Command. His awards include the Navy Meritorious Civilian Service Medal and the U.S. Air Force Exceptional Civilian Service Award. With his son Trent, he wrote *Battle Line: The United States Navy, 1919–1939*.

Dr. Norman Friedman has written more than thirty-five books on naval and national security subjects, including *U.S. Aircraft Carriers: An Illustrated Design History*, *British Carrier Aviation*, and *Carrier Air Power*. He was awarded the Westminster Medal of the Royal United Services Institute for his *The Fifty-Year War: Conflict and Strategy in the Cold War*. His most recent books are *Network-centric Warfare: How Navies Learned to Fight Smarter through Three World Wars* (2009) and *Unmanned Combat Air Systems: A New Kind of Carrier Aviation* (2010). He contributes a monthly column on world naval developments to the U.S. Naval Institute *Proceedings*, and he has written numerous articles for journals worldwide.

Dr. Mark D. Mandeles is founder and president of The J. de Bloch Group, an independent consulting company. He has served as a consultant to the U.S. Joint Forces Command (JFCOM), to the director of the Office of Net Assessment in the Office of the Secretary of Defense, to the Under Secretary of Defense for Policy, and to other Defense Department agencies and private industry. He is the author of *The Development of the B-52 and Jet Propulsion*, *The Future of War: Organizations as Weapons*, and *Military Transformation Past and Present: Historical Lessons for the 21st Century*.

Index

Numbers in bold indicate pages with illustrations

A

A3D/A-3B Skywarrior
- catapult capacity to launch, 99, 100, 103, 108
- characteristics, 177, 178
- on *Forrestal,* **108**
- nuclear weapon delivery by, 99, 139, 163–64
- priority for production of, 108

A3J/A-5A Vigilante, 164, 177

A4D/A-4C Skyhawk, 163–64, 177

A-20A Havoc, 26, 27

AD-1/AD-2 Skyraider
- characteristics, 177, 178
- design and development of, 15, 30, 31, 42
- effectiveness of, 139
- launch and recovery of, 102, 132
- nuclear weapon delivery by, 132–33, 152nn35–36
- photo of on carrier deck, 74, 75, 115
- weight of, 164

aerial strike doctrine, 17

Aeronautical Board, 15–16

airborne aircraft carriers, 136, 158

aircraft
- accidents with, 50, 92, 168, 170, 171n31
- characteristics of and utility of aircraft carriers, 6
- design competitions, 11, 12–15, 17, 18–20, 30
- design of around engines, 11, 31–32, 53, 65, 136
- design of for specific missions, 169–70
- development of, 5, 12–15, 100–101, 182
- exchange of information about, 50–51
- modifications to existing, 23–25
- number of for World War II, 16, 17, 138
- performance improvement of, 13, 14, 15, 21n6
- procurement process, 11, 25
- production of for allies, 3–4, 57
- quantity vs. quality conflict, 23–24, 32nn3–4
- R&D, 16, 23–28, 30–32
- simulations and fleet exercises and design of, 12, 15
- supersonic flight capabilities, 7
- testing of, 139, 182
- unassisted launch of, 101
- *See also* bombers; fighter aircraft; jet aircraft; piston engines and propeller-driven aircraft

aircraft carriers
- aircraft characteristics and utility of, 6
- boilers on and steam temperatures and pressures, 48–49, 114–15, 117–18
- carrier battles, lessons learned from, 42, 75, 134
- carrier-controlled approach (CCA) system, 79
- carrier forces, size and resources of, 65, 67n37, 70–71, 84–85
- construction program for USN, 2
- defense of, 5
- demobilization after World War II, 69

aircraft carriers *(continued)*
    design and development of, 74–77, 134–35, 157–64
    design responsibilities, 5
    exchange of information between USN and RN about, 50–51, 167
    fires aboard, 170, 171n34
    future carriers, committee to discuss, 41–42
    hangar decks and open hangar configuration, 49, 141, 158–59, 163
    jet aircraft, mating of to, 145–46
    land-based bombers, use of carriers against, 45
    modernization of RN carriers, 49–50, 141–42
    modifications to, 6, 134–35, 158–59
    size of, 27, 28
    strategic bombing operations from, 40–41, 71
    strike potential, 17
    technological developments and design of, 78–82
    USN as leader in, 163
    vulnerability of, 28, 35
    weight of aircraft and launch and recovery capabilities, 27, 33n21
    See also angled flight deck; flexible deck/carpet deck; flight decks

aircraft industry and manufacturers
    British aircraft industry, 65, 140, 141
    as BuAer suppliers, 11
    combat operations, observation of by, 38–39
    contacts between BuAer personnel and, 25, 31, 38, 39, 67n23, 161
    contract negotiations with industry, 67n19
    design competitions, 11, 12–15, 17, 18–20, 30
    output cuts from, 4
    procurement of aircraft from, 11, 12–15
    role of in innovations, 2
    superiority of US industry, 65, 140

Air Force, U.S. (USAF)
    flexible deck, interest in, 93–94
    jet engines for aircraft used by, 64
    military aviation, disputes about role and organization of, 4, 71, 72–73
    nuclear weapon delivery by, 41, 129

airlines and airliners, 57

AJ-1 Savage
    catapult capacity to launch, 99, 103
    characteristics, 177, 178
    design and development of, 99, 158–59
    launch and recovery of, 78, 79, 83
    nuclear weapon delivery by, 77, 99, 128–33, 139, 152n35, 180
    photo of on carrier deck, 77
    replacement of, 139
    XAJ mock-up, 130–31, 134, 138

Allis-Chalmers
    contract negotiations with industry, 67n19
    J-36 engine, 63
    jet engine development, 58–59

Allison engines, 60, 64, 174

AM-1 Mauler, 30

American & British Aircraft Carrier Development, 1919–1941, 1, 65, 148, 168, 170

American Locomotive Company (ALCO), 54–55

Anderson, George, 16

angled flight deck
    adoption of, 8, 73–74, **108**, 124, 149, 160, 182
    conceptual justification for, 47
    development and testing of, xiii–xiv, 1, 51, 73–74, 89, 96–97, 124–25, 127, 137, 146–47, 160
    eight-degree offset, 74, 96
    flexible deck and development of, 51, 89, 96–97, 160

technological developments and, 85

use of aircraft carriers and, 73–74

value of, 8, 74, 136, 147, 164

antiaircraft technology development, 118, 127–28

Antietam (CV 36), 124, 125, 125, 146–47, 167

antiship missiles, xiii

Ark Royal (RN), 45, 85, 96, 124, 146

armored-flight-deck carriers, 2, 35, 45, 65, 75

Army, U.S.

bombers for, size and weight of, 26–27

bomb-guidance systems development, 41

bombing operations and end of war, 36

cooperation between USN and, 16

jet engine R&D, 17, 58–59, 60

Liberty engines for aircraft, 53–54

turbojet engine development, 55

Army Air Corps, U.S., 55, 56

Army Air Forces, U.S., 58, 71

Arnold, Henry H. "Hap," 53, 58, 59–60

arresting gear/arresting wire

cooperation between RN and BuAer on, 83–84, 146

development of, 8, 81, 83–84, 135, 137

on flexible decks, 50, 93–94

flight operations pattern, 8

gravitational forces on airplane structures from, 50–51

missing the wire and safe return to the air, 47

powered and unpowered landings, 19

testing of, 182

Ashworth, Frederick L., 129, 131

attack aircraft/fighter-bombers

combat operation observations and design of, 38–39

landing gear/undercarriages, aircraft designed without, 94

landing speeds, 45, 177–78

list of at close of World War II, 177

long-range aircraft, value of, 35–36, 51

long-range and heavy aircraft, development of, 24–28, 30–31, 105–108, 129–30, 134–35, 137, 161–62, 164

mission requirements, 30

ordnance loads, 38, 178, 179

RN use of, 45–46

single-seat aircraft, 24–25, 28, 30, 38, 42

size of, 35, 132, 180

takeoff roll, 178, 179, 180

weight of, 45–46, 132, 178, 179–80

attention as scarce resource, 157

aviation community, information exchange within, 11

aviators/pilots

cooperation between USN and RN, 7

demobilization after World War II, 138

Fleet Air Arm pilot training, 3–4

jet aircraft, training for and experience with, 63, 67n32

number of for World War II, 16, 17

promotion of, 69, 70

training of, 5

B

B-17 bombers, 174

B-25 Mitchell

carrier launch of, 36, 37–38, 101

characteristics, 26, 27, 132

Doolittle Raid, 35, 42–43n1, 101

B-36 bomber, 151–52n34

B-47 Stratojet, 64, 107

Ballentine, John J., 144, 161

barriers and barricades

concept and function of, 12, 19, 49

barriers and barricades *(continued)*
    cooperation between RN and BuAer on, 83–84
    development of, 51, 81, 154n95, 158–59
    tricycle landing gear and, 37, 137

Bartlett, J. L., 90, 96

Bat glider, 40

battleships, 78

Beall, Wellwood E., 25–26

Bennington (CV 20), **126**, 170

Blandy, William H. P., 129, 131

Boddington, Lewis
    angled deck development and testing, 89, 96, 124–25, 137, 160
    catapult development, 47
    exchange of information about aircraft carriers, 50–51, 149
    flexible deck development and testing, 50, 89, 165
    innovation development, role in, 127, 168, 169
    jet aircraft, takeoff and landing requirements for, 123–24, 127, 147, 159–60, 162, 163
    jet aircraft trials, 46–47
    leadership of, 181

Boeing, aircraft design and development by, 25–26, 57

bombers
    carrier-based, importance of and requirement for, 41–42
    carrier launch of, 35–38
    carriers for launch and recovery of, 6
    design of, 27–28, 76
    fighters as escorts for, 17–18, 37–38
    land-based, 41, 45
    launch and recovery capabilities and, 27, 33n21
    long-range aircraft, development of, 27–28, 76
    one-way missions with, 107
    operational range and firepower, 27–28
    ordnance loads, 27, 28, 33n21, 76
    range of, 27–28
    size of, 26–27
    supersonic flight capabilities, 107
    underway replenishment, 27–28
    weight of, 26–27, 33n21

bombs
    German bomb and missile technology, 47–48, 118, 127
    gliders/glider bomb (GLOMB), 39, 40
    guidance systems, 40, 41
    size of, 76
    See also nuclear weapons

Boyd, Denis W., 141

British Air Commission, 65, 140

British Pensacola Veterans, 4

Brown, Eric, 46, 50, 91–92, 95–96, 123, 126–27, 148, 149, 168, 170

Brown, Sheldon W., 114, 115, 117, 143–44, 145

BT2D Sky Pirate, 31, 38–39, 42

BT3D aircraft, 75

BTD/BTD-1 Destroyer, 15, 27, 31, 67n21

Buckingham, Edgar, 54

Bunker Hill, 144

bureaucracies, problem solving in, 181–82

Bureau of Aeronautics, U.S. Navy (BuAer)
    aircraft design competitions, 11, 12–15, 17, 18–20, 30
    aircraft designers, constraints on, 154n93
    authority and influence of, 5, 6, 7, 71–72, 86n16, 133–34, 157, 162
    command of, 11, 12, 15
    contacts between industry and, 25, 31, 38, 39, 67n23, 161
    contacts between OPNAV and, 161

Doolittle Raid, role in, 36

exchange of information with British team, 50–51, 167

function and mission of, 5, 11, 133–34, 152n38

funding for, 159

innovation development and organizational factors in, 145–47

modifications to existing aircraft, information sources for, 24–25

Naval Aircraft Factory, responsibility for, 5, 11

organization of, 12, 32, 71–72, 86n16

personnel in, 15–16

R&D responsibility of, 5, 16–17

Ten-Year R&D History, 57

testing, commitment to, 139

Towers as chief of, 3, 15, 139–40, 167

turbojet engine development, 55

war preparations by, 16–17

See also research and development (R&D)

Bureau of Ordnance, U.S. Navy (BuOrd)

antiaircraft technology development and adoption, 118, 127–28

cooperative relationship with RN, 80–81

foreign innovation, adoption of by, 118

guided weapons development by, 40

Bureau of Ships, U.S. Navy (BuShips), 5, 69–70, 82

Bureau of Standards, U.S., 54, 58

Burke, Arleigh, 148

Bush, Vannevar, 58

BX-52 bomber, 151–52n34

C

C-2 carriers, 76–77

Cambell, Dennis R. F.

angled deck development and testing, 96, 124–25, 160

exchange of information about aircraft carriers, 149, 167

flexible decks, limitations of, 49–50, 124

innovation development, role in, 127

jet aircraft, takeoff and landing requirements for, 127, 147

mirror and lighted landing aid development and testing, 125–26

Carney, Robert B., 6

carrier aviation

development of, 12, 147, 148, 157–64

nuclear weapons and, 4–5, 6, 41, 42, 51, 71, 76–77, 84, 107, 128–33, 142, 152nn35–36, 163–64, 166, 171n27, 180, 182

rocket-assisted takeoff equipment, 45

role and organization of, disputes about, 4

simulations and fleet exercises of capabilities of, 12

World War II lessons and, 41–42

catapults

aircraft takeoff into wind and, 100

all aircraft, catapult need for, 83, 101

development of, 8, 29, 47–49, 81, 100–110, 118–19n3, 120n24, 120n26, 137, 142–44, 153n76, 158–59, 160–61, 170

direct-drive and indirect-drive types, 104, 113–14, 115–17, 120n33

electric-driven types, 103–104

explosive fuel for, 81, 105, 106–107, 116, 120n26

funding for development, 107

German-built, 48, 81, 101–102, 119n5

hydraulic-pneumatic types, 29, 48, 81, 99, 100, 102–103, 109, 110, 113, 117, 118–19n3, 119n8, 170, 171n34

internal-combustion type, 99, 105

launching aircraft with, 77, 84

linear-turbine type, 104

more-powerful, specifications of, 101, 105–106, 107–108, 109, 110, 115, 116, 119n4

catapults *(continued)*
    popgun types, 48
    powder (explosive-driven) types, 104, 106–107, 111–12, 113, 116–17, 119n18, 120n26, 143–44
    requirement for, 46–47
    seaplane launch with, 29, 102–103
    slotted-cylinder/slotted-tube types, 29, 48, 81, 83, 101–102, 103, 104–10, 111–12, 119n5, 119n8, 120n24, 120n26, 120n33, 137, 142–44, 153n76, 158–59
    solid-piston types, 108–109
    support for use of, 46
    takeoff roll and, 178, 179, 180
    testing of, 182
    Type K (flywheel), 47, 48
    weight of, 116
    See also steam catapults

cavity magnetron, 3, 16, 57
Chafee, George B., 158–59
Chance Vought aircraft manufacturing, 50
Churchill, Winston, 57
Clarke, Ralph S., 113, 143
Coe, C. F., 80
combat information center (CIC), 7
combat operations, observation of, 38–39
Combs, Thomas S., 138, 143
communications
    antennas for equipment, 79
    CCA systems, 79
    information exchange and innovation, 167
    problems on flight decks, 149
Congress, U.S., 4, 16
convoy escort operations, 73
Cook, Arthur B., 18
Coral Sea (CV 43), 74

Coral Sea battle, 7, 23
Cunningham, Andrew B., 46
Curtiss-Wright J65 engine, 132
CVB-X carriers, 76–77

D

DC-4 aircraft, 55
death rays, 5
deck landings
    experiments with aircraft, 19
    landing speeds, 18–19, 20, 45, 49, 83, 84, 146, 177–78
    powered landings, 19, 47
    separate landing and takeoff decks, 47
    unpowered landings, 18–19, 20
    See also barriers and barricades
deck park, 12, 19, 47, 49, 51, 101
Defense Aid program, 3
deflectors, jet-blast, 77
de Havilland Goblin engine, 61, 63
Denfeld, Louis E., 106
Deputy Chief of Naval Operations for Air (DCNO [Air])
    carrier design and development, 74–76, 134–35
    catapult development, 111
    creation of and organization of, 71–72, 86n16, 133, 152n38
    innovation development and organizational factors in, 145–47
Deputy Chief of Naval Operations for Logistics (DCNO [Logistics]), 76, 78–79
Devlin, Leo, 25
DH-100 Vampire fighter, 63, 91, 91–93, 148
Diehl, Walter S., 21n6, 25
dive-bomber aircraft, 13–15, 25, 30, 38, 42
Doolittle Raid, 27–28, 35–36, 42–43n1, 101

Douglas Aircraft
    aircraft design and development by, 57
    aircraft development cycle, 39
    contacts between BuAer personnel and, 25, 38, 39
    exchange of information with British team and, 50
    turbojet engine development, 55

Dove bomb, 40

Dreyer, Frederic, 140

Driggs, Ivan H., 132

drones and unmanned/pilotless platforms
    advances in, xiii
    development of, 39–40, 159
    number produced, 39–40
    opposition to, 135
    speed of, 39
    target drones, development of, 29, 39

Durand, William F., 58, 60, 61–62

E

E28/39 aircraft, 58, 59–60

electronics, 7, 79

Electropult (electric-driven catapult), 103–104

elevators, deck-edge, 49, 74, 75, **108**, 134, 135, 141, 158–59, 163

Engen, Donald D., 93–94, 126, 161, 168

Engineering Aerodynamics (Diehl), 25

Engineering Division, Bureau of Aeronautics
    attack aircraft development, 30
    Design Coordination and Contract Airplane Design Section, 16, 130
    fighter design, 18–20
    function and mission of, 12
    personnel in, 30

engine manufacturers, 61–62, 67n19

engines
    design of aircraft around, 11, 31–32, 53, 136
    development of for carrier operations, 19
    Liberty engines, 53–54
    suppliers of, 53
    turbine engines, 54–55
    turbo-superchargers for, 54–55, 57, 60–61, 66n10, 174
    See also jet propulsion/turbojet engines; piston engines and propeller-driven aircraft

Enterprise (CVAN 65), 12, 13, 99

escort carriers
    aircraft for, 25
    catapults for, 29, 101
    construction program for USN, 2
    jet aircraft for, 63

Essex (CV 9) and *Essex*-class carriers
    aircraft design for launch from, 27, 30, 166, 171n27
    aircraft landing on, 73
    aircraft takeoff into wind, 100
    aircraft takeoff weight limitations, 83
    catapults for, 102, 109, 110, 111–12, 115, 117, 119n8, 120n33, 145
    modifications to, 74–75, 134–35, 160–61
    weight of, 119n8

experimentation, value of, 96–97, 166

F

F2H/F2H-1 Banshee, 59, 74, 75, 146, 179

F3D Skynight, 64, 100, 102

F3H Demon, 63–64, 100

F4D Skyray, 63–64, 100

F4F Wildcat, 26

F4U Corsair, 26, 28, 62, 174–75, 177, 178, 179, 180

F6F Hellcat, 26

F6U Pirate, 63

F7F Tigercat, 26, 27, 28, 37, 42, 75, 177, 178, 180

F7U-1/F7U-3 Cutlass, 63, 83–84, 177, 178, 180

F8F/F8F-1 Bearcat, 19, 26, 60, 62, 66, 67n23, 139

F9F-1/F9F-2/F9F-5 Panther, 64, 67n35, 73, 83–84, 177, 178, 179–80

F9F7 Cougar, 94–95

F-14 fighter, 164

F15C fighter, 60, 63

F-84G Thunderjet, 94

F-86 Saberjet, 64

Fahrney, Delmar S., 39

Fairey, C. R., 65

FD/XFD-1/FD-1/FH-1 Phantom, 60, 63, 67n21, 135, 179

Fechteler, William M., 114, 127, 143, 153n79, 169

fighter aircraft

    armament requirements, 20

    design competitions, 12–13, 17

    design of, 17–20, 65

    escort function of, 17–18, 37–38

    landing speeds, 18–19, 20, 177–78

    modernization of fleet, 139

    ordnance loads, 28

    performance improvement of, 13, 14, 15, 21n6

    powered and unpowered landings, 18–19, 20

    range of, 20, 25–26

    RN use of, 45–46, 140–42

    size of, 26–27, 45–46, 81–82

    speed needs, 18, 19–20

    strike potential, 17

    supercharged fighters, 18–19

    weight of, 19, 20, 26–27, 45–46, 81–82, 83–84, 179–80

    weight of aircraft and launch and recovery capabilities, 27, 164

FJ-1/FJ-4B Fury, 63, 146, 163–64

Fleet Air Arm (FAA)

    aircraft carrier experience for, 167

    aircraft for, 70

    aviation organization to support, 141

    club for U.S.-trained pilots, 4

    pilot training for, 3–4

    reconstruction of, 181

fleet air defense, radar use for, 3

fleet problems and exercises, 7, 12, 15, 18, 157–58, 168

flexible deck/carpet deck

    angled deck development from, 51, 89, 96–97, 160

    arresting gear/arresting wire on, 50, 93–94

    concept behind and construction of, 89, 90, 91, 91, 95

    development of, 80–81, 89–91, 123–24, 159–60, 165

    flight operations pattern, 50, 89, 92–94, 93

    landing on, skill needed for, 50, 95

    limitations of, 49–50, 51, 80, 124, 136

    proposal for, 46, 47

    RN offer to BuAer to fund and manage program for, 80–81

    testing and assessment of, 47, 49–50, **91**, 91–96, **93**, 150n1

    USN following RN lead on, 96–97

flight decks

    armored-flight-deck carriers, 2, 35, 45, 65, 75

    deck-edge elevators, 49, 74, 75, **108**, 134, 135, 141, 158–59, 163

    flight operations pattern, 12, 47, 49, 50, 51, 62, 84, 101, 137, 141 flush-deck carriers, 77, 79, 125

jet-blast deflectors, 77

separate landing and takeoff decks, 47

sortie volume and deck arrangements, 75

wooden decks and jet engines, 55

See also angled flight deck; flexible deck/carpet deck

Flight Division, Bureau of Aeronautics, 12

Forrestal (CVA 59) and *Forrestal*-class (CVB 59) carriers, 108, 112, 145, 147, 162, 163, 168

Forrestal, James, 70, 128

FR-1 Fireball, 59, 60, 65, 67n21, 67n24

France, 3, 57

Frisbie, William Z., 16, 130

Future Building Committee (FBC), 45–46, 140–41, 165, 181

G

Gallery, Daniel V., 129

Gargoyle missile, 40

Gates, Artemus, 70

General Board, U.S. Navy

aircraft design requirements, 20

authority and influence of, 6–7, 71, 133, 157, 161–62

carrier design and development, 77

function and mission of, 6, 74, 140

hearings on ship design, strategy, and technology, 158

substitute for, 134

technological developments shipbuilding programs, 78–82

General Electric (GE)

contract negotiations with industry, 67n19

I-16/J31 engine, 59, 60

I-40/J33 engine, 60, 61, 63

J35 engine, 60, 64, 151–52n34

J47 engine, 60, 64

jet engine development, 57, 58–60

microwave radar development, 16–17

TG-100 engine, 59

turbo-supercharger development and production, 55, 57, 66n10

Germany

aeronautical research, examination of, 131–32

aircraft designs, 65

bomb and missile technology, 47–48, 118, 127

catapults built by, 48, 81, 101–102, 119n5

high-speed flight research, 56

jet engine development, 58, 61, 65

Mistrel aircraft, 107

gliders/glider bomb (GLOMB), 39, 40

Goodhart, Nicholas, 125–26, 127

Gorgon missile, 40, 59, 136

Grant, Lucien M., 143

Great Britain

adoption of innovations from, 118, 149–50

aircraft, purchase of U.S.-made, 3–4, 57

aircraft industry in, 65, 140, 141

bomb development by, 41

collaboration between U.S. and, xiii, 1

financial condition after World War II, 69–70, 163

high-speed flight research, 56

innovation development in, xiii–xiv, 2, 51, 118

jet engine development, 57–58, 59–61, 64–65, 67n24

special relationship between U.S. and, 4

Green, F. M., 123

Grumman Aircraft Corporation

contacts between BuAer personnel and, 67n23

Grumman Aircraft Corporation *(continued)*

    exchange of information with British team and, 50

    jet aircraft designs, 60

    preferred BuAer supplier status, 67n23

Guadalcanal, 7

Guadalcanal, 129

guided weapons, 40, 41, 159

H

Halford H-1 engine, 63

Halsey, William, 3, 41

Hancock, 77, 143, 145, **160**, 160, **164**

Hayward, John T. "Chick," 130–31, 132–33, 151n25, 151n27, 152n36

He-176 aircraft, 58

He-280 aircraft, 58

Heinemann, Edward

    attack aircraft development, 38, 131–32, 152nn35–36

    catapult capacity, concerns about, 102

    combat operations, observation of, 38–39

    innovation development, role in, 168

    jet engine development, 63–64

    opinions about, 25, 131

    wartime R&D process, 31

high-speed flight research, 56, 174

Hopkins, F. H. E., 38

Horn, Peter H., 113, 143

Hornet, 27–28, 35–36, 42–43n1, 182

HOTFOOT plan, 40–41

hydrogen peroxide fuel, 48, 102, 105, 115, 116, 119n5, 144

I

Illustrious (RN), 126, 161

Imperial Japanese Navy (IJN), 13, 14, 15, 45

innovations

    decision making and, 148–49, 181, 182

    experimentation and, 96–97, 166

    foreign-developed, adoption of, 118

    funding for, 159

    individuals, role of in, 1–2, 123–33

    information exchange and, 167

    institutions, role of in, 2, 147–50

    organizations, role of in, 1–2, 133–47, 157–60, 168–70

    serendipity and, 160

Intrepid, 145

Italian Academy of Sciences, 56

J

Japan

    bombing operations and end of war with, 36

    Imperial Japanese Navy, 13, 14, 15, 45

    operational challenges of fight against, 127–28

    radar development by, 37

    strategic bombing operations against, 40–41

    Tokyo, raid on, 41

jet aircraft

    assisted takeoff requirements, 46–47, 49, 101, 123, 135

    on carriers, concerns about, 136, 138, 139

    carriers, mating to, 145–46

    combat operations, simulation of, 139

    development of, 46, 49, 138–39, 158–59

    landing speeds, 49

    launch and recovery methods for, 51, 84, 101, 123–24, 127, 147, 148, 157–60, 162

    pilot training for, 63, 67n32

    piston-engine aircraft, engagement of by, 139

    size of, 99

speed of, 54

takeoff speeds, 47

undercarriages/landing gear, aircraft designed without, 46, 47, 50, 90–91, 92–93, 93, 96, 123, 159–60, 163

weight of, 99

jet-assisted takeoff (JATO) units, 29–30, 81, 118, **128**, 128

jet propulsion/turbojet engines

acceleration of, 62

adoption of, 53

aircraft design to accommodate, 65

axial-flow engines, 59, 60–66

centrifugal-flow engines, 58, 60–64

clustered small engines, 59

development of, xiii, 4, 7, 8, 11–12, 57–66, 151–52n34, 174

development of as focus of BuAer efforts, 100–101

evaluation of applicability of, 57

exchange of information about, 3, 17, 57–58, 59–60

fuel consumption by, 62

funding for, 16, 53

gas turbines, evaluation of, 57

mixed piston-jet aircraft, 60, 67n24

obstacles to development of, 53–57

physics of, 57, 173–75

pressure to develop, 174–75

reliability of, 135

research into, 17, 57

thrust, 62, 63, 173–74

Johnson, Felix, 143

JUPITER, Project, 136

K

Kearsarge, 110

King, Ernest J., 6–7, 42, 42–43n1, 127–29, 131, 161–62

Komer, Robert W., 181–82

Korean Conflict, 163

Kraus, Sidney, 16, 18–19

L

L-133 fighter, 58

La Guardia, Fiorello H., 54

Lake Champlain, 110

Langley, 12, 135

Lark missile, 136

Lend-Lease Act, 3, 58, 65, 70, 150

Lewis, George W., 56

Lexington, 12–13

Leyte (CV 32), 170

Liberty engines, 53–54

light carriers, 2, 29

Limbo antisubmarine weapon, 118

Lockheed L-1000 jet engine, 55, 58

Long Range Objectives Group (Op-96), 164

Lonnquest, Theodore, 131, 151n27

M

magnetron, 3, 16, 57

Malta-class carriers (RN), 85, 163

Marine Corps, U.S.

aircraft and pilots for World War II, 16, 17

jet aircraft for, 63, 136

Martin aircraft manufacturing, 57

Massachusetts Institute of Technology (MIT), 11, 16, 55, 58

Material Branch, Bureau of Aeronautics, 12, 16, 18–19

McCain, John S., 71–72, 133

McDonnell aircraft manufacturing, 50

Metsger, Alfred B., 65–66, 138–39

Midway (CV 41) and *Midway*-class (CVB 41) carriers

aircraft takeoff weight limitations, 83

Midway (CV 41) and *Midway*-class (CVB 41) carriers *(continued)*
    catapults for, 107, 108, 110, 145
    JATO launch from, 118, **128**, 128
    jet aircraft development for, 132, 159

Midway battle, 7, 23, 75

military services
    contract negotiations with industry, 67n19
    demobilization after World War II, 4, 69, 149
    military aviation, disputes about role and organization of, 4, 71, 72–73

Miller, Jerry, 128, 129, 133, 152n35

Ministry of Aircraft Production (MAP), 2, 46, 89–91, 92, 140

mirror and light landing aid
    adoption of, **108**, 126, 149, 161, 182
    concept behind, 125–26, **126**
    development and testing of, 1, 125–26, 127
    technological developments and, 85
    value of, 164

missiles and rockets
    catapult launch of, 104–105
    characteristics, 40
    cost of, 40
    development of, 4, 40, 136–37
    engines for, 67n21
    German bomb and missile technology, 47–48, 118, 127
    nuclear weapon delivery by, **164**, 164
    number produced, 40
    rocket motors and guided weapons development, 40

Mitchell, Colin C., 48, 89, 90, 114, 115, 117, 118, 126, 144, 166

Mitscher, Marc A.
    aircraft development for carrier aviation, 12, 162
    BuAer role, 12, 15
    carrier design board, 74–76, 134–35
    fighter design, 18, 21n23
    Hayward, relationship with, 131
    Hornet and Doolittle Raid, 35, 36, 42–43n1
    long-range aircraft, need for, 28

Montgomery, Alfred E., 42

Moore, Henry, 82

Moore, John, 94–95

Moss, Sanford A., 55, 58, 66n10

Murphy, Joseph N., 30–31, 130, 132

Murray, George D., 134

M. W. Kellogg Company, 104

N

National Academy of Sciences, 57

National Advisory Committee on Aeronautics (NACA)
    airfoil sections, design of, 53
    aviation research by, 11
    cowling design for piston engines, 53
    fighter design, support for, 19–20
    innovation development by, 170
    jet-propulsion committee (Durand committee), 58, 60, 61–62
    jet propulsion research by, 17, 57
    turbojet engines, development of, 53, 54, 56
    wind tunnels, 56

National Defense Research Committee (NDRC), 40, 58

Naval Aircraft Design Committee, 46–47, 141, 181

Naval Aircraft Factory
    BuAer responsibility for, 5, 11
    catapult development, 29, 100, 104–105, 116, 118–19n3, 143, 144
    drones, development of, 39
    gliders, development of, 39
    innovation development at, 146, 154n95

production from, 11

reorganization of, 100, 134

Ship Experimental Unit, 29

steam catapult testing, 182

Naval Aircraft Modification Unit, 134

Naval Air Experimental Station, 100, 134

Naval Air Material Center (NAMC)

    aircraft testing for carrier landings, 37

    arresting gear, capabilities of, 83

    catapult development, 99, 100, 103, 104, 109, 111–13, 114, 117, 118–19n3, 119n18, 142–44, 158–59

    funding for, 100, 159

    innovation development at, 145–46, 154n95

    reorganization of, 100, 134

Naval Auxiliary Air Station, 134

naval aviation

    aircraft production for allies, 3–4

    innovations during World War II, xiii, 4

    organizational changes and restructuring, 5, 71–72, 86n16, 168

    plan for, fulfillment of, 140

    strength of after World War II, 70

Naval War College

    authority and influence of, 6, 7, 157, 161–62, 168

    carrier aviation simulations, 12

Navy, U.S. (USN)

    adoption of innovations by, 149–50

    aerial strike doctrine, 17

    aircraft and pilots for World War II, 16, 17

    aircraft development by, 70–71

    aviation policy, 71, 161

    bombing operations and end of war, 36

    carrier force, size and resources of, 65, 67n37, 70–71, 84–85

    committee system in, 142

    competition between RN and, 1, 148–49

    cooperation between Army and, 16

    cooperative relationship with RN, 1, 3–4, 7, 16–17, 50–51, 71, 80–81, 82–85, 127, 146–47, 150, 154n96, 167, 181

    decision making and innovation in, 148–49, 182

    demobilization after World War II, 69–70, 138, 149

    enlisted personnel statistics, 17, 69

    flexible deck, following RN lead on, 96–97

    funding for, 70, 134

    innovation development and organizational factors in, 133–39, 147, 157–59, 165–66

    jet engine development, 58–59, 60

    jet propulsion research by, 17

    Long Range Objectives Group (Op-96), 164

    military aviation, disputes about role and organization of, 4, 71, 72–73

    nuclear weapon delivery by, 41, 129–30, 147–48, 149

    operational challenges of fight against Japan, 127–28

    organization and management of, 157–58

    parallels between RN and, 51

    policy development, 131, 157–59

    professionalism in, 149–50, 167–68

    sortie volume, 73–74

    spread of innovations to, 2

    strength of after World War II, 70

    testing of aircraft and equipment, tradition of, 139, 182

Neutrality Act, 56, 58

Nimitz, Chester, 6, 7, 42–43n1, 72, 105

North American Aviation, 50

Northrop
   Turbodyne project, 57
   turbojet engine development, 55
nuclear weapons
   carrier aviation and, 4–5, 6, 41, 42, 51, 71, 76–77, 84, 107, 128–33, 142, 152nn35–36, 163–64, 166, 171n27, 180, 182
   delivery of by Navy, 41, 129–30, 147–48, 149
   interservice rivalries about control of, 41, 129–30
   missile delivery of, 164, 164
   naval policy on, 131
   size and weight of, 4, 132, 152n35, 163
   survivability of attacks from, 5
   testing of by Soviet Union, 163

O

Office of Naval Intelligence (ONI), 80
Office of the Chief of Naval Operations (OPNAV)
   authority and influence of, 161–62, 168
   BuAer restructuring and authority, 5, 72
   contacts between BuAer personnel and, 161
   naval policy development, 157–59
   quality of officers, 157
Okinawa, 28
operational art, 28
operational surprise, 35–36
optical landing aid. *See* mirror and light landing aid
organizations
   adaptability and problem solving in, 181–82
   change, resistance to, 182
   leadership in, 169
   Navy organizational players, 6–7
   professionalism in, 169
   role of in innovations, 1–2, 133–47, 157–60
   support for innovation in, 2, 165–66, 168–70
Oriskany (CV 34), 83, 100, 109, 110, 146
Ostrander, J. E., 30

P

P2V Neptune bombers, 118, 128, 128, 142
P6M SeaMaster, 169
P-51 Mustang fighter, 37–38
P-61 fighter, 101
P-79 flying-wing fighter, 67n21
P-80/F-80 Shooting Star, 60, 61, 63, 66, 139
Pacific Fleet, 7, 182
Parsons, William S., 128–29, 130, 131
P/A V aircraft, 102
Pavlecka, Vladimir, 55
PBJ-1 bombers, 37
Pearce, James, 130–31
Pelican glider, 40
Perry, J. C., 110–11
Perseus (RN), 48, 111, 113, 114–16, 115, 117, 118, 126–27, 143–45, 153n79, 166, 169, 182
Pirie, Robert B., 138
piston engines and propeller-driven aircraft
   air-cooled piston engines, 62
   alternatives to, interest in, 46, 56
   development and construction of, 11, 12
   limitations of, 139
   mixed piston-jet aircraft, 60, 67n24
   NACA cowling for, 53
   performance improvement of, 13, 14, 15, 21n6
   physics of, 173–74
   reliance on piston engines, 53–54, 174
   speed of, 54
   turbo-superchargers for, 54–55, 57, 60–61, 66n10, 174

Plans Division, Bureau of Aeronautics, 12, 16, 18–20, 30

Pound, Dudley, 140

Pratt, William V., 7

Pratt & Whitney
    J-48 engines, 94
    J57 engine, 64, 132
    jet engine development, 55, 64
    piston engine development, 174
    R-2800 engine, 62
    R-4360 engine, 62
    Tay/J48 engine, 61, 64
    Type 19B/J30 engine, production of, 67n21

Pride, Alfred M., 15, 80, 103, 107, 111, 135–36, 138, 139, 142, 144, 166

Procurement Division, Bureau of Aeronautics, 12, 16

Purnell, William R., 128–29

R

RA-5C Vigilante, 164

radar
    advances in, 80
    airborne, development of, 4
    air-search, development of, 16, 45
    death rays, 5
    ground-based, development of, 4
    Japanese development of, 37
    magnetron and, 3, 16, 57
    microwave radar development, 16–17
    RN's defensive use of, 3
    surface-search radar, 23

Radford, Arthur W., 38, 72, 73, 129, 131, 133, 168

Raisseur, W. T., 75, 134, 135

Ramage, James D., 84

Ramsey, DeWitt, 16, 28, 37, 76, 133

Ranger, 12–13

Reeves, Joseph M., 18

Regulus missiles, **164**, 164

research and development (R&D)
    aircraft development cycle, 14–15, 23–24, 25, 30–31, 38, 39
    BuAer responsibility for, 5, 16–17
    funding for, 16, 17
    improvement of facilities for, 4
    peacetime aircraft R&D, 16, 23, 26, 30
    priority of projects, 137–38
    wartime aircraft R&D, 23–28, 30–32

Research and Development Master Program, 136–38, 142

Richardson, Lawrence, 16

Rickover, Hyman, 118

Rivero, Horacio, 129, 131

Rolls-Royce engines
    Nene engine, 61, 64, 135–36
    Tay/J48 engine, 61, 64

Royal Aircraft Establishment (RAE)
    catapult development, 47–49
    decision making and innovation in, 148–49, 181
    flexible deck development and testing, 89–92, 93–94, 150n1
    jet aircraft trials, 46–47
    jet aircraft without landing gear, proposal for, 92–93, **93**
    jet engine development, coordination of, 61–62
    Naval Aircraft Department, 46–47, 96, 123, 150n1
    role of in innovations, 2

Royal Air Force (RAF)
    aircraft development by, 70
    aviation mission from RN, 140
    jet aircraft without landing gear, proposal for, 90–91, 92–93, **93**
    Whittle jet engine development, 61

Royal Navy (RN)

    aircraft carriers, modifications to launch and recover bombers, 6

    aviation doctrine of, 141–42

    aviation mission to RAF, 140

    carrier force, size and resources of, 65, 67n37, 70, 84–85

    committee system in, 142, 147, 165

    competition between USN and, 1, 148–49

    cooperative relationship with BuOrd, 80–81

    cooperative relationship with USN, 1, 3–4, 7, 16–17, 50–51, 71, 80–81, 82–85, 127, 146–47, 150, 154n96, 167, 181

    decision making and innovation in, 181–82

    decline in, 69–70

    fighter aircraft performance, 13, 14, 15

    fighter aircraft use by, 45–46, 140–42

    fleet doctrine, 181

    flexible deck, USN following RN lead on, 96–97

    government policy on, 150, 167

    innovation development and organizational factors in, 139–47, 159–60, 165

    jet aircraft, takeoff and landing requirements for, 147, 148, 157–60

    jet aircraft without landing gear, proposal for, 90–91, 92–93, **93**, 159

    mission of, 73, 138, 147–48, 149, 150, 163

    nuclear mission, lack of, 133, 147–48, 163

    parallels between USN and, 51

    purchase of aircraft by, 65, 140

    sortie volume, 73–74

    See also Fleet Air Arm

Russell, James S., 74, 138, 167

S

Sallada, Harold B., 76, 134–35, 162

Saratoga, 12, 13, 112

SB2A Buccaneer, 13

SB2C Helldiver

    characteristics, 24, 27, 177, 178

    design and production of, 13, 24, 32n3

    modifications to, 36

    strategic bombing operations with, 40

    successors to, 24–25, 31

    takeoff roll, 179

SBD/SBD-1 Dauntless, 13, 21n6, 31, 131

Sea Hornet fighter, 46

Sea Mosquito fighter, 46

seaplanes, 29, 102–103, 174

Sea Vampire fighter, 93–94

Shangri-La (CV 38), 37, 38, 101, 132

Sherman, Forrest P., 107–108, 139, 153n79, 169

ships

    hearings on ship design, strategy, and technology, 158

    submarine capabilities and surface ships, 5

Sims, William S., 7

Slattery, M. S., 90

Small, James D., 124

Smith, Abel, 147

SO3C Seamew aircraft, 131

Soucek, Apollo, 35, 113, 118, 138, 143, 152n79, 161, 169, 182

Soviet Union

    financial condition after World War II, 163

    nuclear weapon testing by, 163

    sea power use against, 41, 100

    threat from, 5, 163

Spaatz, Carl A., 72

Spangenberg, George

    aircraft design requirements, 25

    aircraft development cycle, 39

    aircraft for nuclear weapons delivery, development of, 130

BuAer role, 16
F8B aircraft development, 25–26
jet engine and aircraft development, 62, 63, 65–66, 138–39
Spangler, Selden B., 66
speed
fighter aircraft speed needs, 19–20
high-speed flight research, 56, 174
landing speeds, 18–19, 20, 45, 49, 83, 84, 146, 177–78
stall speed, 177–78
takeoff speeds, 47, 83
Stack, John, 54
steam catapults
adoption of, 99, 100, 117–18, 126, 142–45, 160, 160–61
advantages of, 116
BuAer design program, 112–13
capacity of and steam plant on ship, 99, 105, 111, 115
development of, xiii–xiv, 1, 48–49, 99, 100, 105, 110–11, 112–18, 119n18, 127
direct-drive and indirect-drive types, 113–14, 115–17
launch intervals with, 105
organizational factors and development of, 142–45
steam temperatures and pressures, 48–49, 114–15, 117–18
testing of, 113, 114–17, 126–27, 143–45, 153n79, 166, 182
weight of, 115, 116
Stevens, John, 143
Stevens, Leslie C., 30, 38
submarine aircraft carriers, 158
submarines
Limbo antisubmarine weapon, 118
missile deployment from, 164

postwar developments, 42
rafting nuclear submarines, 118
U-boat capture, 129
U-boat technology, 41, 42
Sullivan, John L., 6
Super Gorgon missile, 136
swept-wing aircraft, 50, 65, 100, 136, 139

T

Tactical Orders and Doctrine (PAC-10), 182
takeoff roll, 178, 179, 180
TB2F aircraft, 36–37, 169–70
TBD Devastator, 13, 14
TBF/TBM Avenger
characteristics, 14, 27, 177, 178
design and production of, 13–14, 24, 32n4
launch of, 101
strategic bombing operations with, 40
XTBF-1 Avenger, 13
technology
advances in after World War II, 78–82
development of during World War II, xiii, 4, 7, 78
exchange of during Tizard Mission, 3, 16–17, 57–58
hearings on ship design, strategy, and technology, 158
innovation developments and, 85
Pandora's box of, 85
thrust, 62, 63, 173–74
Tizard, Henry, 3, 16–17, 57–58
torpedo planes, 12–14, 27, 30, 36, 38, 42, 130
Towers, John H.
attack aircraft, development of, 30
BuAer command, 3, 15, 139–40, 167
Fleet Air Arm pilot training, 3
R&D funding, attitude toward, 17

Towers, John H. *(continued)*
    RN, respect for, 4
    war preparations by, 16–17
Trapnell, Frederick M., 38, 50, 131
Triumph (RN), 125, 147
Truman, Harry, 6
Tunnell, R. W., 110–11
turbine engines, 54–55
Turbodyne project, 57
turbojet engines. *See* jet propulsion/turbojet engines
turboprop engines and aircraft, 46, 55, 57, 58–59, 62, 75, 76, 132, 134, 139, 151–52n34, 173

U

Ubee, S. R., 92
United States, 76, 77, 83, 103, 107, 146, 162
United States (U.S.)
    collaboration between Great Britain and, xiii, 1
    financial condition after World War II, 70
    Navy, policy on, 150, 167
    special relationship between Great Britain and, 4
unmanned/pilotless platforms. *See* drones and unmanned/pilotless platforms

V

V-1 missiles, 47–48, 101–102
Volta Congress on High Speed Flight, 56
von Kármán, Theodore, 56, 57

W

war gaming, 7, 12, 15, 18, 157–58, 168
Warrior (RN), 49–50, 95–96
Wasp, 110
Weitzenfeld, Daniel K., 119n18, 144
Westinghouse
    24C engine, 64
    contract negotiations with industry, 67n19
    electric-driven catapult development, 103–104
    failure as engine builder, 63
    J46 engine, 59
    Type 9.5/J32 engine, 59
    Type 19/19A/19B/J30 engines, 59, 62–63, 67n21
    Type 24/J34 engine, 59, 62
    Type 40/J40 engine, 63, 66, 100, 132
Whittle, Frank, 3, 17, 53, 61, 174
Whittle jet engine, 3, 17, 53, 58, 60, 61, 174
wind tunnels, 56
Wood, Hugh, 171n31
Woodhull, Roger B., 130
World War I, 1, 4, 5
World War II
    aircraft and pilots for, 16, 17
    carrier battles, lessons learned from, 42
    demobilization after, 4, 69–70, 138, 149
    financial conditions after, 69–70, 163
    lessons from and carrier aviation, 41–42
    naval aviation after, 4–5
    promotion during, 30
    relationship between Great Britain and U.S., 1, 3–4
    strategic bombing operations, 36, 40–41
    technological developments during, xiii, 4, 7, 78
Wright engines, 174

X

XA2D Skyshark, 171n31
XB-47 bomber, 151–52n34
XBT-1 aircraft, 13
XBT2D-1 Sky Pirate, 15, 31
XBTC-1 aircraft, 23
XBTC-2 aircraft, 23, 24, 27
XBTK-1 aircraft, 24–25, 31

XBTM-1 aircraft, 24, 27, 31
XF4U-1 aircraft, 20
XF5F-1 Skyrocket, 26
XF5U-1 Flying Flapjack, 26
XF8B-1 aircraft, 25–26, 27
XFY-1 Pogo, 169
XP-59A/P59A Airacomet, 38, 63, 131, 135
XSB2A-1 aircraft, 13
XSB2C-1 aircraft, 13

XSB2D-1 aircraft, 14–15
XSB3C-1 aircraft, 14, 24
XTB2D-1 aircraft, 36
XTB2F-1 aircraft, 27, 33n21, 36–37
XTB3F-1 aircraft, 28
XTBU-1 Sea Wolf, 13–14

Y

Yorktown, 3, 12, 13

The Newport Papers

Defeating the U-boat: Inventing Antisubmarine Warfare, by Jan S. Breemer (no. 36, August 2010).

Piracy and Maritime Crime: Historical and Modern Case Studies, edited by Bruce A. Elleman, Andrew Forbes, and David Rosenberg (no. 35, January 2010).

Somalia . . . From the Sea, by Gary Ohls (no. 34, July 2009).

U.S. Naval Strategy in the 1980s: Selected Documents, edited by John B. Hattendorf and Peter M. Swartz (no. 33, December 2008).

Major Naval Operations, by Milan Vego (no. 32, September 2008).

Perspectives on Maritime Strategy: Essays from the Americas, edited by Paul D. Taylor (no. 31, August 2008).

U.S. Naval Strategy in the 1970s: Selected Documents, edited by John B. Hattendorf (no. 30, September 2007).

Shaping the Security Environment, edited by Derek S. Reveron (no. 29, September 2007).

Waves of Hope: The U.S. Navy's Response to the Tsunami in Northern Indonesia, by Bruce A. Elleman (no. 28, February 2007).

U.S. Naval Strategy in the 1990s: Selected Documents, edited by John B. Hattendorf (no. 27, September 2006).

Reposturing the Force: U.S. Overseas Presence in the Twenty-first Century, edited by Carnes Lord (no. 26, February 2006).

The Regulation of International Coercion: Legal Authorities and Political Constraints, by James P. Terry (no. 25, October 2005).

Naval Power in the Twenty-first Century: A Naval War College Review *Reader*, edited by Peter Dombrowski (no. 24, July 2005).

The Atlantic Crises: Britain, Europe, and Parting from the United States, by William Hopkinson (no. 23, May 2005).

China's Nuclear Force Modernization, edited by Lyle J. Goldstein with Andrew S. Erickson (no. 22, April 2005).

Latin American Security Challenges: A Collaborative Inquiry from North and South, edited by Paul D. Taylor (no. 21, 2004).

Global War Game: Second Series, 1984–1988, by Robert Gile (no. 20, 2004).

The Evolution of the U.S. Navy's Maritime Strategy, 1977–1986, by John Hattendorf (no. 19, 2004).

Military Transformation and the Defense Industry after Next: The Defense Industrial Implications of Network-Centric Warfare, by Peter J. Dombrowski, Eugene Gholz, and Andrew L. Ross (no. 18, 2003).

The Limits of Transformation: Officer Attitudes toward the Revolution in Military Affairs, by Thomas G. Mahnken and James R. FitzSimonds (no. 17, 2003).

The Third Battle: Innovation in the U.S. Navy's Silent Cold War Struggle with Soviet Submarines, by Owen R. Cote, Jr. (no. 16, 2003).

International Law and Naval War: The Effect of Marine Safety and Pollution Conventions during International Armed Conflict, by Dr. Sonja Ann Jozef Boelaert-Suominen (no. 15, December 2000).

Theater Ballistic Missile Defense from the Sea: Issues for the Maritime Component Commander, by Commander Charles C. Swicker, U.S. Navy (no. 14, August 1998).

Sailing New Seas, by Admiral J. Paul Reason, U.S. Navy, with David G. Freymann (no. 13, March 1998).

What Color Helmet? Reforming Security Council Peacekeeping Mandates, by Myron H. Nordquist (no. 12, August 1997).

The International Legal Ramifications of United States Counter-Proliferation Strategy: Problems and Prospects, by Frank Gibson Goldman (no. 11, April 1997).

Chaos Theory: The Essentials for Military Applications, by Major Glenn E. James, U.S. Air Force (no. 10, October 1996).

A Doctrine Reader: The Navies of the United States, Great Britain, France, Italy, and Spain, by James J. Tritten and Vice Admiral Luigi Donolo, Italian Navy (Retired) (no. 9, December 1995).

Physics and Metaphysics of Deterrence: The British Approach, by Myron A. Greenberg (no. 8, December 1994).

Mission in the East: The Building of an Army in a Democracy in the New German States, by Colonel Mark E. Victorson, U.S. Army (no. 7, June 1994).

The Burden of Trafalgar: Decisive Battle and Naval Strategic Expectations on the Eve of the First World War, by Jan S. Breemer (no. 6, October 1993).

Beyond Mahan: A Proposal for a U.S. Naval Strategy in the Twenty-First Century, by Colonel Gary W. Anderson, U.S. Marine Corps (no. 5, August 1993).

Global War Game: The First Five Years, by Bud Hay and Bob Gile (no. 4, June 1993).

The "New" Law of the Sea and the Law of Armed Conflict at Sea, by Horace B. Robertson, Jr. (no. 3, October 1992).

Toward a Pax Universalis: A Historical Critique of the National Military Strategy for the 1990s, by Lieutenant Colonel Gary W. Anderson, U.S. Marine Corps (no. 2, April 1992).

"Are We Beasts?" Churchill and the Moral Question of World War II "Area Bombing," by Christopher C. Harmon (no. 1, December 1991).

Newport Papers are available online (Acrobat required) at www.usnwc.edu/press/.

www.ingramcontent.com/pod-product-compliance
Lightning Source LLC
Chambersburg PA
CBHW050459110426
42742CB00018B/3307